Anti-nuclear protest

Other works by Alain Touraine

published by Editions du Seuil

Le Pays contre l'Etat (with François Dubet, Michel Wieviorka and Zsuzsa Hegedus), 1981
Lutte étudiante (with François Dubet, Michel Wieviorka and Zsuzsa Hegedus), 1978
La Voix et le regard, 1978
La Société invisible, 1976
Au-delà de la crise (under the author's supervision), 1976
Lettres à une étudiante, 1974
Pour la sociologie, 1974
Vie et mort du Chili populaire, 1973
Production de la société, 1973
Université et Société aux Etats-Unis, 1972
Le Mouvement de Mai ou le communisme utopique, 1968
La Conscience ouvrière, 1966
Sociologie de l'action, 1965
Ouvriers d'origine agricole, 1961

by other publishers

Solidarité (with François Dubet, Jan Strzelecki and Michel Wieviorka), Fayard, 1982
Mouvements sociaux d'aujourd'hui (edited by Alain Touraine), Editions Ouvrières, 1982
L'Après-Socialisme, Grasset, 1980
Un désir d'histoire, Stock, 1977
Les Sociétés dépendantes, Duculot, 1976
La Société post-industrielle, Denoël, 1969
L'Evolution du travail ouvrier aux Usines Renault, CNRS, 1955

Anti-nuclear protest

The opposition to nuclear energy in France

wwwwwwwwwwwwwwwwwwwwwwwwwwwwwwwwwwwwwwwwwwwwwwwwwwwwwwwwwwwwwwwwwwwwwwwwwwww

ALAIN TOURAINE

ZSUZSA HEGEDUS

FRANÇOIS DUBET   MICHEL WIEVIORKA

TRANSLATED BY PETER FAWCETT

CAMBRIDGE UNIVERSITY PRESS

Cambridge

London   New York   New Rochelle   Melbourne   Sydney

EDITIONS DE
LA MAISON DES SCIENCES DE L'HOMME

Paris

Published by the Press Syndicate of the University of Cambridge
The Pitt Building, Trumpington Street, Cambridge CB2 1RP
32 East 57th Street, New York, NY 10022, USA
296 Beaconsfield Parade, Middle Park, Melbourne 3206, Australia
and
Editions de la Maison des Sciences de l'Homme
54 Boulevard Raspail, 75270 Paris Cedex 06

Originally published in French as *La Prophétie anti-nucléaire* by Editions du Seuil, Paris,
1980 and © Editions du Seuil 1980

First published in English by the Maison des Sciences de l'Homme and Cambridge
University Press 1983 as *Anti-nuclear protest*
English translation © Maison des Sciences de l'Homme and Cambridge University Press
1983

Printed in Great Britain at the University Press, Cambridge

Library of Congress catalogue card number: 82-17666

British Library Cataloguing in Publication Data
Anti-nuclear protest.
1. Antinuclear movement–France
I. Touraine, Alain   II. La prophétie anti-
nucléaire. *English*
333.79′24   HD9698.F8

ISBN 0 521 24964 3
ISBN 2 7351 0020 0 (France only)

SE

Contents

Contents

Translator's note

The present translation is an abridged version of the original French, the sections to be omitted having been chosen by Alain Touraine. While this version is to be considered as a new edition of the original, the Chronology indicates the full extent of the research carried out in France.

PART ONE

SEARCH FOR A SOCIAL MOVEMENT

1

vvvvvvvvvvvvvvvvvvvvvvvvvvvvvvvvvvvvvvvvvvvvvvvvvvvvvvvvvvvvvvvvvvvvvvvvvvvvvvvvvvvvvvv

The stakes of the research

THE BIRTH OF A SOCIAL MOVEMENT

In our search amongst the social struggles of today for that social movement and conflict which might tomorrow take over the central role played by the working-class movement and the labour conflicts of industrial society, we look to the anti-nuclear struggle to be the one most highly charged with social movement and protest and most directly productive of a counter-model of society.

Perhaps this is because the continuing influence of the working-class movement leads us to view the struggle against the means of production, and especially of energy production, as a more fundamental form of action than opposition to the centralising State, student protest or the women's liberation movement.

Or more simply because the production of electricity from nuclear power is such a lengthy enterprise and one which mobilises considerable material and political resources – supporters of the fast-breeder quite happily extend their calculations over half a century, whilst every year many billions are invested in the construction of nuclear power stations.

Or finally because successive administrations, and in particular the government of M. Pierre Messmer a few months after the massive increase in oil prices, have presented their energy programmes as vital for foreign trade, national independence and industrial growth.

Other struggles merge to a greater or lesser extent with an appeal to modernity and a call for the destruction of outmoded forms of social organisation and archaic customs, but in the anti-nuclear struggle the opposite is true: the dominant image of modernity is challenged, our whole future is cast into the crucible of debate, our economic organisation, our way of working and living, are called into question. This, surely; is where the popular social movement will take shape, in opposition to technocratic power, to the domination of a whole sector of social life by a system able to create and impose products and forms of social demand serving only to reinforce its own power.

The anti-nuclear struggle also appears as the spearhead of the ecology movement, which transforms a scientific and cultural apprehension into a specifically social conflict, whilst finally, in July 1976, when the present research programme was being set up, the anti-nuclear movement had developed to the point of carrying its crusade to Malville itself, site of the future fast-breeder.

In short, the anti-nuclear struggle emerges as the leading figure of the new social movement.

It will be seen that we distinguish between social movement and struggle. A social movement is defined as the actor in the class war for control of historicity, in other words of those models of behaviour from which a society produces its customs and practices. There is only one social movement for each class in each type of society. In industrial society, it was the working-class movement. What is to take its place in the post-industrial, programmed society now taking shape?

A struggle, on the other hand, is any type of conflict. It may represent a social movement, or it may simply reflect institutional pressures or social and economic demands. Anti-nuclear protests, such as the demonstrations organised at the sites of projected power stations, are clearly struggles. But the sociologist has to ask whether they embody a new social movement, or whether they are situated at some other, less elevated, level of social life. The hypothesis presented here is that, in a society where the largest investments no longer serve to transform the organisation of labour, as in industrial society, but to create new products, and, beyond that, new sources of economic power through the control of complex systems of communication, then the central social conflict has shifted. It no longer opposes manager and worker, subjected to the rationalising process of the workplace, but rather the people and those apparatuses which have acquired the power to impose patterns of behaviour upon the people according to their own interests.

Initially, the people resist this interpretation of their behaviour in terms of demand for the goods and services produced by the system. They fall back defensively upon so-called natural or basic needs. But at the same time they launch a counter-offensive by giving those needs a social form at variance with the one that the system seeks to impose upon them, and by striving to extend the field of democratic control to areas which had previously seemed beyond the sphere of politics.

The opponents of the nuclear industry are motivated firstly by the fear of accident, of damage to the genetic capital and the destruction of the essential balances of the eco-system. But they also fight against it by proposing an alternative model of development, and sometimes even denounce the false modernisation of the nuclear industry in the name of a more profound modernisation which would create the social and cultural conditions needed to go from a society which is a heavy consumer of energy to a more sober society which would be a heavier consumer of information. By joining with the trade unions, the scope of their action is further extended from the cultural to the economic sphere.

A struggle which had begun as a defensive movement, sometimes even protective of established situations, is thus transformed into a confrontation with a technocratic apparatus all the more powerful for belonging to the State, and proposes an alternative model of development based on scientific ideas and the latest techniques and types of consumption.

This combination of the movement to protect nature with the struggle to overthrow technocracy and the fight to establish a different, more modern, type of development, provides the definition of that popular social movement which will come to dominate the whole stage in our programmed society, as we move more completely into the post-industrial era.

OR BREAKDOWN?

But this image, which was taking shape as we set up the research programme, may have seemed inappropriate when, two years later, we proceeded to the sociological intervention and the analysis of the results.

The wave of anti-nuclear protest had subsided, especially after the death of a militant during a demonstration against the power station under construction at Malville, on 31 July 1977, whilst the ecology movement, after a remarkable run of successes in the local elections, found itself divided and weakened in the general elections and was reluctant to become involved in the European elections. At Le Pellerin, near Nantes, or at Plogoff, near La Pointe du Raz, various groups fought on against plans to build nuclear power stations, but the resistance became scattered precisely as the government was committing itself more clearly to an energy policy strongly in favour of nuclear power. The fear of an energy shortage was growing, whilst the electoral defeat – if that word is strong enough – of the Left had affected the social and cultural struggles more seriously than might have been expected. There were those who thought that the crisis of the Left might give greater initiative to the feminist, regionalist or ecology groups, but those movements were too weak by themselves and had pinned all their hopes on a victory of the Left even as they were criticising the very parties they wanted to succeed. Even a whole year after the general elections, these new protest movements had been unable to organise any significant kind of action. On the other hand, the gravity of the recession, finally recognised for what it was and no longer imagined by anybody to be a mere hiccup in the economy, was diverting attention from the more general, more ideological, questions. Public opinion, preoccupied by unemployment, no longer seemed so concerned with problems relating to the so-called quality of life, problems which apparently pose no threat to immediate survival.

Everything suggests that we have just lived through a brief period, beginning with the May 68 movement, in which the crisis in the values of industrial society was a prelude to awareness of economic crisis. The intervening time allowed the creation of a movement of counter-culture and ideological critique which was impassioned and contagious, but fragile, and which is now fading rapidly before the harsh realities of economic depression.

This cultural crisis may last for a long time yet, but it will not always be able to produce a movement of social protest. The latter may be no more than the ephemeral flickering caused by the draught of counter-cultural protest through the embers of dying social movements, and the ecology movement just a stirring in the ashes of leftism. The environmental defence movement may already be no more than a handful of pressure groups and associations with a limited outlook, especially since the leftist climate of the years immediately after 1968 has given way in France to a liberal or anti-State ideology more directly opposed to the totalitarian States than to the French State, which may be imperious and bureaucratic but is still comparatively respectful of human rights.

Could it be that the anti-nuclear struggle was no more than an episode in history which is already drawing to a close and which has therefore to be explained in terms of a specific economic situation, or even of the characteristics of a particular social class – the malaise of the teachers and educationalists who provide a large number of its militants? Could it be a movement motivated more by an ideology of rejection than by political and social aims?

For ten years, the ideological scene in France has been dominated by a revolutionary discourse increasingly divorced from the social practices of the masses, as the trade unions have turned more towards negotiation and the Communist Party has ceased to attract the intellectuals, who no longer believe in the role it offers them as interpreters of the meaning of history. This discourse has become a form without a content, dogmatic in some, terrorist in a few, a mere password for the majority, but above all a search for other commitments, firstly to the national liberation movements and then to the new currents of social and cultural protest. The breakdown of the communist model has led to the coexistence and often the coalescence of a language of objectivity, denouncing the relentless mechanisms of bourgeois domination, with a call for subjectivity which is more an expression of revolt or anguish than of revolution.

This language in search of objects to name and these feelings in search of political meaning may sometimes come together in a brief encounter, as in the anti-nuclear movement, but there is nothing to make the union durable. The counter-cultural protest has already diluted into a simple desire to live differently, whilst the language inherited from the working-class movement, like a balloon soaring too high, has exploded in the rarefied atmosphere. The brief illusion of struggle seems already to have faded.

If we now turn our attention from the most ideological and politicised of the militants to the local groups, other hypotheses on the nature of the struggle come to mind, equally remote from the idea of a social movement. We have all seen how quite isolated and fragile communities resist the major industrial projects that bring chaos to their lives, seize control of the land and force prices into an upward spiral. But this resistance, intensified by the secrecy and the brutality of the public or private firms with the power to crush a local community, would be no different if the nuclear power station were replaced by a plan to build a chemical works, a dam or a motorway. The resistance, it seems, is provoked only by the building of the power station and tends to fade away once it is operative. There would even seem to be no real link between these local defence committees and the more general, cultural or political, movements of opinion.

If these hypotheses are correct, then after 1980, when a quarter of electricity will be generated from nuclear power, the anti-nuclear struggle will have disappeared. Like the student revolt, it will have lasted no more than a few years. Its leaders will have moved on to launch new campaigns, against computerisation, genetic engineering or the private car, or to embark upon a specifically political action for an ecology programme which will be so general that the anti-nuclear movement will gradually be reduced to a minor theme.

THE WORK OF THE STRUGGLE

These two images seem contradictory, and yet they both correspond so obviously to important aspects of the struggle that they need to be combined. That may not be so difficult. The practical struggle might be seen as a kind of work to transform the behaviours of defence, crisis and breakdown into a social movement, and that work would consist, in a first phase, in the creation of a utopia proposing a model of society counter to the one being resisted, but without defining the resistance in properly social terms and without being able to name the relationship of domination which is being suffered and rejected. Unlike the working-class movement, which opposes capitalist and exploited worker, this utopia does not oppose an actor and an adversary, but rather the concepts of life and death, sense and nonsense, happiness and crisis.

Such a utopian mode of thought permeates the whole of the ecology movement. It repeatedly asserts that industrial society has crossed the threshold beyond which growth becomes negative and self-destructive, and that strength of community and the protection of the natural balances must replace a society blindly devoted to the cult of change; a society of machines and signals, which inevitably becomes a society of surveillance, must give way to communication and happiness; necessity must give way to freedom.

There are those who have already withdrawn from a world gone mad from productivism, overcrowding, pollution and dwindling natural resources, and who are trying to live more simply by reconstructing neighbourly relationships, protecting the natural environment and rejecting the lure of a society which transforms need into merchandise and production into waste.

Beyond these laudable but limited experiments are to be heard the warnings of those who denounce the absurdity of a growth without end or aim, people such as the experts in the Club of Rome, or Ivan Illich proclaiming the counter-productive effects of the car, the school or the hospital.

These are not criticisms turned towards the past and calling for a return to the quieter life of old, but turned rather towards the future and finding their most receptive audience in the most 'modern' professional and social milieux. Their strength derives, in fact, from their being a first form of denunciation of the nascent technocracy.

But utopias never become forces of social struggle. They may become strident or degraded, but they never change. They bear witness, but they never fight. Sometimes they lead to overt violence, sometimes to the retreat and perhaps even the mass suicide of some sect, but they never define a social relation or conflict. They may prepare the way for such a conflict, but they may also turn it awry.

In like manner, we must ask if the anti-nuclear struggle will manage to raise itself to the level of a social movement, or if it will collapse back exhausted into a reaction of fear and defence in the traumatic memory of Hiroshima and Nagasaki. Between the crisis in the values of industrial society and the utopian confrontation with the State or the order it imposes, is there, in fact, room for a social movement? More simply still, does there exist a central class struggle in the programmed society now taking shape?

Class conflict occurs only when the defensive action of the dominated class, protecting itself from domination by the enemy, comes together with a counter-offensive action which attempts to regain control of historicity and destroy the power of the ruling class. If the defensive action is isolated, it becomes no more than a behaviour of self-protection and crisis, whilst the counter-offensive action may reduce to a mere utopia if the actor is identified with the cultural stake, the enemy no longer being defined in social terms but rejected as meaningless. Thus, the formation of a social movement, of a class action, presupposes the integration and surpassing of behaviours of both crisis and utopia. Consequently, it is through the social movement, through the various struggles for the control of historicity, that all other forms of collective action are to be understood.

The object of the present study is to see how the generalised rejection of a social and cultural order can be transformed first of all into a creative utopia, and then elevated to the level of a social conflict, in which identifiable opponents fight for a stake which they both accept as cultural orientation but to which they both give entirely different social interpretations. There are three aspects to this transformation.

Firstly, it has to be asked whether the fear of catastrophe, which does not concern a particular social actor but the whole species, can be replaced by a call to the defence of an actor as clearly defined as were the working classes in industrial society, or the people and the nation in an age when the struggle was essentially legal or political.

Secondly, we must ask whether the system which is being opposed, sometimes called industrial society or even modernity and which is in reality always identified with the State, can be replaced by the definition of a specific adversary. Can the dominated classes name those who control historicity and equate it with their own interests? Can they successfully point to a ruling class?

Thirdly and finally, can the opposition between growth and balance be replaced by the struggle of two conflicting social representations of modernity and the society of the future?

The answers to these questions will tell us whether the anti-nuclear struggle carries within itself the popular social movement of the programmed society, or whether it is simply the expression of a crisis, the exacerbated form of a counter-cultural retreat and refusal which may either wither away as rapidly as it developed, or linger on but only on the fringes of the major social conflicts.

But even more is at stake. We are living in a time when social facts are no longer analysed socially, when power can no longer be identified with economic domination, as in the capitalist industrial society, but does not yet seem to have found a new incarnation and hovers uneasily above us in a socially indeterminate space. Even as I speak of historicity and social movements, our society seems indifferent to its future, entrenched in defensive positions or enfolded in dreams and desires that it makes no attempt to transform into modes of social life. Perhaps this apathy is the sign of an irreversible decadence, as wealthy societies yield to the mellow sweetness of a long autumn in the belief that they are still secure from internal and external catastrophe. Perhaps we are even witnessing the end of societies, in this small corner of the world which invented them, and which, over a few brief centuries, evolved areas of social relations free from the conquests and the commands of States.

9

Such an event would fulfil the prophecies of liberals like de Tocqueville, according to which the networks of groups, interests and conflicts would be replaced by a central power ruling over a decomposed and atomised society. In that case, the time for social movements would be past, and Marcuse would be right to say that henceforth revolt will come only from the excluded.

Such ideas are well attuned to the present period, and I am aware that my own analysis seems, in contrast, to be far removed from observable contemporary practice. But it could yet well be that after a period of confusion similar to that which heralded the dawn of industrialisation, we shall finally discover that invisible society which is to be ours, free ourselves from dead languages and learn to name the actors, the arena and the stakes of the new conflicts and innovations through which it will create its practices. And if there really is a social movement taking shape today, it must surely be opposed to the energy policy and the consequent model of economic development imposed by the dominant centres of production and decision.

As the present research is being written up, history, as they say, has not yet decided. Perhaps because the events under study are too recent, or because the anti-nuclear struggle, although no more than a relatively brief episode, really does carry within itself the central social movement of our society and is helping to reinforce it, even though it will later take on other forms. But if the sociological analysis is to be of any use, the question of the significance and meaning of the anti-nuclear struggle must be answered now. Hence the need for a direct study of the movement, whose meaning, which is not clear from its history, has to be discovered from a study of the collective action itself, its directions, forms and organisation.

HISTORY OF THE INTERVENTION

NB: The method of *sociological intervention* used here and devised for this research programme consists in intervening by incitement or hypothesis in the actors' self-analysis of their struggle. The main stages can be summarised as follows:

1. Two *intervention groups*, each composed of a dozen participants in the anti-nuclear struggle, hold discussions with *interlocutors* chosen by themselves: allies, opponents, experts, politicians, trade unionists, industrialists, ecologists, and so on.

2. The researchers, called the *agitator* and the *secretary*, encourage the groups to analyse the conditions and the meaning of their action.

3. The researchers formulate their hypotheses and tell the groups what

seems, in their opinion, to be the *highest possible meaning* of their action and help them to understand that action from such a vantage point.

This central phase is called the *conversion*.

4. After drafting their initial conclusions, the researchers discuss them with the intervention groups and other interested parties and study the ability of the actors to transform this analysis into a programme of action.

This phase is called *permanent sociology*.

The present intervention was conducted with two groups, one made up of militants from Grenoble and the region of Malville, the other composed of militants from Paris, La Hague, the region of Nogent, and Lille. It is through the work of these intervention groups that we shall analyse the anti-nuclear struggle, but the history of the intervention must first be sketched out.

Preparation

The history of the intervention began in early 1976 when Zsuzsa Hegedus established initial contacts with the different components of the anti-nuclear struggle. During the two years before the beginning of the intervention (April 1978), she was in touch with the Réseau des Amis de la Terre (RAT, Network of the Friends of the Earth), the GSIEN (Grouping of Scientists for Information on Nuclear Energy), the *Gazette nucléaire*, the Confédération Française et Démocratique du Travail (CFDT, a mainly social-democrat trade union confederation), trade unionists from the CEA (Atomic Energy Commission), and militants from the Malville Committee in Grenoble. Thanks to her own role in the movement, she was able to create highly favourable attitudes towards the research programme amongst the militants and to obtain their active participation in the intervention, whilst the part played by Alain Touraine in the Commission des Sages, set up at the request of François Mitterrand in 1977, helped in establishing contact with several of the interlocutors. However, the intervention itself was organised around Zsuzsa Hegedus.

Given the date of its creation, at the end of 1977, the choice of locality was an easy one. The importance of the struggle at Malville and the nature of the general components of the action – ecologists, trade unionists and scientists in particular – were a strong inducement to set up two groups, one in Grenoble and Malville, and the other in Paris. The two groups were necessarily different, with the local militants from Malville wishing to work on their own to analyse the action against the fast-breeder, whilst in Paris it was tempting to form a group composed entirely of scientists and ecologists. The disparity would have been too great, however. Consequently, the Malville militants agreed to work with trade unionists, ecologists and scientists from Grenoble, whilst the Paris group was expanded to include

11

two trade unionists from La Hague, two militants from the Nogent region, and one ecologist from Lille. As a result, the two groups, whilst still very different from one another, were equally able to experience within themselves the main problems of the anti-nuclear action.

The groups

The Paris group was formed initially of leaders of the ecology movement: Hannibal, an engineer and founder of the Energy Commission of the Réseau des Amis de la Terre; Georges Flamand, head of the Amis de la Terre in Lille, but also one of the main personalities in the Réseau des Amis de la Terre; Emmanuel Kropo, an engineer given this pseudonym to emphasise his anarchist tendencies; Piccolo, the linchpin of a local anti-nuclear group in Paris, whose sense of humour was to help the group through some difficult moments; Sophia, a painter; Alice, a former official of the Amis de la Terre, and Jacqueline Monceau, an actress, both of whom tended to be thought of, by themselves as well as the others, as 'the women' of the group; they were both to leave the Amis de la Terre in Paris at the same time after the general elections. To these was added a scientist, Jean-Philippe Pharisca, one of the signatories of the Appel des Quatre Cents [see p. 20] and one of the founders of the GSIEN. The trade unionists from the CFDT were Cotentin and Haggar, union officials at the reprocessing plant at La Hague whose union section had produced the film *Condemned to Succeed*, and Roland Maire, an engineer at EDF (French Electricity Board), an active member of the CFDT and one of the editors of the *Gazette nucléaire*. He was to play a very important part in the group. Saint-Hilaire, a technician with the SNCF (French Railways), represented the militant anti-nuclear movement of the Nogent region, as did Provins, a farmer from the same region. Pelot, a manual worker and member of the LCR (Revolutionary Communist League) left the group halfway through.

The other group was made up initially of militants from the Malville region who had all played a major part in the campaign against Super-Phoenix. There was François Delain, a farmer; Esther, a teacher, who, in spite of her links with the region and the Malville Committee, felt isolated; Marie-Jeanne Vercors, secretary to the Malville Committee, responsible for its links with all the anti-nuclear groups in France and abroad, and also a militant Catholic; Marie-Jo was so active in her region that she decided to leave the group halfway through to devote herself to the local struggles. Of the people from Grenoble, Jean-Jacques Rodrigo was one of the main organisers of the Malville Committee until the summer of 1977. He felt responsible for the dramatic events of 31 July and denounced those who had taken the Committee in a direction of which he himself disapproved, and in particular Valence, an anarchist whose participation in the group was

12

sporadic but whose attitudes made a marked impression. Yves Le Gall, on the other hand, was close to Rodrigo but had kept his distance from the Malville Committee and was thus less marked by its internal dissension and therefore more easily able to adopt an analytical attitude. Like Valence, Leforestier belonged to the 'diversified' tendency in the Malville Committee, which meant that he did not reject violent action. Claudine had come to the action through her children; she was strongly attached to the Malville Committee and wanted to keep it open to all tendencies. The trade unionists from the CFDT were Christophe, an engineer at the CEA who was to play a unifying role in the group, and Bourguignon, who came from Marcoule every week to take part in the group but who was conscious of the distance between the world of the workers and that of the ecologists. Véronique Uri was a physicist but also and above all a militant from the LCR as well as being an active member of the Union of Researchers and the Malville Committee. Antoine Villars was, like her, a member of CUSPAN, a group of anti-nuclear scientists, but nonetheless much less hostile to the nuclear industry.

THE GROUPS

Paris

Alice	Official, Amis de la Terre (Friends of the Earth), Paris, 1977–8
Haggar	Worker from the CEA (Atomic Energy Commission) at La Hague, CFDT trade unionist
Hannibal	Engineer, Energy Commission of the RAT (Network of the Friends of the Earth)
Saint-Hilaire	Technician, Amis de la Terre Committee of Nogent
Cotentin	Worker from the CEA at La Hague, CFDT
Emmanuel Kropo	Engineer, RAT
Georges Flamand	Official, Amis de la Terre, Lille
Roland Maire	Engineer, CFDT, GSIEN (Grouping of Scientists for Information on Nuclear Energy)
Jacqueline Monceau	Actress, Amis de la Terre, Paris
Pelot	Worker, LCR (Revolutionary Communist League)
Jean-Philippe Pharisca	Physicist, GSIEN
Piccolo	Executive at ORTF (French Radio and Television), Anti-nuclear Committee of the 14th Arrondissement of Paris
Provins	Farmer, Anti-nuclear Committee of Nogent
Sophia	Painter, Amis de la Terre, Paris

Grenoble–Malville

Bourguignon	Worker from the CEA in Marcoule, CFDT
Christophe	Engineer, CENG (Grenoble Centre for Nuclear Studies), CFDT

13

François Delain	Farmer, Malville Committee of Meypieu
Esther	Teacher, Malville Committee of Polleyrieu
Leforestier	Engineer with the National Forestry Commission, Malville Committee of Grenoble
Yves Le Gall	Researcher, economist, Amis de la Terre, Grenoble
Marie-Jo	Mother of five, Malville Committee of Bouvesse
Jean-Jacques Rodrigo	Teacher, Amis de la Terre, Grenoble, leader of the Malville Committee of Grenoble
Claudine	Mother of four, Malville Committee of Grenoble
Valence	Printing worker, Malville Committee of Grenoble
Marie-Jeanne Vercors	Mother of three, Malville Committee of Morestel
Véronique	Physicist, LCR, Malville Committee of Grenoble
Antoine Villars	CUSPAN (University and Scientific Committee to Stop the Nuclear Programme)

2

vvvvvvvvvvvvvvvvvvvvvvvvvvvvvvvvvvvvvvvvvvvvvvvvvvvvvvvvvvvvvvvvvvvvvvvvvvvvvvvvvvvvvvvvvvvv

The anti-nuclear struggle

BIRTH OF A POLITICAL ECOLOGY

In France, as in neighbouring countries, the anti-nuclear movement began as a defensive movement directed against the dangers of accident and contamination created by the nuclear industry for the population, and more especially for those who work in and live near the power station. But the size and importance of this campaign cannot by themselves explain why we should have looked to it for the formation of a movement capable of attacking the principal centres of social domination. And if we analyse the circumstances of that great fear which links the nuclear industry with the atomic bombs dropped on Hiroshima and Nagasaki, the search for a social movement in this domain seems even more surprising, since the catastrophe we fear so much threatens the whole of humanity and thus ought to provoke a moral rather than a social reaction in so far as it does not pit one group of social actors against another. Moreover, as we shall see, the anti-nuclear movement is turning more and more consciously away from the problem of the military use of atomic energy and, more generally, from the reactions of fear.

If we thought we would be able to find a social movement in the anti-nuclear struggle, it was because that struggle took on a political orientation almost from the beginning, in the sense that it has constantly sought to transform an ecological current of opinion into a true social struggle, with a precise definition of its adversary. To talk of anti-nuclear action is, by definition, very different from a call to defend a humanity whose survival is threatened by insane and criminal adventures. Of all the many campaigns for cultural liberation or social equality, for the rights of a given category of people or a region or again for the independence of a nation, the anti-nuclear action seems the one best able from the outset to define its social adversary, challenge a social and economic policy and at the same time call upon a precise population, that which is threatened by the nuclear installations.

What are the origins of this political orientation to the anti-nuclear struggle, an orientation which seems more marked in France – but also in

15

Germany – than in the United States or England, where the struggle is more directly integrated into the defence of the environment and a movement of counter-culture?

1. We must look first to the *May Movement* for the origin of this orientation. since the student protests constantly linked social revolt, political confrontation and cultural uprising. The crisis in university organisation sparked off both a challenging of knowledge and its transmission and a rejection of Gaullist power, to which the revolutionary groups added the reference to the working-class movement, whilst the police intervention provoked a violent reaction against the State. After the violence of the spring, this union of diverse elements broke down. Worker control became a doctrinaire discourse which largely dominated the social sciences and other sectors of the university, in particular through the militant action of the LCR and the 'Marxist-Leninist' groups, whilst the cultural revolt went outside the university to be briefly embodied in certain revolutionary groups such as Vive la Révolution which published the short-lived *Tout* (Everything). This revolt rejected the industrial society, but it did not try to identify the new economic and social forces which control it. Many anti-nuclear militants, even those too young to have taken part in the events of May, appeal to its spirit and its forms of actions. The PSU (Unified Socialist Party) has been one of the constantly privileged places where particular cultural or social struggles have been given a general political meaning through reinsertion into the tradition of the socialist and revolutionary working-class movement, in conformity with the spirit of May. This continuity of the May Movement right through to anti-nuclear ecology is symbolised by Brice Lalonde in France and by Daniel Cohn-Bendit who became a militant ecologist in Germany. The shifting of the struggles towards new ground also attracts those who, like Cohn-Bendit himself, rebel against the domination of revolutionary forces by the traditional parties and especially by the Communist Party, which is the zealous champion of a strong State, accelerated growth and authoritarian productivism. The militants of the political ecology are first and foremost the children of May 68.

2. Their struggle is not directed against nuclear energy alone, but also, and almost from the beginning, against the nuclear policy, so continuing the struggle against Gaullist power begun in May 68. But other social forces were also sensitive to these criticisms of the bureaucratic and authoritarian centralising State. On the one hand there are those categories which are forced onto the fringes of society by the accelerated industrialisation and the concentration of power. Frequently, although never for very long, young revolutionaries will unite with public figures or local populations who feel endangered by the upheavals threatened by the formidable apparatus of nuclear production. On the other hand there is a new generation of leaders

and experts who are highly suspicious of an industrialisation which seems to them to involve too many uncertainties and who would like to move towards a more flexible, more open mode of organisation often identified with American society. The political ecology is more threatened than strengthened by this confluence of such contradictory currents, amongst which the revolutionary current may be the most visible but is not necessarily the most influential. Its importance is obvious, but so too are its ambiguities.

3. The ambiguity was masked, however, during most of the period by the growing union of the Communist and Socialist parties under the banner of the *Programme Commun* signed in 1972. Even those political groupings and associations which wished to remain independent of this powerful political bloc considered its victory to be a necessary condition for the success of their own action. Many militants from the small parties and extreme left organisations were even swept up in the dynamics of this union. Such was the case for a section of the PSU which followed first of all Gilles Martinet and then, in 1974, Michel Rocard in their transfer to the Socialist Party, and also for a number of trade unionists from the CFDT who joined the party at the same time through the Assizes [see p. 25].

The political ecology contains various tendencies, but the political situation in France has marked it to the Left. René Dumont's campaign in the presidential elections of 1974 was not directed against François Mitterrand and even made clear reference to themes of the Left, especially, for example, in his analysis of famine and non-development in the Third World. It was only later, as the gap widened between the two main parties of the Left, that the political ecologists began to criticise them almost as vigorously as the Right, either to reject the old traditional vocabulary, or to present themselves, not without some artifice, as the only true expression of the Left.

Such was the political context in which we observed the anti-nuclear struggle. We would probably not have looked to it in the same way for the social movement that it carries within itself if we had encountered it elsewhere, in another country or at the time of its first successes. We must be aware of the choice made at the outset. We could have concentrated on the associations for the defence of nature and looked to the themes of their militants for the signs of a cultural change, but in fact our intervention groups were composed mainly of political ecologists since we were looking for a social conflict and movement rather than a new image of culture, by which we mean the relationship between a society and its environment.

It may be that we have made the wrong choice and missed the most important meaning of the anti-nuclear struggle, but at the time of our research that would seem unlikely. The environmentalists are gradually finding their place within the existing institutions and it is only the political ecologists who are striving to unite cultural protest and social conflict. Above all, they were and still are the only ones striving to breathe new life into an action for the defence of nature and the rejection of industrial civilisation which rapidly lost ground in every country as people became increasingly aware that they were living through the worst economic crisis since the thirties. If we concentrate on the political ecologists, it is because they are the only ones struggling to prolong the anti-nuclear explosion and transform it into a movement of social criticism and political initiative.

THE GRAND NUCLEAR POLICY

In 1974, France reacted like other countries to the quadrupling of oil prices by speeding up its electro-nuclear programme. This programme had begun slowly in the sixties, in France as elsewhere, because electricity from nuclear power could not compete with the low price of oil. As a result of the oil crisis, however, electro-nuclear programmes changed dramatically in every Western country except the United States, where orders for power stations peaked in 1972–3. Elsewhere, orders doubled between 1973 and 1974, and forecasts for 1985 are for 45,000 MW in Germany, 60,000 in Japan and 50,000 in France.

It was not only in France, then, that the programme was speeded up, but whereas in many countries this sudden acceleration gave way a year later to a deceleration brought on by the difficulties involved in going over to the industrial stage, in France the oil crisis removed the major obstacle to the carrying out of the grand nuclear project already prepared by EDF and the CEA long before 1974.

The French government was the only one, in 1975, to authorise a process in which *every stage* of the nuclear cycle went directly over to a stage of massive industrialisation. The French electro-nuclear programme corresponds to a twofold strategy: first to ensure France's energy supply – EDF presents nuclear electricity as the vehicle of progress and national independence – but secondly to create a powerful nuclear industry capable of *exporting* not only reactors but nuclear fuel and related services. The development of uranium mines, of enrichment and reprocessing under the authority of the CEA goes well beyond purely national needs.

THE RISE OF THE ANTI-NUCLEAR STRUGGLES IN FRANCE

The anti-nuclear wave

The Messmer government's decision provoked a massive reaction, specific to France like the country's electro-nuclear programme, but also set in a

18

wave of protest against electro-nuclear programmes throughout the Western world in general in the years 1970–5, a wave of protest which was formed everywhere in the same circles and met the same obstacles but achieved different results in each country.

The unity of this anti-nuclear wave derived from the object of its attack: the nuclear power stations. In spite of its name, the protest of 1970–5 was not directed against nuclear power in general. First of all, it did not raise the problem of the military use of nuclear power, even though the dangers of explosion and fallout, associated with the image of the bomb, were widely used to alert the public. Not only did this wave of protest have no link or continuity, even in a country like Japan, with the movement of the fifties, which had been directed mainly by scientists and pacifists against the military use of nuclear power, but also the electro-nuclear programmes which provoked the protest of 1970–5 were, in a way, the culmination of the 'peaceful atom'.

Nor did the civilian nuclear industry, in its beginnings, provoke any protest. The electro-nuclear programmes which existed in several countries from the sixties onwards nowhere aroused mass reaction. The sporadic outbursts of protest, of which the most famous was the one against the first fast-breeder in the USA (Enrico Fermi in 1964), were limited in scope, had no consequences, and, above all, never at any time led to a challenging of nuclear energy itself.

Between 1972 and 1975, however, the programmes for developing the electro-nuclear industry to replace oil as the engine of growth in production and energy consumption sparked off a massive protest which everywhere centred on the same themes: refusal of dangers and risks considered unacceptable and doubt as to the reliability of nuclear technology and even the rationality of a development policy based essentially on the massive production of electricity from nuclear power.

The second general characteristic of this anti-nuclear movement relates to the identity of those circles which were the first to react in different countries. Everywhere the protest emerged both in the populations directly affected by the building of a reactor and in scientific circles close to nuclear research. In the United States, as in West Germany later, the grass-roots groups began to oppose the building of power stations at the very time when the first scientific criticisms began to appear, first from Tamplin and Goffman, and then from the Union of Concerned Scientists and the Committee for Nuclear Responsibility, whereas the AFL-CIO, which had joined in the opposition to the fast-breeder in 1964, became one of the main defenders of the electro-nuclear programme. The working-class organis- ations as a whole did not adopt an anti-nuclear stance and it was mainly the teachers, social workers, scientists and students who led a fight which also mobilised the populations directly affected by the building of nuclear plants.

But everywhere the anti-nuclear protest also suffered from the same weakness, the same inability to organise. In spite of the more or less strong links which existed between them, the different elements of the protest were nowhere integrated into an anti-nuclear struggle which directly challenged a social domination.

The protest movements developed differently in each country. In the United States, after a beginning marked everywhere by marches, site occupations and denunciations of the risks and dangers of the nuclear industry, the movement became increasingly associated with the vast number of groups which, under the aegis of Ralph Nader, worked within the institutional system to exert strong pressure on legislation. In West Germany, on the other hand, the struggle of the inhabitants gradually acquired its own organisation (*Bürgerinitiative*) and clashed with the police, but was unable to integrate itself into a much wider range of struggles.

In France, as in the United States, the first electro-nuclear programme, which began modestly in 1969, provoked reactions from the population, especially in Alsace where it was directly affected by the Fessenheim project, the first power station of the PWR type, and in scientific circles, but these reactions remained isolated. The struggle of the Alsatians, whose defence committee, the CSFR, mobilised 10,000 people for the second march on Fessenheim in 1972, had no imitators in the other regions of France. Similarly, the criticisms of nuclear power which appeared from 1972 onwards in the review *Survivre et Vivre* (Survive and Live), founded by scientists concerned with the problem of the function and social utilisation of the sciences, aroused no echo until 1974. The great demonstrations against the power station at Bugey in July 1972, like the criticisms in the ecology review *La Gueule ouverte* (Open Gob), suggested the beginnings of an opposition, but it remained limited. As in other countries, however, affected populations and scientific circles reacted immediately to the speeding up of the nuclear programme in 1974.

Scientific criticism

In February 1975, 400 scientists addressed themselves directly to public opinion to draw people's attention to the 'ill-considered' nature of the Messmer government's decision, 'the consequences of which could be serious'. The appeal, which by the end of the year had been signed by 4,000 scientists and was followed immediately by the distribution of the pamphlet 'Risks and dangers of the electro-nuclear programme', cast doubt on that programme in the name of the very science and rationality to which it appealed.

With the creation of the GSIEN and the publication of the *Gazette nucléaire*, the scientists took on the task not only of criticising the programme but of informing the public, something they had called for in their appeal. In public debates throughout France, they brought to the anti-nuclear protest not only the guarantee of knowledge but also the necessary competence to challenge the electro-nuclear programme on the adversary's own ground.

The CFDT

Unlike other countries, however, the protest created by the electro-nuclear programme was not limited in France to the affected population and the scientists. The global nature of the French programme brought reaction from the CFDT which did not reject nuclear power but was opposed to the 'all-nuclear' nature of the programme, to the methods of decision-taking in energy matters, to the type of development implied by the 'all-nuclear' programme and to its technical, economic and social consequences. As early as October 1974, the CFDT organisations involved in energy production (Federation of Gas and Electricity, Federation of Miners, Atomic Energy Union) gave a national press conference to demonstrate their opposition to the Messmer programme and to denounce its dangers, in particular for the workers in the nuclear industry. In November 1975, a series of brochures which had been published from 1974 onwards by the CFDT union of atomic energy (SNPEA) were republished in book form under the title *L'Electro-nucléaire en France*. France is the only Western nation in which one of the large union confederations has declared itself opposed to the electro-nuclear programme.

The political ecologists

It was above all the ecologists from the Amis de la Terre and *La Gueule ouverte* who, as early as 1971, declared the nuclear conflict to be the central conflict which today most directly challenges the system of social domination. These militants, situated at the intersection between the political critique of May 68 and the ecological critique, posed the problems of growth as themes which directly challenge the relationships of domination and around which, therefore, a political action of protest representing new social aspirations can be created. The nuclear problem was chosen with this objective in mind.

The argument of the political ecologists against nuclear power focuses on opposition to authoritarian, centralised, technicist conceptions of society, the extreme expression of which would be the 'nuclear society'. The problems and dangers of the nuclear industry and the type of growth it imposes are analysed as political and social problems. The ecologists dispute the idea that the nuclear industry is a strictly technical, neutral and

21

progressive solution and try to show that the imposition of nuclear power means the imposition of a type of society which not only continues our present society, based exclusively on criteria of growth and market consumption, but which, because of the conditions under which nuclear energy itself is produced, becomes increasingly centralised and controlled. However, like the struggle of the Alsatians and the first scientific criticisms, the anti-nuclear campaign launched by the ecologists, the most famous of which demanded a five-year moratorium on the electro-nuclear programme in 1973 and attacked the military tests in the Pacific, did not manage to mobilise the population until 1974.

The demonstrations against the nuclear plants

By contrast, the new plan for the construction of nuclear power stations triggered off a vast movement. Whereas before 1974 Alsace was practically the only region where the population had mobilised, the publication in early 1975 of the map of future power stations (see map) was the signal for a massive protest in several regions, Brittany and the South-West in particular. The posters 'No to Nuclear Power' and 'Reactor Spells Death' sprouted everywhere and there was a succession of demonstrations involving tens of thousands of people.

Those who mobilised to occupy sites came together in an ever-increasing number of defence committees. Thus, the forming of a first CRIN (Regional Committee for Nuclear Information) by the inhabitants of Erdeven in Brittany in November 1974 was imitated immediately at other sites and culminated in the formation in May 1975 of the Brittany Federation of CRIN and CLIN (Local Committees for Nuclear Information).

The action to prevent the building of nuclear power stations by demonstrating, occupying sites or refusing to take part in public inquiries, brought the population into direct conflict with EDF which, as the protest grew, was increasingly obliged to have recourse to the judicial and police apparatus of the State. The police intervention in Brittany and at Braud-et-Saint-Louis, together with the trials which often followed them, revealed not only the political nature of the nuclear debate but also the impotence of elected representatives and the inadequacies of institutional recourse against EDF and the State. New posters appeared alongside the ones bearing the death's-head: 'Stop nuclear power any way we can', 'EDF and the bosses make the decisions, the riot squads do the rest'.

This tendency towards confrontation with the State was reinforced by the cultural or political protesters themselves, for whom the anti-nuclear action was an opportunity to demonstrate their opposition to political power. The anti-nuclear demonstrations became rallying points for all sorts of protests, but the link between local defence and the more general

22

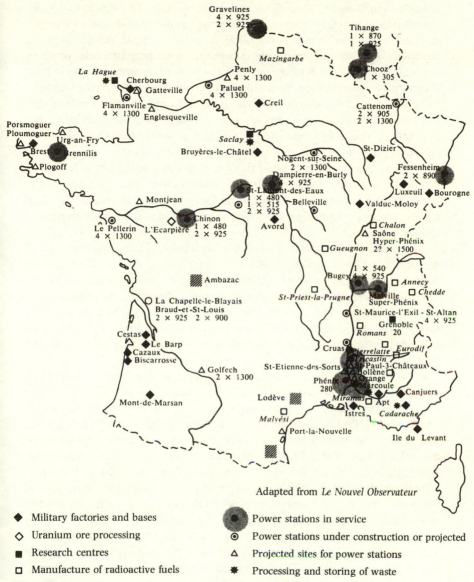

Gravelines
4 × 925
2 × 925

Tihange
1 × 870
1 × 925

□ *Mazingarbe*

La Hague
✶■ Cherbourg
◆△ Gatteville

Penly
△ 4 × 1300
Paluel
4 × 1300

Chooz
1 × 305

◆Creil

Cattenom
2 × 905
2 × 1300

Flamanville △
4 × 1300 Englesqueville

Porsmoguer
Ploumoguer △
Urg-an-Fry
△ Brest Trennilis
△Plogoff

■ *Saclay* ✶
Bruyères-le-Châtel ◆

St-Dizier
◆

Nogent-sur-Seine
2 × 1300
Dampierre-en-Burly
× 925

Fessenheim
2 × 890

Luxeuil ◆ Bourogne

△ Montjean

St-Laurent-des-Eaux
1 × 480
1 × 515 Belleville
2 × 925

◆ Valduc-Moloy

Le Pellerin
4 × 1300 L'Ecarpière
◇

Chinon
1 × 480
2 × 925

Avord

□ *Chalon*
△ *Saône*
Hyper-Phénix
□*Gueugnon* 2? × 1500

Ambazac

1 × 540
Bugey 4 × 925

□ *Annecy*
□ *Chedde*

La Chapelle-le-Blayais
Braud-et-St-Louis
2 × 925 2 × 900

St-Priest-la-Prugne

ville
Super-Phénix
◉ St-Maurice-l'Exil - St-Altan
4 × 925
Grenoble
Romans 20

Cestas ◆
◆ Le Barp
Cazaux
Biscarrosse

△ Golfech
2 × 1300

St-Etienne-des-Sorts

Cruas

Pierrelatte *Eurodif*
castin
Paul-3-Châteaux
ollène
Orange
arcoule
Canjuers

Mont-de-Marsan

Lodève

Phénix
280
Miramas
Istres *Cadarache*
□ Apt
✶✶

Malvési

△ Port-la-Nouvelle

Ile du Levant

Adapted from *Le Nouvel Observateur*

◆ Military factories and bases
◇ Uranium ore processing
■ Research centres
□ Manufacture of radioactive fuels
▨ Uranium mines

● Power stations in service
◉ Power stations under construction or projected
△ Projected sites for power stations
✶ Processing and storing of waste

objectives of the ecologists proved difficult to establish. In Brittany, in spite
of the presence of some 15,000 demonstrators on the dunes of Erdeven at
Easter 1975, the anti-nuclear struggle was conducted almost entirely by the
local population. The heavy mobilisation of the inhabitants caused the local

politicians in Erdeven, Plogoff, Ploumoguer and later Le Pellerin to declare themselves opposed to plans to build power stations and also to join the population in direct opposition to EDF and the power of the State. Faced with this opposition from whole communities prepared to take physical action to prevent access to the sites, EDF withdrew temporarily, switching the planned power station from one site to another over the next two years.

Things were very different in the case of Braud-et-Saint-Louis in the Blayais where local ecologists played a major part in mobilising the population. The defence committee which was set up (SYDAM) began an active struggle in 1974, first flooding the public inquiry with a quarter of a million letters protesting against the power station, and then in July 1975 physically opposing the beginning of construction. But contrary to the expectations of the militants who camped all summer in the region, the trial and conviction of several farmers did not trigger off another mobilisation of the population.

At Cruas-Meysse in the Ardèche, where information provided by the ecologists led to a heavy mobilisation of the population, relationships between the latter, united against aggression from outside, and the militants, themselves from outside, became strained. At Nogent, the somewhat conservative population showed suspicion and even hostility towards the 'long-haired Parisians', even though the latter were yet again the ones who, through the provision of information, had begun the mobilisation.

By contrast, the demonstration at Malville in the Isère in July 1976 brought together the ecologists and a population not yet sensitive to the nuclear debate, as well as large sections of public opinion. On the day when the demonstrators, mainly ecologists, arrived in the region to occupy the site of the fast-breeder as a symbolic expression of their opposition to everything that Super-Phoenix and the 'all-nuclear' programme represented, *Le Monde* published the appeal entitled 'No to Super-Phoenix', which condemned political and economic concentration, the type of development it imposes and the irresponsibility and dangers involved in the fast-breeder. Amongst the signatories who declared their solidarity with 'those wishing for a peaceful occupation of the site' were to be found, alongside the GSIEN, the Amis de la Terre and the anti-nuclear committees of various regions, the CFDT represented by several national secretaries and various trade unions, especially the EDF union, and the Socialist Party represented by several members of the central committee and several sections.

At the same time, the violence of the police repression mobilised the local population, and several local politicians set up the 'Interdepartmental committee of local representatives against Super-Phoenix'. The Socialist Party, after condemning the repression and declaring itself opposed to

Super-Phoenix, did not simply demand suspension of work on the site and the opening of a public debate, but actually took the initiative of beginning the debate. After the first free debate that had ever taken place in an elected assembly at that level, the General Council of the Isère voted in favour of the motion put down by the Socialist Party calling for the suspension of work on the site. The Council of the Savoie followed suit a month later.

Over the next few months, Malville Committees were formed not only in the region itself but in the whole of France and beyond. Malville became the symbol not only of the anti-nuclear struggle, but also of the struggle against a State considered responsible for the electro-nuclear programme. The dynamics of the protest within the nuclear industry took a decisive step forward with the strike of the workers at the reprocessing plant in La Hague in the autumn of 1976. Strikes in the CEA had begun in 1969 when the decision to abandon the graphite-gas system led the management to seek 3,600 redundancies.

The industrial orientation of the CEA, the privatisation of reprocessing, and the deterioration in working conditions merely served to aggravate the identity crisis of the 'creators of the French nuclear industry'. The dynamics of the protest developed from the defence of work and the firm towards a questioning of the aims of the work and of nuclear power. It was expressed not only in strikes, but in the growing importance of the role of the CFDT, which was the first to inform the public of the real state of the technical difficulties encountered by the Messmer programme and its consequences for working conditions in the nuclear industry.

With the strike, which began in September 1976, it was possible for the first time to bring together the demands of the workers in the nuclear industry and those of the population. The workers of La Hague wanted their factory to stay within the CEA in order to ensure the safety of both workers and population. The Cherbourg Assizes, which they organised in November 1976, provided the first forum for all those – workers, ecologists, anti-nuclear committees, scientists, the CFDT and the Socialist Party – who were opposed to the government's nuclear policy and who, in the final meeting, passed a resolution condemning the electro-nuclear programme.

The local elections

During this period, which saw the ecologists achieve their aim of forming a mass struggle, the local elections seemed to offer a good opportunity for demonstrating and intensifying public sensitivity towards ecological themes.

The most political amongst the militants saw the local elections as a suitable terrain for the new political action which they represented in opposition to traditional politics. In the words of the Amis de la Terre of Lille:

'The local elections represent the coming together of two visions of politics: the classical view, for which these elections have scant importance, and the vision in which the commune represents the major political stake. These elections must show a new vision of social life at work . . . Counter-powers must be formed in the commune which will be the only guarantee of a living democracy.' The unexpected success of the 96 ecology candidates, who obtained in general between 5% and 13% of the vote, demonstrated the influence of their themes. The candidates in Paris polled on average more than 10% of the vote and in Alsace Solange Fernex was elected with 62% of the vote.

The anti-nuclear struggle was a major theme in the election campaign. The *Gazette nucléaire*, with the help of ecologists, scientists and political militants, devised a series of questions, to be put to the candidates from the political parties, which used the case of nuclear power to raise the problems of technology, energy and society. And although in Paris the success of the candidates was the result of ecological awareness, in several regions it was the opposition of the ecology or left-wing candidates to nuclear power which ensured their success. Anti-nuclear candidates already elected had no difficulty in holding on to their seats in Brittany, whilst in the Rhône–Alpes region, several communes voted for left-wing candidates who adopted an anti-nuclear position.

It should be recalled that this great upsurge of anti-nuclear action occurred in 1976 and 1977, in an atmosphere charged with expectations of a victory of a Left which did not seem insensitive to the aspirations represented by the anti-nuclear militants.

THE COLLAPSE

Malville 1977 and the elections of March 1978

The events of 31 July 1977 at Malville and the results of the March 1978 elections revealed, however, that the formation of a great anti-nuclear struggle was more apparent than real. The ecologists' attempt to set up a mass movement around the nuclear conflict met with failure. The reason was that the upsurge of 1976–7 had concealed the ambiguities which were to cause the struggle to break up.

The months following the Malville demonstration in 1976 were increasingly dominated by 'direct actions' which, together with civil disobedience, became one of the main watchwords at the Morestel Assizes in February 1977. These Assizes, which were attended by 3,000 militants from the whole of France and several European countries, as well as representatives not only of the unions but also of the parties of the Left, were dominated by the debate over the means to be used – violent or non-violent – in the struggle against EDF and the State: never at any time was there any discussion of the aims of the demonstration planned for the following summer. The watchword of the Assizes, 'Legitimate defence against Super-Phoenix', was justified in the following way:

The aim of our struggle is clearer than ever: to ensure the protection of our own and future generations against the insane risk and also against the model of society which is being imposed upon us by force . . . We must give the green light to all forms of action which will hold up work . . . And challenge the Super Phoenix project from all possible sides by preventing it in every possible way and place from being built. EDF has turned Malville into a fortified camp with barbed wire, electric fences and police dogs; we must strike at the fortress from all sides.

This coming together at Morestel of local defensive action and the general opposition to the social order and the State created a dangerous confusion. The attempt by some ecologists to bring organisation into a struggle with clearly defined objectives came up against the refusal, shared by libertarians, anarchists, and local militants, of any kind of organisation. The various forces each maintained their own objectives and accepted coordination only for one-off actions. The demonstration of 31 July was more a gathering of diverse protests than an action oriented and organized by precise objectives. This refusal of organisation was directly counter to the wishes of the political ecologists.

The drama of 31 July 1977 began well before that date. In spite of the arrival of 60,000 militants from the whole of France and several European countries, the hope for a great social struggle against nuclear power was already compromised. The CFDT and the Socialist Party, which had initially taken part in preparations for the day, withdrew in concern over the absence of any control of the demonstration. On 31 July, the demonstrators clashed with the police, without preparation of any kind, without ever having discussed the objectives and the strategy of the demonstration. The fields became a battleground where the demonstrators left one dead and several wounded. Their stunned retreat in the rain was followed the next night by a police manhunt.

It was in just the same way that the ecologists launched into the general election campaign of March 1978. The setting up of Ecology 78 after the local elections had favoured the creation of a vast current of opinion at the expense of an action defined by a programme and an organisation. Despite obvious divergences between some militants and some groups, there was no debate on the objectives of the campaign or of the ecology movement in general. The warnings of some and the last minute withdrawals of others did not change the main fact: the ecologists were going into the electoral battle as no more than a current of opinion, formed on a theme of central importance and around a general sensibility, but offering no real choice to an electorate which knew that the great confrontation of Right and Left would have profound consequences for the future of society. The failure of the ecology candidates (there were three times as many as in 1977 but their share of the vote was cut by half) demonstrated the inability of the anti-nuclear current to organise itself into a political force.

PART TWO

HISTORY OF THE RESEARCH

vvv

A conflict of cultures

THE ANTI-NUCLEAR EXPLOSION

The great refusal

Denied by some, stressed by others, accepted or rejected by the same militants according to the precise state of the debate, fear underlies the anti-nuclear action. But fear of what? Certainly of the risk of accident, of a 'nuclear excursion', of the possible failure of a complex tool, and on several occasions these themes were broached from a highly technical viewpoint. But there was much more to it than that. The idea of a breakdown belongs to a certain kind of rationality, enables one statistical calculation to be opposed to another, and the enormity of the risk or the number of potential casualties to be emphasised in answer to those who invoke the infinitesimal probability of an accident.

This rational version of the fear was common amongst those who came to the struggle through scientific or union practice. It is far less common amongst militants less well equipped with scientific knowledge of nuclear matters. In their case, beyond the precise risk of accident looms the spectre of a much more general threat to life. The human species is in mortal danger. Nuclear power is the plague, a cancer, a mysterious and terrible disease: 'People are still shit-scared', said Jean-Pierre Provins, a farmer from the Nogent region who was a member of the Paris group. The sentiment was broadly echoed by Piccolo: 'We've been publishing tracts for two years, and we tell people: it's going to kill you.' In Malville, the feeling was expressed very well by Claudine: 'I got into the action to defend my kids' future, the future of mankind.' In her opinion, with nuclear power society was collapsing into aberration, madness, no longer respecting the laws of nature. With nuclear power, according to Georges Flamand of the Amis de la Terre in Lille, 'we feel threatened in our most basic being'. Fear is not only the feeling by which some people are drawn into the struggle. As a pure reaction, it calls upon an instinct which does away with the need to think of the action in terms of social relations. To evoke it is to appeal to humanity, the species, or civilisation, to locate oneself before or beyond a social conflict.

By contrast, when the Paris group came to analyse the search for a social adversary and to embark on a critique of power, Roland Maire, an engineer at EDF and a trade unionist with the CFDT, but also Emmanuel Kropo, a scientific researcher, and the three women in the group, Sophia, Alice and Jacqueline Monceau, vigorously rejected the theme of danger and fear that they had all accepted until then.

More generally, the language of fear which was present at the beginning of the intervention became blurred and tended to fade away as the research advanced. Although it was never abandoned entirely, the militants recognised themselves less and less in the references to danger. They were well aware of the role that the theme played in the practice of the movement, but they themselves moved away from it as they progressed in the search for a social definition of their action which could not rest content with an appeal to a socially indeterminate emotion.

This instability of the theme of fear, which disintegrated only to resurface from time to time, led us to associate its emergence with the image of a crisis: fear would seem to be the subjective translation of a situation of crisis.

Such a hypothesis first required a return to history: has the atom always been associated with the images of death and destruction on which the nuclear anguish feeds? Many members of the public associate the image of the bomb with the image of nuclear power stations, and the works of C. Guedeney and G. Mendel (see bibliography) clearly demonstrate the constant presence of anguish, latent and repressed more often than expressed in the regions affected by the building of a power station.

But in the groups this association was to break down. Bourguignon, a CFDT unionist, explained to the Malville group that the workers at Marcoule and the population in general had always come to terms with reactors built to manufacture plutonium for bombs. Furthermore, both in Paris and Malville, militants like Leforestier, Jean-Philippe Pharisca or Hannibal, referred on several occasions to the fifties and sixties when everybody thought that the civilian use of nuclear power would 'redeem the atom'. The civilian atom was not always felt as a threat, and the fear of nuclear power is a social phenomenon which is set in a very precise historical context.

The anti-nuclear struggle developed at the end of a period of growth. With economic crisis and unemployment came the doubt, the image of a society unable to master its own change. In that case, might not the anti-nuclear movement be one of the expressions of a general crisis of a world which has lost control of itself?

In the early stages of the intervention, everybody, with variations, expressed their feeling of disarray before what was still described as a dominant order, a system which is no longer comprehensible, which crushes and alienates, which is beyond even those who are supposed to be directing it.

Sometimes the fear was not related to a crisis of civilisation but, in a much more limited way, to the risk of upheaval in a local way of life.

Saint-Hilaire, in Paris, who worked at the SNCF and owned a garden in the Nogent region, told the group how he had tried to mobilise the population of Nogent-sur-Seine: the projected power station would bring the atom, but behind the atom would come the industry with its cortege of immigrant workers, a source of anxiety to some of the inhabitants.

Such resistance is useful for the defence of very precise interests, and, in some cases, brings higher prices for the sale of expropriated lands, but it would be too restricting to stop short at an analysis which would make the movement no more than an expression of a localised rejection of the administration. If resistance there is, then it is far more global, appealing to life against death, to the great balances, and ultimately to nature. Naturalism and fear go hand in hand and determine an asocial vision of the action but also of the actor, of whom Philippe Lebreton, in Malville, gave a striking version: this interlocutor, one of the national leaders of the movement, called for the reconciliation of man with nature and appealed to the biological constants found in all species. Initially, his argument was accepted by Jean-Jacques Rodrigo, Marie-Jeanne Vercors, who was for several months secretary of the Malville Committee, and François Delain, a farmer who was very well known in the movement. Bourguignon speculated: 'Yes to the hypothesis that at certain stages of our development, the species, all species, might be able to evolve brakes for self-preservation. Perhaps the anti-nuclear movement is one such brake?' It is the species which is at stake, humanity in its relationship with nature.

But Philippe Lebreton's argument very soon encountered a strong resistance which testified to the group's ability to go beyond the reduction of social problems to biological problems that the interlocutor was trying to make them accept. Christophe was the first to show indignation: to follow Lebreton was to see only the relationship of humanity with nature, to close one's eyes to social inequalities, to make no distinction between the Left and the Right, ultimately to resign oneself to impotence. He was far from being alone in the group which was united in loud laughter when Christophe pointed out the contradiction between Lebreton's language of impotence and certain calls to militant action on a poster signed by the same Lebreton.

The group did not want to become imprisoned in a biological view. Confronted with the demands of the struggle, the language of fear and the instinct for survival crumbled, opening the way to other hypotheses.

The crisis in the values of industrial society

In this phase of the intervention, the 'we' of the group was not constituted by fear and even less by the feeling of belonging to a renegade social class, but by a common rejection of the values of industrial civilisation.

The rejection of industrial values

The idea of an almost natural evolution of societies along the path of progress was called into question. On this point there was unanimity in both groups: 'Ten years ago', recalled Hannibal, 'when people talked about progress all you could do was keep your trap shut.' Nowadays, everybody is in agreement in challenging the image of social progress through growth. In opposition to the Marxist model which postulates the potentially unlimited development of the productive forces, everybody is receptive to the idea of finite resources and the idea that there are thresholds and limits which cannot be passed: industrial civilisation is on the edge of the abyss, it is auto-destructing, producing more pollution than wealth, bringing a factitious progress, as deceptive, said Christophe, as the calculations of government experts who are unable to see that the GNP is rising because pollution and waste are increasing. Both groups provided a flood of examples drawn from the demonstrations of Illich and daily life: the use of industrial techniques in agriculture is ruining the land, the household gadgets which were supposed to liberate women are in fact forcing them to work relentlessly, and so on.

There was general agreement in the groups over this challenging of the values of industrial society, even though it was expressed differently by different people, progressively by some and as nostalgia for the past by others.

Claudine was the most sensitive to the regressions concealed by the cult of progress and pointed out that before the French Revolution there had been 450 schools of music in France, whereas today there were only 120 conservatoires: 'So I don't see how you can claim that the level of culture has gone up as a result of industrial growth.'

Others were turned more towards the future: Georges Flamand asserted that our society 'has several possible futures'; Yves Le Gall, using the specific case of agriculture, with which he was well acquainted, explained: 'It isn't a question of saying: let's stop progress or let's go back to the good old days, but of trying to imagine a different kind of progress . . .; one can imagine other paths for progress.' But the solitary voices of Georges and Yves elicited little reaction from their respective groups; the rejection of industrial values was stronger than the interpretations, retrospective or progressive, that might be given of it.

The crisis of science

From the very beginning, the anti-nuclear movement attracted a fair number of militants or sympathisers who came from the world of science but whose participation in the movement was motivated by a questioning of science related to the rejection of the values of industrial society.

The great hope of the fifties was a thing of the past: Leforestier told the group how he had learned about radioactivity at school: 'It was great, it was the future . . .; but after a while we realised it was one almighty cock-up.' It was not society as such that was in question but its inability to solve the problems of society and in particular to adapt to the demands of industrialisation: we know in theory how to reprocess radioactive waste but industrially we can scarcely manage it. And how can one not be filled with doubt when an installation as sophisticated as a nuclear power station is still at the mercy of ordinary human carelessness, as in the case of the technician who almost caused a terrible catastrophe at Browns Ferry with a mere candle? This was a level of criticism which commanded wide agreement and was argued energetically by Véronique Uri, a researcher and a militant from the LCR, the Union of Researchers and the Malville Committee in Grenoble: it is an illusion, she declared on several occasions, to believe that we will manage to dominate all the technical or scientific difficulties; there is no single person who has an intellectual grasp of the whole of the electro-nuclear process.

The debates of the Paris group during its first weekend provided the best opportunity for analysing the nature of the movement's criticism of science.

At first the group resisted anti-science, the appeal to nature or to knowledge not recognised by the scientific establishment. Piccolo, who defended such ideas and, in particular, supported alternative medicines such as homoeopathy against the orthodox medicine of the official institutions, was listened to but tended to be relegated to the fringes of the group, largely because, in the realm of energy policy, it is difficult to set nature against technology and alternative science against orthodox science. The real temptation for anti-nuclear militants lies rather in the opposite direction: using science to construct an alternative social model. That, after all, is something that scientists, like the mathematician Courrèges, have themselves tried to do, with the *Alter* project, for example, which proposes a model of consumption that can be satisfied without recourse to nuclear energy and which considerably reduces the need for oil. The authors of such a project might claim that the group's discussion of it did not do them justice, but the important point was that the actors emphatically rejected a purely 'scientific' project which ignores the political and social determinants of any energy policy and which is dangerous because it leads to the authoritarian imposition of a mode of consumption.

35

The ecologists, naturally Rousseauists, did not want to invent a new Geneva subjected to the imperious dictate of science. In opposition to a conception in which society is submitted to science, Jean-Philippe Pharisca, a physicist at the CNRS (National Centre for Scientific Research), subjected the scientistic illusion to a criticism which frequently echoed the themes of the review *Impascience*. He was concerned at the development of a science which no longer seemed to have even knowledge as its objective, but rather to be mesmerised by the power of the means themselves. He remarked, together with Roland Maire and Véronique, both of whom also had scientific training, on the compartmentalisation of scientific work.

Pharisca: 'The present development of science is so impetuous and so closely linked to political and ideological questions that you end up wondering if what we know has any usefulness for the scientific problematic itself. There are fundamental mechanisms, for example in high energy physics, which might occur at a less macroscopic level and which could be discovered "softer" research using weaker means.' He then elaborated on the classic theme: 'The development of science at all costs can no longer be considered as beneficial when science has been integrated into a power structure and a development which looks more like forward retreat.' Jean-Philippe Pharisca carried the group along with him and thereby contributed to the development of a social movement, for nothing could be more contradictory than a movement which, instead of making technological and scientific knowledge the stake of a social conflict, opposes one model of society to another in the name of scientific arguments, as if, for example, nuclear power led straight to dictatorship and solar energy to democracy, a form of reasoning which some members of the group often came close to but which, in the end, they managed to avoid. Thus the way in which the Paris group handled the theme of science was original: in the movement's press and in the practice of many militants the idea of a 'solar' solution receives a great deal of attention and in terms which suggest that a science or a technology induces a type of society, but the Paris group strongly rejected such a technological determinism in order to pursue a critical analysis of scientific knowledge and its use which restored science to the realm of political and social relations.

The meetings with the communist interlocutors
During the sessions in which the groups met Communist Party officials, there was opposition between the values of industrial society, defended with conviction by the communist interlocutors, and the counter-values presented in the preceding section. The Communist Party is not only the left-wing political force which defends nuclear energy. It counters the theme of waste with the under-consumption of millions of workers, the criticism of science with absolute confidence in the possibilities of the scientific and

technical revolution, the idea of finite energy resources with the unlimited prospects of nuclear fusion, the questioning of Concorde and more generally of the social usefulness of certain industrial projects with the protection of jobs, the image of a growth which generates social inequalities with another kind of growth . . . The representatives of the Communist Party were opposed to the government's nuclear programme and in particular to the strengthening of the power of private industrial monopolies, but this was not the ground on which disagreement emerged and discussion took place. For the anti-nuclear militants, the communist position was no more than an attitude of principle favourable to massive reliance on the nuclear industry. The communist representatives, for their part, supported some of the anti-nuclear demands, but did not hide their opposition to their general orientation, which seemed to them to ignore the urgent need for another, democratic, type of growth in production, as far removed from the present policy as from the utopias of non-growth.

Both groups united against the interlocutor. The opposed values which they were defending gave them a strength and homogeneity that were never to be seen again in any other session. All their members were united by a profound solidarity, a consensus which demonstrated their acute awareness of being the bearers of common ideas and a common sensibility.

Neither side was able to claim victory. In both camps, each person argued his convictions and staked out his territory, rejecting the other side into non-sense. In Malville, there were mutual accusations of mysticism and wishful thinking. In Paris, the clash was more violent. Hannibal, in a state of great irritation, accused the communist interlocutor of not knowing Carnot's second principle. Monsieur Metzger was not to be outdone: he asked what chapel he was in and expressed amazement at hearing a sermon for a new religion. Tendential lowering of profit margins versus the second law of thermodynamics . . . as Roland Maire fully realised: 'The paradigms of explanation are totally different.'

The behaviour of the two groups showed that the anti-nuclear movement had very much left behind the ideological categories of the working-class movement. It also showed a rejection of the political model represented by the Communist Party, but above all it conveyed a declaration: the intention of an actor to become a social movement, to return to a radical critique of society to which the Communist Party would become increasingly alien. In Paris, Georges Flamand was the main accuser: 'For me, the anti-nuclear movement is an expression of the class struggle in the sense that it is a cry from the little people without power, who see decisions about energy, which are enormous decisions, being taken without consulting them . . . I'm absolutely amazed, I don't understand how the Communist Party can't see that.' In Malville, Leforestier went much further in this split over the question of belonging to a popular class. As Véronique Uri stressed, not only does the Communist Party never agree to attend unitarian meetings, but it is also on the side of law and order, of the forces of repression, of the Ministry of the Interior, whereas 'when *we* say anything, you understand, we get our faces kicked in by the fuzz'. And when Marc Blachère retorted that in that area the Communist Party had nothing to learn from anybody, Leforestier was more specific: 'There *was* a time when the cops used to beat you up, but now they go easy on you.' Both in Paris and in Malville, there was a very keen sense of belonging to a nascent social force, in contrast with a Communist Party which defends a largely institutionalised working-class movement.

The anti-nuclear movement had proven its desire to establish itself as a historical actor on the basis of the great refusal which gave it birth. All that remained now was for it to turn this determination, which was still pure subjectivity, against a social rather than ideological and political adversary.

AN ANTI-TECHNOCRATIC STRUGGLE?

We had wanted to know if the actors were capable of defining their action socially and politicising a cultural movement, whose vitality we have seen, by engaging in a struggle in which the adversary is the author of the nuclear programme and its technology. The answer had to be no, for the sessions in which the groups met interlocutors embodying the technocratic adversary were, from this point of view, a failure.

Experts and counter-experts

We had wondered whether the groups would set themselves up as counter-experts, challenging the energy policy of EDF or the CEA in economic or technical terms. Roland Maire in Paris immediately attacked Monsieur Gauvenet, head of security at the CEA, on this ground. He raised the question of the CEA's policy on safety studies, the way in which, according to him, the results were published, the inadequacy or the lack of freedom of the security services, the total lack of knowledge of the mechanical problems of container cracking . . . A barrage of questions that Monsieur Gauvenet answered with precision, showing the group beyond doubt that Roland Maire, relayed briefly by Hannibal, had chosen the wrong terrain.

In fact, the group was in no real position to oppose an interlocutor who displayed such a clear awareness of his responsibilities, and a determination never to allow the imperatives of profit or production to interfere with those of safety. The Paris group reserved a rather friendly welcome for Monsieur Gauvenet, whose professional logic favoured the interests of the workers in the nuclear industry. Roland Maire's polemic at the beginning of the session finally caused irritation in the group. Georges Flamand gave voice to an annoyance that had been visible for some time. Feeling that the debate was getting nowhere, he wanted to leave aside its technical aspects. The problem 'has nothing to do with the in-fighting between those responsible for building and those responsible for safety. It's political.' Nor was it a question of whether people do their work seriously and conscientiously: 'at the political level, that argument is totally inadequate'.

With Monsieur Boiteux, the group avoided economic or technical debates. The criticisms, coming mainly from Jean-Philippe Pharisca, Hannibal and Roland Maire, did not get very far because the group refused to follow. In particular, when Monsieur Boiteux declared that nuclear energy can be shown to be the least costly, the least polluting and the least dangerous or, at least, the least deadly of energy forms, Emmanuel Kropo retorted: 'That subject has taken up whole public debates, and I don't know if there's any real interest in discussing it.' The Paris group, then, was most reluctant to follow those who, perhaps because they had real competence, were momentarily tempted to set themselves up as counter-experts. Here the anti-technocratic protest was not to be conducted on purely technical grounds. The debate was elsewhere, political and social.

But it was precisely this refusal to engage in a debate in which the advantages and disadvantages of nuclear energy would be judged on the basis of just such an argument over facts and figures which most concerned the interlocutor. For Monsieur Boiteux, the real danger of the protest was not its opposition to nuclear energy but the refusal of the militants to become involved in a rational debate and their appeal to the most irrational fears and anxieties to mobilise people nowadays against nuclear power. In this way, according to Monsieur Boiteux, the protest ran the risk of rejecting not nuclear power but the world of reason and rationality itself, a world to which he himself wished to remain attached and which he defended from the point of view of coherence of choices, against a world which would be completely dominated by the irrational.

He did not present himself as an unconditional defender of all the forms of the nuclear industry. Nor did he think that EDF was imposing a policy on the country; the company was applying government decisions and on its own, if it was not to abuse its powers, it could only make technical choices dictated by economic and industrial considerations. As a producer of electricity, EDF had no reason to be opposed to the search for other methods of generating electricity or, more generally, for energy other than nuclear energy. His position was resolutely set far below the objectives attacked by the members of the group, which were global and social rather than technical.

In Malville also the debates occasionally took a technical or economic turn. Véronique Uri and Jean-Jacques Rodrigo, who was one of the principal leaders of the Grenoble–Malville Committee, challenged the way in which

EDF did its economic sums and François Delain showed that he was well informed in technological and scientific matters, but both Monsieur Daurès and Monsieur Thiriet were on favourable ground and developed a line of argument which was only really disputed when Monsieur Thiriet declared his conviction that science can solve the problems of reprocessing at the industrial stage.

Clearly, the movement was not fundamentally involved in a dispute of experts who could develop counter-propositions to the government's energy policy. Certainly, it called for technical solutions other than nuclear power, but, faced with interlocutors who were the authors or the managers of a programme they were disputing, the groups did not see their task as proposing a programme or discussing the technical means of putting research into practice. They tried rather to define a conflictual relation which did not, without collapsing almost immediately, involve technical debates.

This refusal of wholesale commitment to counter-expertise represented a departure from the usual practice of the militants, who, in the groups, discarded the scientific or technical discussions and demonstrations which are so frequent in the day-to-day life of the anti-nuclear movement. In return, the interlocutors in no way denied the importance of the anti-nuclear protest and in particular never simply opposed economic or technical necessity to unrealistic ideas. They all believed they were serving social and economic progress whilst still being aware of the difficulties of the nuclear enterprise. In this way, as well as by their presence, they agreed to situate the discussion at the level of general conceptions of social life and so recognised the seriousness of the anti-nuclear position, even though they rejected it. But the anti-nuclear militants were unable to show that, in the presence of the representatives of the nuclear industry, they could go beyond a global protest, offer a more precise criticism and define other modes of development.

The intervention had shown us what the movement did not want to be, but we still did not know what a positive definition of its social commitment might be.

The rejection of the adversary

If the anti-nuclear movement is to establish itself as a historical actor opposed to the technocratic adversary, it must first accept the idea itself of a social and not purely ideological or cultural conflict, and that implies that it must not place itself solely in the realm of values. Then it must extricate itself from a critique of the dominant order which dissolves the adversary into a 'system' without actors.

Can one really reproach EDF and the CEA for representing values disputed by the movement? In Paris, it was mainly Hannibal, Jean-Philippe Pharisca and Roland Maire who criticised Monsieur Boiteux for the model of growth in which EDF's policy is set. But they did not get very far: EDF's general manager declared that EDF's forecasts tended towards a 'less materialist and less energy-oriented' development, that he was not a partisan of growth at all costs, that the graphs had been interpreted wrongly and that 'pronouncements about nuclear power' were generally distorted; he turned the debate towards other problems and nobody resisted.

In Malville, even more clearly, the group was willing not to dwell purely on the conflict of values. When Monsieur Thiriet declared: 'If you think economic growth isn't necessary, then there's no debate, obviously. We can stop right now', Christophe answered: 'The basic problem is not whether we want economic growth, but whether we want to reduce social inequalities, create another kind of life, another kind of consumption, another kind of production.' The interlocutor was confident that science could solve the technical problems and thought, with qualifications, that economic growth and more especially energy growth would lead to progress and the reduction of social inequalities. It was on these premises, on the basis of this social analysis, that he was attacked.

Whether they were the deciders or the managers of the French electro-nuclear programme, the officials from the CEA and EDF were above all for the protesters the embodiment of a system, of a dominant order which, through nuclear power, is leading society down the path of police repression and totalitarianism, a vision which was less strong in Paris than in Malville, where the group was composed of the actors, and to some extent the organisers, of a struggle which had clashed head-on with police repression.

We had reached an important stage in the intervention where we did not know if the militants would develop a language, common in the movement, denouncing a technology and the damage it causes, or rather confront an adversary which imposes the nuclear technology, attack nuclear power or the technocrats, condemn a technology for the society it creates or declare that a type of social relations leads to technological choices which exclude alternative solutions. In this respect, the two groups behaved in different ways which foreshadowed the opposite ways in which they were to behave in the central phase of the intervention.

The meeting of the Grenoble–Malville group with Monsieur Daurès, the director of the Bugey power station, was not a success for the anti-nuclear militants. Christophe, Jean-Jacques and Véronique saw the massive recourse to nuclear energy as a source of increasing inflexibility and inertia. The policy imposed by EDF could not be changed, and so we found ourselves on a course that leads to irrationality, since we do not at present know how to store radioactive waste for extremely long periods of time. Monsieur Daurès rejected this fatalism and technological determinism; he did not even believe that our society was going to trust itself to the 'all-nuclear' concept; the share of nuclear energy in consumption would be smaller than the share of oil now.

In the course of this long and very important discussion, Monsieur Daurès constantly emphasised the political determinants of technological choices whilst his adversaries stressed the momentum effect both of technologies and of the inertia of the apparatuses. Likewise, several members of the group described the constant stepping-up of police surveillance measures in and around the power stations, whereas Monsieur Daurès thought such measures were connected with the present social and political tension and were likely to disappear once the power stations were no longer seen as a political stake. Overall, the difference in attitudes was similar to the one found in the special issue of *Que Choisir?* (Which?) which set out the arguments of the supporters and opponents of nuclear power: the former were mainly concerned to defend a social and political analysis, whilst the latter were afraid of the constraints arising mainly, as they saw it, from the technologies themselves or from the ability of the great productive apparatuses to function more like machines than centres of political decision. Without exaggerating this opposition, it did at least testify to the great difficulty experienced by the anti-nuclear militants in transforming their anxiety into a properly social critique precisely when their interlocutor had no difficulty whatsoever in dissociating himself from technological determinism.

The group's reaction to this embarrassing situation was to suspend discussion with their interlocutor, ignoring him completely whilst they talked amongst themselves. There was no longer conflict, but distance and division. The group, and more especially Leforestier and Valence, embarked upon a critique of the State whilst Monsieur Daurès talked to his wife and his colleague. This breakdown of the debate was pointed out by the secretary who asked what it meant. Esther, a militant from the local Committee, on the one hand, and Monsieur Daurès on the other were in agreement: it was an opposition of two different worlds, two different languages. Thus the critique of the 'all-nuclear' policy and the repression it implies seemed to be the negation of the social conflict, leading the movement towards a division which prevented it from considering the technocracy as a social adversary.

In Paris, Monsieur Gauvenet and Monsieur Boiteux stood up just as well to the attacks on the CEA and EDF, but the group adopted a very different perspective which revealed its ability to develop a properly social critique of the nuclear policy.

Georges Flamand accused the CEA of developing 'without observation and participation from outside', an argument which was to be frequently reiterated by different people: the CEA and EDF were considered to be motivated by a logic which evolves without any possibility of democratic control. But why should this type of logic be criticised? Because it is contrary to the general interest, but also because it increases the distance between the world of the decision-makers and what Roland Maire called the social body. Roland Maire, Jean-Philippe Pharisca and Hannibal pointed this out in Paris: the transition of nuclear power to the industrial stage was an insane undertaking that the 'social body' was no longer prepared to follow. It was not a matter of rejecting development but of ensuring, in some way or other, that it was submitted to popular choices. 'Behind the choice of a technology', said Roland Maire to Monsieur Boiteux, 'there is a sort of choice of a model of development and society. And I deny EDF the right to make that choice. It isn't for them to decide but the social body. By what method I don't know.'

In Paris, this rejection was expressed in moderate terms which defined a conflict, but in Malville the nucleocrats were accused of leading the world blindly towards catastrophe, of being irresponsible or lunatic, so that the fight against them was no longer a social struggle but the crusade of Life against Evil.

Christophe accused Monsieur Daurès of self-alienation whilst Leforestier claimed that the technocrats know nothing. Claudine, pushing to its extreme this logic of rejecting the interlocutor into non-sense, declared that 'with technocratic rationalisation, we end in the absurd' and even went so far as to compare Monsieur Daurès to a Nazi doctor. Thus the image of conflict was disintegrating before us; we were in the presence not of two social actors locked in struggle for control of the same stake, but of people who thought they represented life, the species and reason and saw in front of them only the absurd, plague, self-alienation and barbarity.

The final attempt

The groups endeavoured to overcome this failure by stressing the directing role of EDF and the CEA in defining and setting up the electro-nuclear programme. At every turn, the interlocutors replied that the power to take decisions belonged to politicians and the government, that EDF and the CEA merely clarified the decision and, once it was made, respected it; and was it not exaggerated to reproach them with not opposing a programme which corresponded to their vocation? But this argument was never accepted. In Malville, Christophe, Jean-Jacques Rodrigo and Yves Le Gall were the ones who reacted most strongly to it: they recalled the existence of the PEON Commission (Commission for the Production of Electricity of Nuclear Origin) and the way in which, according to them, the Messmer plan had been dictated by EDF. In Paris, it was mainly Roland Maire, Jean-Philippe Pharisca and Georges Flamand who put forward an identical argument.

43

The groups thus showed themselves able to develop their opposition to those whom they were now designating as the technocrats. But the success was fragile; neither group advanced beyond a comparatively undifferentiated view of the nucleocratic adversary, whom they located as much in government as in EDF and the CEA without being able to define the real centre of decision-taking. The dominant image was the one developed by Roland Maire of 'occult relations and nobody knows where the balance of power is located', an image which included the idea of a domination of the politicians by the technocrats – 'the technician prepares the decision in such a way that responsibility circulates without anyone ever knowing who has assumed it'.

The interlocutors did not just resist these representations by maintaining their positions firmly and insisting that EDF and the CEA were subordinated to the government; they counter-attacked on the very terrain of democracy itself. Monsieur Daurès could scarcely get an answer from Christophe when he asked him: 'How can we and how have we the right to go and impose in Bouvesse a choice made at the national level? Not a single party, union or democratic organisation has given me an answer to that question which I have asked over and over again.' The group was thrown into utter confusion.

The researchers concluded from this that the strength of the anti-nuclear action was not to be found where it appears first and most vividly: in the denunciation of a technology and an industry. It was a purely negative conclusion but indispensable to the further progress of the analysis. The groups themselves were to be pushed in a new direction by the results of these meetings.

EXEMPLARY COMMUNITY AND UTOPIA

Exemplary action

Malville. On the previous evening the group had met Monsieur Daurès and Monsieur Thiriet in succession. Its reactions showed that it had realised its failure.

Marie-Jo: 'As electricity consumers, we have our share of responsibility. That might seem a bit strong, but it'll be true as long as we haven't found a way of getting people to understand that we're going to cut down on our personal consumption of electricity and find other ways of living.'

Marie-Jeanne Vercors: 'Yes, we're always looking for scapegoats, but we've got to come down to the fact that we're all in it.'

We must challenge ourselves: the adversary, the State or the system are first and foremost in our heads: the search for a social adversary can only conceal an inability to challenge oneself.

This belief in the virtues of exemplary action, of challenging oneself and one's life-style as a possible means of acting on society, came to light in Paris in similar conditions, during closed sessions and thus in reaction to the debates of the open sessions.

Emmanuel Kropo and Jacqueline Monceau insisted on the idea of a coherence between the way one lives and the way one talks. Georges Flamand illustrated this idea from his own experience in a commune and stressed the need for anyone who wants to be fully responsible, and that meant the anti-nuclear movement, to free themselves of the social-State, the insurance-State which offers assistance. Hannibal saw in the anti-nuclear movement people who had come to testify, to alert others to problems and 'not to win something'. He thus brought a messianic dimension to this ethic of conviction. Roland Maire saw in this theme of exemplary action a means of demonstrating the incoherence of those who organise and manage society. They were all to varying degrees sensitive to this image of a peaceful power which, purely through witness, ought to lead to victory. But it was Haggar who expressed this ethic most forcefully. For a militant trade unionist, his words were surprising: 'Organisations make demands. But when you get down to it none of those demands change anything . . . That's why the anti-nuclear movement is so important, and that's why, if you're a convinced anti-nuclear supporter, you have to begin by challenging yourself . . . and that's what embarrasses the rest of society.' For Haggar, the force of example transcended union action, of which he was nonetheless one of the most active supporters in La Hague, since it ensured the transition to a different society and will allow us to 'shake the whole system'.

It should be pointed out that Haggar was not an exception in the CFDT. Although they might not always go quite so far, there are many in the confederation who would recognise themselves in the positions he defended. A few months after the intervention itself there was a meeting over the first version of this text of several officials from the CFDT, Roland Maire and three of the researchers from the team. The first reaction of one of the CFDT militants was to confirm the determination to link, 'as complements, with the one feeding the other', the realm of political action and the realm of exemplary action.

Located at the very heart of a philosophy which has the utmost confidence in the force of conviction, exemplary action seems able to inspire a strategy for struggle around the concept of non-violence which, in theory at least, allows the reconciliation of ethic and efficacy.

The ethic of conviction enabled the groups to rally after sessions in which they had scarcely been able to affirm themselves as a social force. A tension towards the future and a personal commitment rather than a guideline for a strategy, it can be an all too convenient refuge, but also the force which sustains an action not yet able to define itself in a practical way and which is not yet in the realm of the possible but only in that of sincerity and moral exigency.

A community sensibility

The further away the actors moved from the idea of a social conflict, the more they expressed a community sensibility which provided an anchorage for the cultural protest and a privileged domain for the exercise of the ethic of conviction.

In Paris, Georges Flamand, who had experienced the cultural drift of the years after 68 in experiments in communal living in which, without bitterness, he saw the 'isolation of a circle of drop-outs', refused to judge it negatively. 'I had the possibility of acting and intervening . . ., the feeling of possessing my life.' Faced with very strong resistance from Pelot, for whom the community sensibility clashed with the demands of the struggle and its organisation, Emmanuel Kropo and Jacqueline Monceau defended the importance of the commune experiments. Emmanuel was the most precise: for him they were a form of grass-roots organisation which sprang up 'without waiting for the great mobilisation, without ritualising and mediatising political action'.

More generally, in the Paris group, those who advanced the community themes presented them as the starting point for action. Georges Flamand insisted that it was in a commune that he had realised, along with others, that nuclear energy made it possible to have a commitment. Likewise, Haggar and Hannibal stressed the importance of practices which challenge a 'life-style'. None of this, in fact, was properly developed, and the Paris group gave no more than a pallid account of this community dimension. That might have been due to the agitator, who did not encourage debate on this level – to the extent that several months later in the meeting to discuss the first version of this book, the members of the Paris group bitterly reproached him with having always tried to minimise this component of the action. But it also meant that this group went much further than the Malville group in the search for a social movement.

In Malville, by contrast, we were witness to a clear process in which the concept of community emerged and unfurled to the detriment of the previous day's debates which became blurred and forgotten. It was the day after the sessions with the managerial interlocutors, whom the group had rejected into the realm of the absurd and non-sense, turning in upon itself in search of its own responsibilities. Now it began to invoke the warmth of communal life, the idea of a richer, more convivial collective life.

Leforestier: 'We're each of us shut away in our own little house, in our own little flat, each in front of our own little telly.'

Marie-Jeanne Vercors: 'I couldn't agree more . . . Because you could very easily get together with ten other people for a washing machine, we can change our way of living . . .'

The debate was launched, and Marie-Jo, who was there for the last time because she preferred to devote herself to the local action, explained that for her it was more a matter of creating different relationships between people than of living communally: 'I prefer to say collective life.' Esther and Marie-Jeanne accepted the formulation which Christophe interpreted: 'A commune is a closed group, whereas collective life is more open, each individual is in communication with everbody.'

But there is a considerable difference between advocating community principles and seeing the struggle as a social movement, set in a network of social relations. The direction the group was taking not only brought out that distance but increased it, tô the point of challenging the sociological method itself which allows for meetings with social partners and adversaries: why bother with such meetings if what the movement expresses can disregard the outside world, if the really important things are the ones that take place amongst the militants themselves?

This gave us the measure of the great distance from the interlocutors of the day before. The group fenced itself off in community withdrawal, became immersed in debates which diverted it from the effort of analysis which is at the heart of sociological intervention and lapsed into a dynamic which gave expression to internal tensions alien to the struggle. The end of the session was, in fact, dominated by the problem of who was to be allowed to speak and when. We were then furthest away from the search for the social movement, in a group which had become a natural group, turned in upon itself, a fact criticised by Yves Le Gall, who denounced it as a 'functioning of the Malville Committee type'. At this stage of the intervention, the community dimension, as it was expressed in the Malville group, seemed to be drawing the militants towards a break with society rather than towards action.

There are very few interventions in which the actors leave the realm of the values which inspire them in order to give a precise and concrete definition of the kind of society they want.

Three themes dominated the references to this ideal society. Some emphasised the conviviality and the richness of collective life, the use of increased leisure time to create more communication. 'All sorts of things just start to happen all over the place', said Jean-Jacques Rodrigo, emphasising the creative capacity of this society in which, according to Christophe, 'people will express themselves more'.

This image implied the suppression of hierarchical relationships of any kind: 'The day we toss out these hierarchical relationships of men/women, parents/children, and so on . . .', said Christophe, 'there'll be different needs.' There would be no more society but people living interpersonal relationships, 'no more woman trouble – I'm speaking as a bloke', said Jean-Jacques Rodrigo, 'no more trouble with the kids, no more hostile relationships'. Meaning will be defined not by a social group but by the individual, his desires, his thirst for experience and balance. We had come to the heart of the ecologist utopia, the one which, in the very first session of the Malville group, had moved Yves Le Gall to say: 'I call on nobody. I call on myself alone', linking his refusal to express himself in anybody else's name to the reference to 'deep and latent aspirations'.

A second theme, close to the first, stressed the need to retain control over the tools which will be used in this society. Those who advanced this theme did so in backward-looking rather than progressive terms. They rejected the complexity of the modern world. Hannibal, Jean-Jacques Rodrigo, Claudine, Esther, Piccolo, Yves Le Gall to some extent, but also Pelot and Véronique Uri – anxious that the workers should have intellectual mastery and effective control over the means of work – wanted simple, robust tools: 'small is beautiful'. The rejection of gigantism was in this case the necessary condition for a simple life, but also for the control of the people over the material means around which existence is organised.

A third theme, represented mainly and almost exclusively by Leforestier, came from the projection into the future of pure opposition to the system and especially to the State. Leforestier described nomadic societies which have no private property, and was led to imagine 'an ideal society where there would be no delegation of power . . . The Indians had chiefs, but they were chiefs without means of coercion.' His utopia was one of a society without State and without power, rather than the utopia of an ecologist society reconciled with nature.

Resistance to utopia

Yves Le Gall reacted against the societal utopias which he had nonetheless just helped to define. He did not want a future 'which would be a multitude of communities, of minorities, and in which in the end there would be practically no more society'; he rejected the idea of a society without a State and wondered whether the existence of a State, 'with clearly delimited functions', was not precisely the condition for the existence of 'those umpteen minorities'. He was later to clarify his idea: this society apparently without State and without social conflicts could only be a Spartan or Cambodian style of society.

But it was mainly the attitudes of Leforestier which contributed to challenging the utopian blue-prints that the Malville group had begun to elaborate. He described the society of his dreams in basically negative terms – with neither powers nor State – which led Jean-Jacques Rodrigo to wonder what would happen if a social group rejected this new system. This question about the methods of change in such a society remained unanswered: 'What interests me is that there should be no more structured, organised power controlled by a group. As for the strategies for change in society, I myself have no theory, I'm incompetent.'

The Malville group, much more than the Paris group, had tried to give substance to a utopia shared by all the actors; but it very quickly became aware of the ambiguous nature of any societal model from which the very idea of conflict would be excluded. On the eve of its first weekend, it broke away from the language of pure utopia, but, as Bourguignon remarked in the eighth session, it was still a long way from defining 'the means needed to bring out concretely, in social practice, another mode of development'.

THE CRITIQUE OF THE STATE

The 'all-nuclear' programme

A first form of opposition to the State consists in condemning it as a machinery of oppression and integration; such an opposition grants no specificity to the anti-nuclear action. Valence was the one who went furthest in this direction. He described society as a vast plot to stifle the expression of desire. For him, civilian and military nuclear power represented the same reality, that of the authoritarian State, whilst the computerisation of society was just one more step towards repression and social control. Nuclear power interested him only as an expression of the violence of the State and its capacity for integration.

This position led to a logic of direct confrontation with the State and caused him to lose interest in the group's work throughout the phase when it was meeting social partners and adversaries – he left the group at the second meeting and only returned for the first weekend. But his departure had nothing to do with exclusion, quite the opposite: his critique of the repressive State was, beyond profound political differences, similar to the positions both of Véronique Uri, for whom the anti-nuclear struggle directly raised the question of confrontation with power and its police, and of Esther, who told Brice Lalonde that she represented a movement 'which is the direct adversary of power since it sends its police against us'.

More often than not, however, the denunciation of the repressive State was not dissociated from the nuclear theme, to which it was related through a technicist conception of the stakes according to which nuclear technology contains a centralising logic which implies repression and police control. At this stage of the intervention this conception was rejected by nobody and, as we have seen, prevented the group from thinking out the conflict in the presence of managerial interlocutors. In Paris, Hannibal gave a far-reaching description of the consequences of nuclear power, including references to South America and torture, whilst in Malville, Leforestier and Valence were the ones who most forcefully developed the idea of repression, summed up in the words: 'a system which you can find all over the place, and which leads to the recruiting of more and more rozzers'.

In this case, the critique was liberal, and, as far as Valence and Leforestier in particular were concerned, libertarian, which is why it provoked hardly any resistance in the groups, which, as we saw in the sessions with the communist interlocutors, rejected Leninist models. It combined easily with the remnants of the leftist language which denounces ideological integration by the State and which was used not only by Pelot and Véronique Uri, both militants in the LCR, but also by Christophe and Claudine, who couched it in biological metaphors.

But were we simply dealing with opposition to the integrating police state? Everybody accepted this idea to some extent, but it was not enough to explain the strength of the anti-nuclear mobilisation. Why the tens of thousands of demonstrators at Malville? Why nuclear power and not some other issue which refers just as directly to the repressive State? What gave the movement its mass character was the brutality and the indiscriminate way in which the State had acted to impose its electro-nuclear programme. This State, according to various members of the groups, was conducting a neo-colonial or imperialist policy in its search for uranium; it was signing contracts with foreign countries for the reprocessing of radioactive waste, thereby turning La Hague into an international dustbin; it was selling power stations to Iran even though that country had no electricity network to consume the energy produced. It was intervening on a world-wide scale, but in France it was also deciding on a policy over which nobody, apart from the nucleocrats in the PEON Commission, had any influence.

Yves Le Gall gave a striking description of the way in which the movement had experienced the setting up of the Messmer plan: in the disintegrated atmosphere preceding the death of Pompidou, in the middle of the oil crisis, the plan had been worked out and decided upon in a sudden and final way, without even the Commissariat au Plan, which had been unable to predict the energy crisis, really being able to intervene. Everything had been done, he said, within the PEON Commission and the government. It was a brutal decision but also one of terrifying scope. The movement had interpreted this programme as the will to impose an 'all-nuclear' concept in which many saw the generalisation of State control. The same criticism was levelled against EDF: EDF was trying to impose an 'all-electric' concept and so eliminate all diversification and the very idea of choice.

It was an arrogant and powerful State which was thus imposing its 'all-nuclear' policy. And it was the same State that the militants came up against when, even without contesting the policy as such, they requested as much information as possible on the safety measures which were to accompany the nuclear programme. It was impossible not to be incensed at the secrecy surrounding the ORSEC-RAD (Emergency Service-Radiation) plans which were supposed to define the procedures to be followed in case of nuclear accident. The militants could see only two possible explanations for this refusal by the authorities to publish the contents of these plans: either the government had nothing but contempt for the people, or the plans were not made public because they were ineffective. In the words of Leforestier, 'people are scared of nuclear power, that's obvious. They're even more scared when it's clear that things are being kept from them.' The dominant image was one of a dangerous State whose brutality in the making of the decision was accompanied by an inability or a refusal to demonstrate the validity of its energy policy.

The scientists against the State

The opposition of the scientists to the nuclear policy of the State may have something to do with the very conditions of scientific research. Véronique Uri and Jean-Philippe Pharisca in their respective groups proffered analyses which initially gave some support to this idea. Véronique stressed the compartmentalisation of scientific work – 'each individual controls just one little bit of the thing'. A researcher at the CNRS, she did not believe that 'scientists will control the problems: that seems false to me'. She felt that the scientists did not have command of the whole of the process they might be working on. Jean-Philippe Pharisca added that research, especially in physics, had developed to the point where the researchers had lost control of experiments which had until then been conducted 'on a human scale'; international competition, the economic crisis and the demands of industrial application had done the rest: 'There came a point when funds were reduced and people grew disenchanted with research.'

The comments of Véronique and Jean-Philippe converged with the general attitudes of actors in a struggle set against a background of scientific crisis. More specifically, their comments related to what Haggar and especially Cotentin had said about the development of the reprocessing plant in La Hague: scientific workers, as depicted in the words of Véronique and Jean-Philippe, seemed to be a class in crisis, the victims of a mutation which seemed to be dispossessing them of the intellectual control of their work. The aims of scientific production had become obscure and there was a growing feeling of having become mere pawns in a vast organisation. Now they were 'just like everyone else, like munitions workers, like prostitutes, like everybody; they have a function, a job'. The idea of a social elite, haloed in the prestige of science, had yielded to a feeling of powerlessness to control the social effects of research. 'Scientists', said Jean-Philippe, 'have no influence on politics.'

The result of all this was to define a commitment at two different levels, with some people feeling themselves to be in an unstable position between the two. The scientists developed a critique of themselves which might go in several directions: Véronique recalled that originally the scientists' protest had been essentially ideological, anti-scientistic and political, in opposition to the 'communist mandarins' identified with the scientistic ideology. Jean-Philippe emphasised the absence of democracy in research and denounced the restrictions which prevent any critical expression, calling for the control of scientific production by society.

These sentiments had nothing to do with the anti-nuclear struggle. They even created a difficult situation for the scientists who played the role of counter-experts in the service of the struggle, a situation which Véronique Uri felt deeply: 'When you come down to it, we're anti-scientistic, but in the debates we make full use of the scientistic image people have.'

The critique of counter-expertise betrayed the malaise of those who did not want to deny their professional specificity, who wanted to put their knowledge at the service of the action, but who, at the same time, refused to lapse into the demagogy and the glibness of the scientistic utopia. How could such a contradiction be overcome? Nobody in the group had an answer, and all that was left for Véronique was to express her weariness: 'I'm sick of it. I've given up nuclear physics to go and militate against nuclear physics by practising nuclear physics!' Militants like Véronique felt trapped in an increasingly painful paradox, whilst many gave up militancy altogether and others, like Pharisca, opted for a role of counter-expert which, at a completely different level, was able to coexist with a democratic critique of the functioning of research.

At a time when the struggle was getting off the ground, many scientists had joined a movement to which they brought the technical expertise needed to challenge the nuclear programme and answer the EDF specialists in public debates. They played a cardinal role in sensitising public opinion and vulgarising an information which the authorities refused to make available. But in a slack period of the action, and just when this work of sensitisation and vulgarisation actually seemed to have borne fruit, they gave the image either of withdrawal or of a malaise which was more and more difficult to bear for those who, like Véronique, were trying to continue the struggle.

Meeting the strategists

So far there had been no clear separation in the opinions of the two groups between the generalised critique of the State and the attacks on the energy policy. Should we not, then, at the end of this first phase of the analysis, conclude that the anti-nuclear struggle is directed against all aspects of power? By no means, for the sessions in which the groups met General Buis in Paris and General Poirier in Malville brought an unexpected demonstration of the separation between the struggle against civilian nuclear power and the opposition to the military uses of atomic energy.

In Paris, this demonstration happened rapidly and to general surprise. General Buis had just introduced himself briefly. Cotentin then spoke up after a short silence. He described the good old days when the plant at La Hague was working for the army: 'We had a certain amount of autonomy, we could take decisions, act on our own initiative and put our grey matter to work a bit . . . Now, with the civilian applications, it's all different and our working conditions have got distinctly worse.' A delighted General Buis admitted that the army did indeed have the means to respect the people who work for it. The group was caught off balance: straightaway, faced with an interlocutor who symbolised military nuclear power, Cotentin with his trade unionist reasoning had shown the distance between the protest against military nuclear power and the protest against civilian nuclear power. The two problems appeared to be entirely distinct, and he clarified his idea: 'We had doubts about the use of plutonium for the bomb, it was a bit unpleasant for us to think about, but we'd struck a kind of balance between the fact of producing plutonium for bombs and the fact of having something to do that actually interested us.' The bomb was one thing, power stations another. The idea went dead against the prevalent philosophy of the movement and several members of the group tried to resist it by stressing the many reasons for linking the civil and the military atom. Roland Maire advanced technological arguments: 'Civilian nuclear power is one of the by-products of military nuclear power' and moreover, he reminded the group, civilian nuclear power leads to the manufacturing of plutonium and, consequently, of the atomic bomb. Georges Flamand, reasoning in terms of imperialism, thought there was a convergence between the massive and international development of civilian nuclear power as envisaged by France and the government's involvement in a geopolitical strategy based on military nuclear power. Hannibal mentioned the fallout shelters, which 'are intended for use in both cases'. Other items were brought into the debate, all aimed at reducing the distance which Cotentin's dramatic declaration had created in a philosophy which had until then been undifferentiated: was there not a historical development of protest beginning with pacifism and ending in ecology? Was there not a single and unique logic at issue in both cases, that of the trivialisation of a dangerous technology? Was scientific research not controlled and financed, directly or indirectly, by the army?

In fact, the breach opened up by Cotentin's declaration was not to be closed. Indeed, it grew wider. Georges Flamand was the first to put into words the difficulty that they were all experiencing: 'What hold does a social movement have at present over the military nuclear programme? None. Of course you can always go and bugger up the submarines at Cherbourg or plant radishes on the Albion plateau, but it's all a bit limited.' Jean-Philippe Pharisca joined in: French military policy was something that had no 'impact on daily life', and protesting against civilian nuclear power was different from protesting against military nuclear power. The idea of a separation between the social and the military was more than present in the group: it was widely accepted.

In Malville, the group arrived at the same result but through a different process. Confronted with General Poirier, everybody tried to maintain the idea of a convergence between civilian and military nuclear power. Here, too, there was a real connivance between the group, its agitator and the interlocutor whose rigorous demonstrations met little resistance in their demolition of various people's arguments against the French strategy of nuclear deterrence. The arguments were similar to those used in Paris and there is therefore no need to repeat them. General Poirier's logic was implacable and, unlike the managerial interlocutors, he was not rejected into absurdity or barbarity, but was rather thought to be a decent man who deserved a wider audience for the logic he was defending.

Jean-Jacques and Christophe voiced the full extent of the distance between the two different problems lumped together under the term 'nuclear'. The majority of the group followed hard on their heels: Esther thought that 'with war you feel helpless, whereas with civilian nuclear power you feel you have something to say'. Leforestier made a distinction between the internal problems of a society and the question of national defence: military nuclear power, he explained, concerns the defence of the nation, whereas 'France can still be France without nuclear energy.' Jean-Jacques Rodrigo clarified his own position: 'To my mind, any government in power in any country in the world can only say yes to military nuclear power.' And so it went on.

The distinction was not made without resistance or hesitation, but it was very widely accepted. Beyond pacifism and a common rejection of the hierarchical world of the army and beyond a diffuse anguish which scarcely differentiates between civilian and military nuclear power, the militants had just set up a basic distinction: on the one side was the State, the military, international affairs, national sovereignty, in short, the bomb; and on the other side, less directly linked to the State, ordinary things, peacetime, everyday life, the problems and the conflicts specific to a society, in short, civilian nuclear power. The first image of a cultural split associated with a critique of the State had been shattered and the way was open for an analysis of the struggles and the search for the theoretical conditions for the creation of a social movement.

Nature

The debates of which we have just given an account still supported the image of a division in which cultural critique and critique of the State merged in an absence of differentiation which began to break down only with the military interlocutors. The ideas and values which defined the 'great refusal' had no difficulty in combining with opposition to the State, and the union of the two seemed to repair the rift that had inevitably been created by the efforts of some members of the groups to provide a precise definition of the social adversary. The general atmosphere was one of togetherness and community, and, apart from the incident which had set Jean-Jacques Rodrigo against Valence right at the beginning of the intervention, there was scarcely any decisive event in the internal life of the two groups. Véronique Uri, who gave her action an anti-capitalist meaning, did not, in this phase of the intervention, try to introduce the theme with any force, even though it was decisive from her point of view, whilst in the cordial atmosphere of the Malville group the so-called 'locals' were scarcely differentiated from the militants motivated by such different logics as Valence, Christophe or Jean-Jacques Rodrigo.

This community feeling was not defensive; it did not protect a sect against a hostile world; it did not isolate feeling from decision. The members of the group had all taken part in actions, had all taken initiatives. During the first phase of the intervention they immediately distanced themselves from anti-nuclear fear and anguish as well as from the blanket denunciation of a demoniac power. Their break with the values of industrial society was not divorced from a will to social struggle, even if the latter remained ill-defined. Their acute awareness of the decay and exhaustion of industrial civilisation could be modernist as well as anti-elitist and, in any case, rejected the values that the ruling elite seeks to impose under cover of technical rationalisation or economic necessity. It is true that only the formation of a social movement marshalled against the new ruling forces, and especially the nuclear technocracy, could give the counter-cultural breakaway a meaning of post-industrial modernisation rather than of anti-industrial withdrawal. But it is also true that this social movement could not be formed if the protesters did not mark out the new battlefield and create a new area of historicity as they prepared the new struggles. The break with industrial values can be defensive, but at the same time it can also define both the stake and the actors of the new social movements.

The researchers probably did not at first see the real importance of the cultural themes and underestimated their interdependence with more social and political themes. They interpreted the development of the intervention as a transition from a generalised cultural refusal to the creation of a specific social conflict. This was a judgement which they were obliged to revise, since the counter-cultural refusal turned out to be neither a mere raw material for the formation of a social movement, nor yet an obstacle to its development, but rather a totally new representation of the relationship between culture and nature, one which transformed the realm of social relations, and the cultural revolution involved was probably more fundamental than the still indeterminate social struggle that went with it.

The challenging of the values of industrial society, the crisis of science, and the appeal to the community themes all designated what one might, with Moscovici, call a 'naturalism', whose main features, those which defined a new field of historicity, we shall try to enumerate. This naturalism rejects the traditional opposition between nature and culture, the Manichaean dichotomy of 'good' society and 'bad' nature (or vice versa), in order to declare the unity of society and nature. It thus breaks in particular with the Marxist idea of a contradiction between productive forces and productive relations, with the idea of an autonomous development of natural forces. It postulates another kind of relationship to technology, and, when it manages to shake off a technicist vision of society, it aims to bring man closer to the 'wonderful tools' that science has given him, seeking, as Georges Friedmann wished, to re-establish contact 'where technology dispenses with man'.

Although it is occasionally backward-looking, this naturalism does not stop short at the great refusal of that which is judged to be unacceptable. It aims to be the bearer of a new conception of economics, production and science and is thus capable of looking to the future, trying in particular to investigate and redefine the relationship between town and country or work and leisure. It can refuse to be imprisoned in the ghetto of counter-culture, and, if it stresses the positive value of the fringe, it is because it prophesies a withering of the centre and the reunion of man with nature and himself. The ecological philosophy breaks with an evolutionist conception in which progress lies in the passage from the simple to the complex, from the mechanical to the organic and from community to society, and reverses the terms without necessarily lapsing into reaction or nostalgia for the past, addressing itself rather to the search for new cultural directions and the call to a process of civilisation located at the level of historicity. It points to an upheaval, which it helps to produce, in the cultural model of our present society, and helps to define what may well be the cultural model of the society to come.

The fact remains, however, that this cultural revolution tends, at the level of social and political relations, to take the form of a generalised opposition to Power, in other words the State, which can lead to withdrawal into an exemplary community or to violence. The very diversity of cultural protest makes it difficult to define a specific social relation, or designate a central locus of power.

A conflict of cultures

The militants passed without difficulty from a cultural critique to a critique of the State, from a call for new values and another kind of life to an opposition to the State defined as a system of order, an obstacle to the achievement or realisation of those values or that kind of life. They did not transform their cultural protest into an anti-technocratic conflict. Or at least not directly: the cultural movement was not the first stage in a process culminating in a social movement. The attempt to create a social relation by confronting the militants with interlocutors representing the technocratic adversary led to the acknowledgement of a considerable distance between the two which scarcely perturbed the militants. But the attempt may have been premature or too ambitious: the *direct*, unmediated transition from the great cultural and anti-State refusal to a social movement proved impossible. The image of the conflict had still not been found, and would have to be built up gradually, from an analysis of the struggles.

www

The struggles

In the debates which followed, the warmth and fusion of the common action disintegrated, opinions conflicted, and the different levels of the action came apart. The sociologist, for his part, was no longer the benevolent ally listening to the militants bear witness. Instead, he became the analyst of what we call an image-group, urging each individual to explain his or her position. He took part in the group's work of shattering the too general image of the movement shared by everybody at the beginning of the intervention. Consequently, our analysis has to take on the form more of a history of the intervention. The groups' debates were the 'image' of the problems of the struggle and its attempt to unite the defence of a cultural identity and the fight against a social adversary.

THE CREATION OF A POLITICAL ACTION

The withdrawal into a community was criticised first of all by the trade unionists who thought that it was doomed to turn in upon itself and become ineffectual and marginal. Yves Le Gall, for example, who sympathised with the whole community enterprise and the parallel networks, produced an extremely critical assessment of it. Unlike pure ecological protest which simply rejects a state of affairs, the anti-nuclear movement could, in his opinion, define itself as a political force and confront a social adversary, and so be led to create struggles and seek a rallying point where demands, political pressures and general criticism could take root and bind together.

Local action

Defence
Is local action to prevent the building of a power station situated at the centre of the anti-nuclear struggle? Can it rise progressively towards a contesting of society, its methods of taking decisions, its culture and its forms of power? This idea was shared by the local militants and by ecologists

like Hannibal and Jacqueline Monceau: 'At Cruas, there were women who were concerned about nuclear power because the reactor was in their back yard. So they went to Malville, and nowadays they say: all anti-nuclear struggles are our business. And when you've got that far, you can begin to ask questions: Why do we need energy? What's it used for? What's a growth rate?' In this view of things, the struggle against one's 'own' power station passes over into protest against the whole of the electro-nuclear programme. It was just such a progression that was outlined by François Delain, a farmer from the Malville region: 'At first, it comes from you as a farmer seeing the land mutilated, fields taken away from farming . . . and then you start to study why they're doing all this nuclear stuff, and you suddenly realise that you're questioning the whole of society. I think everybody goes through the same process.'

But we cannot stop at this image, for the local struggles are initially dominated by land problems and the defence of a threatened community. The building of a nuclear power station in a region which is more often than not rural provokes a clash between an industrial world controlled from outside and a local community whose traditional area of community sociability may be destroyed. This was put very well by Valence, who had the ear of the Malville militants: 'We know the village, we know one another; there's a whole load of relationships of that sort that we know very well because they're all around us. And then on top of that, there's a sort of second world which is completely beyond us, it's the world of government, specialists, a whole pack of people out there, organising a certain part of our lives, making us believe things.'

The social changes and the expropriation of land brought about by the building of a nuclear power station are not compensated for by the local economic spin-offs. Saint-Hilaire thought that in the Nogent region the power station would not create local jobs, since the labourers would be mainly immigrant workers and the permanent staff made up of EDF people from elsewhere. François Delain and Marie-Jeanne Vercors were afraid that the canton of Morestel would be invaded by EDF people; all the investment in the commune was for them, they 'live all together, with a mentality of their own and . . . they don't do their shopping in the region'. But when the mayor of Saint-Laurent-des-Eaux painted a more optimistic picture of the economic effects of the power station, the Paris group offered little resistance. Not only was the exodus stopped, but the commune no longer had unemployment problems; the power station had created a few jobs and small industries had been able to expand.

But the economic arguments did not monopolise the stage and it would be wrong to imagine that for the local actors the struggle against a nuclear power station comes down entirely to a problem of land expropriation and community preservation. The idea of the risks and dangers of nuclear energy is a powerful motive in the fight, and it is in fact at the local level that the theme of fear seems to be most deeply rooted.

Didier Anger begins his book on the struggle against Flamanville with a frequently apocalyptic vision of the risks of nuclear power. In the Grenoble–Malville group, François Delain constantly came back to the risks and spoke at length about the transfer of uranium containers and the lethal risks of the fast-breeder. For Saint-Hilaire, 'nuclear power is Hiroshima', the threat of radiation, cancer and death. Saint-Hilaire was defending his way of life: with a power station so close by, he no longer wanted his grandchildren in the house. The question of the risks was one of prime importance in the debates organised amongst the population. Jean-Pierre Provins thought that on such occasions one ought to 'try and frighten people'. Even Roland Maire, who constantly declared that the movement should go beyond the theme of fear, spoke of the dangers of the atom to the mayor of Saint-Laurent-des-Eaux: it was the risks that would shatter the deadly calm of the population and draw them into a generalised criticism of the nuclear programme.

Land appropriation, industrial shock, the dangers, all of these problems were constantly mentioned, but there was also denunciation of the brutal way in which power stations were decided upon, of the pressures that were brought to bear and the politics of the fait accompli. Saint-Hilaire was shocked by the way in which decisions were taken and made known to the public, who learnt about the plans only through the newspapers. Then the whole administration tries to stifle resistance by putting enormous pressure on elected representatives and the people directly affected. The police manoeuvres, the Secret Service intervenes, and the mayor of Saint-Laurent-des-Eaux himself recalled how the Prefecture could bring pressure to bear on local finances. As Pierre Gremion has shown, relationships between the administration and local representatives are directed away from open conflict and the local political personnel does not think it can put up any resistance unless it has the total support of the community it represents. The local struggle would thus seem to be associated with a demand for greater local autonomy, an objective which has little to do with a general anti-nuclear movement.

Long hair and red flags
The militants themselves dismissed the idea of a spontaneous mobilisation rising towards a struggle against the entire electro-nuclear programme. It was the local militants in the groups who insisted most on the gap between the local struggles and the themes and objectives of the anti-nuclear movement. In many cases, the industrial upheaval was more important than the anti-nuclear dimension in this local defence: 'There is no specifically nuclear aspect', said Saint-Hilaire. Roland Maire also thought

that it was by importing militants from outside that the anti-nuclear struggle was brought in. As long as the mobilisation was merely an affair for local farmers, 'it's no different from the fight against a dam', said Georges Flamand. Jean-Pierre Provins said that where he came from the farmers were mainly interested in the expropriation of land and he joined François Delain in stressing that farmers were largely insensitive to ecology themes: they were still profiting from the modernisation and mechanisation of agriculture and believed very firmly in the virtues of mass consumption, since they were profiting from it after the rest of society: 'they don't question consumer society'. Delain and Provins took a certain pleasure in dismantling before the groups the image of the farmer as the natural ally of the ecologists because he is the defender of nature. François Delain went even further and explained that the advantage of nuclear power for farmers struggling to keep possession of their lands was that it allowed them to find outside allies. Jean-Philippe Pharisca also saw the local struggles in this way: they are 'swollen' from outside because there is a new climate in which general meanings of an ecological, nationalist or anti-militarist nature are grafted onto struggles that were previously isolated and which are now becoming the symbols of generalised protest. There is a brief encounter between general movements of opinion and limited defensive local conflicts.

The main problem then becomes one of the link-up between the local mobilisation and the militants from outside who confer an anti-nuclear meaning on the struggle. This link-up is not very successful. Both groups gradually demolished the dream of a spontaneous coming together of local actors and ecologists. A reporter who had covered the struggle at Braud-et-Saint-Louis gave a harsh account of the distance between the peasants and the ecologists from the towns; he referred to the 'Marie-Antoinettes of ecology' who drop in on the peasants. The group hardly protested; Georges Flamand admitted the distance and talked of the ecology militants who go to the battleground like 'explorers all dolled up in their little pith helmets and their khaki shorts'. But the distance was revealed most clearly in the affair of the power station at Nogent. In spite of general anxiety over the reactor, the population of the Nogent region was hostile to any mobilisation and to the arrival of outside militants 'with their long hair and scruffy jeans'. Saint-Hilaire related how the demonstrators had filed past drawn curtains in a climate of fear and how the local press had developed an extremely negative image of the demonstrations.

It seemed as if everything the Paris militants did was doomed to isolation. In June 1977, the demonstration cut itself off completely from the population by bringing out red flags, which Saint-Hilaire thought was a clumsy gesture on the part of the CFDT and the leftists. Piccolo agreed, but Pelot from the LCR thought on the contrary that red flags are not a quaint bit of folklore but the symbol of a class declaration linked to the anti-nuclear struggle, an idea quite remote from the meaning of the struggle for the locals. The discussion between Piccolo, Pelot and Saint-Hilaire was a perfect expression of the distance which existed in the Nogent region between a will to general and political anti-nuclear struggle and the defensive action of a suspicious and largely unpoliticised local population. The silence of Provins and Saint-Hilaire in most of the general debates, in the discussions which had no bearing on the local domination of a power station, reflected this distance. In the Grenoble–Malville group, François Delain occupied a similar position.

Democratic protest

The weakness of the politicians
The debates and meetings with the local politicians brought out one component of the anti-nuclear action that was not clear at first: a democratic protest. The mechanisms of democracy are blocked and the technocratic State imposes its will on elected representatives who are powerless to react and who shelter behind their technical incompetence. In this way, vitally important decisions are taken without proper democratic control and without due political process. Consequently, the movement has set itself the aim of recreating political life, opening up democracy and decentralising decision-making.

When the militants of the Grenoble–Malville group met Monsieur Durand, the mayor of Morestel, a commune directly affected by the Malville fast-breeder, it was not to launch into a technical debate with him: there was little mention of the dangers and the advantages of the power station. Basically, Monsieur Durand was accused of not having played the political role which ought to have been his and of having allowed the reactor to be imposed upon him. According to Christophe and Jean-Jacques, the local representatives had not been consulted; faced with the fait accompli, they had become cogs in the administrative machinery. Monsieur Durand answered like a good manager: he had every confidence in nuclear technology, and it was necessary for France to convert her system of energy production. But that was not the question, since the voters of Morestel were not hostile to the fast-breeder which represented a golden opportunity for a region in decline: the exodus would be halted, jobs would be created and the licence fee paid by EDF would enable the commune to expand and refurbish its amenities and facilities. He was told in answer that it was precisely this confidence and this tacit agreement between the administration and the local representatives that had to be broken in order to open up information, bring out issues that were not purely local and initiate a political debate. Monsieur Durand, however, did not consider himself to be a politician, since he answered: 'You must argue that with the politicians, not with me.' Jean-

Jacques Rodrigo and Christophe were all the more unwilling to accept this position since the risks created by the fast-breeder affected a much greater population than just Malville and since Super-Phoenix was a central plank in the French nuclear programme. It was totally unacceptable for Monsieur Durand to take refuge in the neutrality of management and the tranquillity of his good relationships with his fellow citizens; he was rendering local power completely inactive and impotent. Christophe reproached him with being a mere cog in the works: 'How can you be a local elected representative in those conditions, when you are left no means and when everything is imposed from the top, with no information and no debate?' No doubt the mayor had been elected and re-elected, but what was the value of a system, asked Jean-Jacques, in which an elected representative could allow himself to be neutral in a matter which affected much more than his commune alone?

There was much the same kind of criticism in Paris. Monsieur Rubline, the mayor of Saint-Laurent-des-Eaux, was engrossed in management problems and fearful of the difficulties he would face when the EDF licence fee was reduced. Roland Maire, Hannibal, Georges Flamand and Haggar immediately denounced the gilded cage that EDF had built around the commune which was, in a way, the prisoner of affluence, of comparative luxury, of the feeling of being privileged. 'You've got a lot of money but you've lost your freedom', said Haggar. So what margin of autonomy did Monsieur Rubline enjoy? Cotentin offered to find out by showing the CFDT film *Condemned to Succeed* in Saint-Laurent.

Messrs Durand and Rubline were mayors of small communes and it was after all easy to understand why they should behave primarily as managers concerned with maintaining a local consensus; they were far away from the real political centre where the problems of the French electro-nuclear programme are debated. The disparity between local government and the omnipotence of EDF was too great. Consequently, when local politicians were criticised, it was always with a reminder that their possibilities for action remained limited. In the eyes of the militants, the national politicians, deputies and senators, especially the government backbenchers, had an entirely different responsibility and their almost total absence from the nuclear debates was a much clearer demonstration of the disappearance of politics.

Monsieur Y—, a member of the parliamentary majority, in his meeting with the Paris group, gave a lengthy account of the lack of interest in parliamentary debates on nuclear energy; Parliament had been incapable of taking control of the French energy policy; the 'nucleocrats' could impose their objectives without control by the political system. 'That's the first time I've heard a member of Parliament say political life is useless', exclaimed Emmanuel Kropo. Pelot recognised in the description the image of members of Parliament who 'play at politics' while the serious matters are being decided without them. The discussion became bitter and Monsieur Y— grew irritated, since, even if EDF is too powerful, one still has to trust the technicians, and then all the constitutional rules had been respected in these nuclear matters . . . But, came the reply, if there had been no real centre of debate on the question of nuclear power, if it had remained within the domain of experts favourable to nuclear energy, if the public had never been consulted, was it surprising when ecologists disrupted meetings organised by EDF and sometimes became violent, as the interlocutor had seen for himself? Those were the only ways to make oneself heard in a simulacrum of democracy. Monsieur Y— brought grist to the mill of the militants when he explained how, at EDF's request, he had sent customers a text in favour of a nuclear power station with the EDF mail. The entire group was unable to conceal its joy at seeing the real face of submission to the system unveiled in this way. Each and every one accused the interlocutor of being a servant of EDF, of renouncing any political role and so creating the conditions for violence by depriving social demands of recourse to institutional means.

Thus the militants called for democracy, for the creation of a political space where energy problems would be debated and technocratic logic prevented from working without constraint. But the democratic demand was not the dominant theme for all the militants, even though they all supported it, and especially Jean-Phillipe Pharisca.

Criticism of institutional paralysis
In Pharisca's opinion, the anti-nuclear struggle should fight bureaucratic obstructionism and the way in which the State maintained its grip on society: 'In France, everything is controlled by the government, and the institutions don't accept any internal debate which would, in fact, help to get things into better perspective and be beneficial. We have a totally blocked society.' Unlike the political system in Germany, England or the United States, the French system has no counter-power structure, so its opponents have the choice between relegation to the fringes and silence or choosing the path of violence. Officials are chosen more for their political docility than their scientific qualities. 'People are appointed not to represent or defend a policy vis-à-vis the administration, but to represent the people at the top vis-à-vis the people at the bottom.' This happens without conflict, since bureaucrats believe in the virtues of civility and have a distaste for public outbursts, but EDF had exceeded its role to the benefit of its own development.

Pharisca was a scientist and was, moreover, frequently irritated by the scientific naiveties that the ecology movement sometimes hawks about, but he also thought that scientists themselves were too ready to become cogs in the bureaucratic system and bore a heavy responsibility for the setting up of the electro-nuclear programme. 'The vast majority accept work no matter where the money comes from.' Pharisca had joined the ranks of the protesters but did not want to use the prestige of science to play the part of the 'great priest'. Basically, he wanted 'independent scientists who are listened to'. The system must be unblocked, criticism allowed and society's control over scientific research increased.

This critique was essentially democratic and did not challenge the legitimacy of science. As a result, the position of independent expert claimed by Pharisca was challenged by some ecologists. The reproach was made by Georges Flamand, followed by Roland Maire: Pharisca's approach 'was an attempt to set himself up as a judge'. In Hannibal's opinion, the movement had, in fact, gone beyond the scientific critique. The scientists in the movement might have played an important part at the beginning, but they serve no purpose now, added Jacqueline Monceau. Pharisca waxed ironic and rejected these points of view. The movement needed the scientists to open up a breach in the solid block of pro-nuclear certainties. They were the ones who had given the movement legitimacy and enabled it to take on a national dimension. Against the closed universe of the scientists, Pharisca appealed to democracy and society and attacked the technocratic utopia of a scientific policy which relegates its adversaries to the realm of absurdity.

Pharisca set himself apart from most of the cultural expressions of the movement and the utopia that it was striving to develop. This was shown by his distance from the group; he felt remote from the community experiments and was suspicious of attempts to stir up confrontation with the State. He thought it would be difficult to go beyond an ecological awareness that was by now quite widespread in order to launch into general political struggles. In his opinion, they should be fighting to unblock and open up the French institutional system.

Against war on the State
Pharisca's isolation in his group might suggest that democratic protest is a kind of afterthought tacked onto or running parallel with the anti-nuclear movement, but in the Grenoble–Malville group Jean-Jacques Rodrigo also represented this democratic protest and showed it to be at the heart of the group's debates. He identified himself with the democratic demand when he violently opposed those who had turned the anti-nuclear movement into a force mainly for struggle and confrontation with law and order, with the State. Nobody was quite so forceful as he was in declaring that we must demolish the rhetoric directed against a supposedly totalitarian adversary. The battle cry of war upon the State, which calls on the one hand for community withdrawal and on the other hand for violence, was not acceptable in a society like ours where it is not true to say that we 'have nothing to lose and everything to gain'.

In the very first meeting of the Grenoble–Malville group, Jean-Jacques had clashed bitterly with Valence on the subject of the violence at Malville, a conflict dominated by the trauma of Malville 1977. During the meeting with Monsieur Sigoyer, one of those who thought the confrontation at Malville justified, the debate was less tense and Rodrigo was more easily able to enlarge upon his attitudes. Sigoyer was in favour of 'all forms of action and all methods'; he was fighting the 'imperial form' of the State and had taken part in every struggle since the Algerian war. For him, Malville was just one moment in this struggle between the people and the State. Yves Le Gall criticised this attitude, which is interested in nuclear power 'only if there's police repression'. Neither did Bourguignon think that the anti-nuclear militants wanted 'a head-on clash with the State'. Véronique Uri had a more qualified attitude: there had to be a favourable political power relationship before there could be military confrontation. By contrast, the local militants, like Claudine, thought the men of violence had their place in the struggle, so pointing the way to an axis of alliance that was to be clearly confirmed later in the research.

During this lengthy debate, the image of the adversary remained the State and its police, a will and a bloc to be confronted, demolished or bypassed according to the individual analysis of the situation. Jean-Jacques suddenly broke off this discussion between warriors, violent and non-violent, and said to Sigoyer: 'What you say seems odd to me, because the power we're up against isn't a single, solid block that's always going to react in the same way. If this were the Soviet Union or Mexico, they wouldn't use tear gas to tell us to piss off but real bullets. Depending on how you behave towards the authorities, you know more or less what you're going to get back in return. So you can't act in the same way towards the French State as you would towards another State. The situation here is specific to France and quite favourable compared with other countries . . . I prefer to be in France . . .' He maintained that the movement should accept the rules of democracy, that the system can be opened up, and later, out of provocation, he declared himself a supporter of Giscard. The movement should get away from the logic of war, the logic of all or nothing, and enter the field of political reforms. It is perfectly possible to influence decisions and experiment with new ways of living and consumption without going straight to extremes which end in defeat and the reinforcement of law and order. We should make our society fit to live in, reject stereotyped slogans, take far more initiatives and dissociate ourselves from forms of action which are meaningless in a relatively open society.

Rodrigo was at the centre of the ecology movement and the fight over Malville, so his call for political pressure could not be identified with a sort of middle-of-the-road, reasonable strategy; rather his rejection of war on the State was motivated by the search for another image of the adversary and for new forms of struggle.

The struggles

Society versus the State

The meeting with Solange Fernex, one of the organisers of the ecology movement in Alsace, showed that the anti-nuclear movement in that region was firmly established, coherent and capable of waging protracted war against nuclear power and in defence of the environment. The action of the Alsatian militants was rooted in the democratic critique but went much further by calling for community responsibility and autonomy in place of the society of the masses. The movement was also impelled by strong moral conviction. Although it could not be identified with an existing social movement, the Alsatian movement went beyond both the democratic critique and the simple cultural breakaway of the community experiments. For Solange Fernex: 'Nuclear power is a caricature of all that is wrong in our society, at the ecological, environmental, political and sociological levels, but our fight is in no way restricted to nuclear energy. That's why I find it too limiting to talk about the anti-nuclear movement.' Nuclear energy is only one, and not the strongest, of all the forces which have the power to 'concrete over and completely transform the world we live in'. Alsace has been destroyed by motorways, agriculture has been industrialised, the Rhine is an open sewer; all this went way beyond the electronuclear programme alone. What was at stake 'is a society in which people become mere cogs, with artificial feelings and where, beyond a certain point, they become harmful . . . We no longer have all the beauty of nature, the spontaneity, the freedom . . .' It was a moral and ethical struggle in a region which is itself religious, a struggle dominated neither by the Churches nor the priests, but founded on an ethic, since they were fighting for a certain representation of nature and humanity. It was much more than a simple local defence such as the one in the Nogent region, since in Alsace the defence of the community was greatly reinforced by more general cultural stakes, by that cultural experience which was the crucible of the movement. Solange spoke of the fight for the survival and the dignity of Humanity whose capacities for initiative and communication are endangered today, but this acute awareness of a crisis of civilisation by no means caused her to withdraw into an isolated and experimental community turned in upon its own convictions. On the contrary, she declared that the movement must open itself up to local struggles and politics and defend democracy and initiative against a powerful, centralised State which dominates the local community, as in Alsace. It was clear to her that it is not enough to open up the institutional system; we must also loosen the hold of the State in order to develop the autonomy of society: the social groups must assume responsibility for their own destiny. Against the Parisianism of ideas and the blindness of the central powers, Solange Fernex constantly appealed to the regional community: in her opinion, we must break the identification of society with the State. Rather than creating the movement in a conflict, we must build upon community autonomies where they still exist – she spoke of the fields and the villages against the towns and the factories. For these very broad aims there are corresponding forms of struggle which are highly pragmatic and always rooted in local life.

The reasoning was profound and prestigious, but some militants in the Paris group were unwilling to recognise in it the image of the movement to be created, since it seemed to them that in the Alsatian struggle the image of the adversary was either missing or vague. The fight against EDF was no longer central to it; the Alsatian militants were too remote from the great ideological and political debates. As Georges Flamand said with some loftiness: 'The Alsatians have represented a tendency which I would call not so much apolitical as anti-ideological.' For example, the movement fielded candidates in every election, which Georges found 'a little bit naive' since the pragmatism which uses elections as a convenient platform masks the ideological and social stakes of those elections: 'I don't want to get into an analysis of where the ecologists stand in the political spectrum, but what you're doing is centrism, anti-nuclear radicalism, a mixture which allows you to avoid the full range of debates.' For Georges Flamand, such very general ideas and such apolitical pragmatism made excellent bedfellows with the politics of wheeler-dealing. Solange Fernex countered this argument with the ability of the villagers to manage their own affairs by themselves, without the need to set up a political or union apparatus or create a new class of public figures.

The fact remained that yet again the image of a widening and generalising of the local struggles had been broken. All that could be seen were local actions attacking the State in the name of a democratic demand for the political system to be opened up. Community defence and the democratic critique were linked, especially in the Alsatian movement, but the group had shown how limited such a conception was in relation to the aspirations of the anti-nuclear movement: the transition from cultural protest to conflict, and from indignation to a social project, is fraught with difficulty. Might an alliance with other movements, and especially that of the workers, as such, make it possible to create other fields of struggle?

THE LINK WITH THE TRADE UNIONS

The CFDT is opposed to the French electro-nuclear programme and had led the fight at Marcoule and especially La Hague in conjunction with the ecologists. More immediately, there were numerous links between the anti-nuclear militants and the CFDT militants in both intervention groups. Did all of this suggest the possibility of trade union action being one of the places where an anti-nuclear protest could develop, or was the trade union born of industrial society incapable of taking upon itself the struggles of post-industrial society? A third possibility was that the CFDT might be an ally, a political operator for the anti-nuclear demands, but not the principal actor. To these central questions was added a doubt related to present circumstances: was the impact of the economic crisis tending to unite unionists and ecologists or separate them more clearly than before?

A climate of opinion

There could be no doubt that the characteristic demands and general orientations of the CFDT were greatly enriched by the ecology climate. Haggar and Christophe were strongly attached to the struggle against dependence and manipulation and to every struggle for new values and a new sociability. Christophe envisaged a more collective life, new needs, different relationships between men and women, the whole universe of 'qualitative' demands, whilst Haggar was searching for a new way of living and thought that union action should take an interest in every aspect of social life. All this led to the critique of a growth which has not only not reduced social inequalities but has, in fact, emphasised them. On this point, the analyses of Christophe, the unionist from Grenoble, matched exactly those of Piccolo, the ecologist from Paris. The groups as a whole shared these feelings to a greater or lesser degree and were opposed on these themes to the representatives of the CGT and the Communist Party. In Christophe's opinion, trade unionism should form an alliance with the ecology movement against a mass consumption which had nothing to do with needs and everything to do with the search for status symbols, 'as if producer and consumer had nothing to say to one another . . . The worker produces goods which he himself has no desire to consume.'

In a more concrete way, the problem of the risks involved in nuclear power could easily be linked with the problem of the dangers and the working conditions faced by workers in the nuclear industry. On this point, local actions could be undertaken in concert. For Cotentin, this link was much wider since nuclear technology is so complex that it leads to an increased control, a reinforcing of hierarchy, a loss of initiative on the part of the workers, so that the technology is incompatible with the project for a self-managed society. If the workers were increasingly reluctant to accept the risks and the control, it was because the game was no longer worth the candle and because they were increasingly aware of the crisis in the values of industrial society and progress. The ideology of the redemption of the atom through civilian nuclear power was collapsing. This climate of opinion had contributed greatly in the fight at La Hague to the alliance of the workers and the inhabitants who did not want to live in the 'dustbin of Europe'. At EDF also, there was a beginning of doubt: 'it began with the little shock we got from the outside world, from people who came to ask questions as a result of their reading', said Roland Maire. Fournier's articles

69

in the satirical *Charlie-Hebdo* were not without influence here. The problem was thus raised of the aims of energy production; critical thinking began to creep into a world which had until then been convinced of its legitimacy. According to Roland Maire, this critique was aimed at the objectives of nuclear policy rather than the techniques, because 'the way you make nuclear power is no worse than the way you make oil, and it may even be better'.

Worker demands

Cotentin criticised the working conditions imposed at La Hague by the COGEMA (General Company of Nuclear Materials), but it was difficult to see how these worker demands, which did not specifically concern nuclear power, were related to the radical critique of the ecologists. Hannibal was dubious: he could not really see the link between the fight against industrialisation and the themes of the anti-nuclear struggle. Roland Maire replied that a struggle always develops from a work situation and that he himself was not at all surprised by the apparent lack of connexion. But Hannibal could not really accept Cotentin's argument that there was nothing specifically anti-nuclear about the struggle at La Hague because there were struggles against the deterioration in working conditions everywhere. Piccolo also pointed out that Taylorisation, shift work and job risks are not specific to the nuclear industry: the miners had fought for better working conditions without ever opposing the 'coal society'.

Haggar was reluctant to stop short at this separation between worker demands and the ecology protest. He tried to outdo Cotentin in ecology and stressed the theme of the specific risks of nuclear power. He explained that he was afraid not of a disaster, but of the small doses of radiation absorbed each day, and he related how the 'dirty job' of decontamination is still given to temporary workers and how the latter had deteriorated psychologically: 'The bloke who's caught his dose, the bloke who's had a sample, goes downhill very quickly; there's a definite effect.' He recalled that union action and the anti-nuclear protest had supported one another in the fight over the norms for dumping waste at sea, with some fighting against the forced pace of industrialisation and others against pollution. But Cotentin maintained that the worker resistance had been concerned above all with the fact that the administrative management of the CEA was to be replaced by the more industrial management of the COGEMA.

The separation

The distance between the anti-nuclear action and union demands was even greater than suggested by this debate about La Hague. All the trade unionists in the groups emphasised the lack of support for anti-nuclear positions amongst the rank and file. It was only the leaders who were sympathetic to anti-nuclear themes. Thus, two actions, the unionist and the ecologist, which had initially been merged in a same climate of opinion, became increasingly separate as the group's work progressed. For their part, the leaders of the ecology movement brought out this separation by dissociating themselves in the clearest possible way from representations of society in which the working class and labour conflicts occupied a central place. In their opinion, the workers were no longer invested with a privileged historical destiny; they had become allies amongst others and were no longer the ones who conferred a historical meaning on an action conducted mainly without them. The workers could not be the natural allies of the ecologists, according to Philippe Lebreton, a leader of the ecology movement: 'At first, I thought the bulldozers sent by the Rt. Hon. What's-his-name were simply an expression of money, power, and so on. Then I realised the bulldozer in question was being driven by a bloke who was a proletarian who got a kick out of screwing up "nature".' Leforestier agreed: one should not 'whitewash' the workers at Dassault, for example, on the grounds that they were 'just poor working-class sods'.

Christophe, of course, protested, but a large section of the group felt some affinity with Lebreton's attitudes: as a producer, the working man is a cog in the destructive industrial machine; he identifies with it and becomes the adversary of those who defend nature. Christophe and Bourguignon countered this idea with a concept of class relations and social domination more fundamental than the destruction of nature, but they remained isolated. The group would have nothing to do with a definition of society based on the relations of economic production. Already on the day following the meetings with Monsieur Daurès and Monsieur Thiriet, Rodrigo had spoken out vigorously against trade unionism. He was not hostile to the working-class movement, and indeed he belonged to a union himself, but in his eyes the workers were involved in a conflict which was no longer central in today's world and which avoided the challenging of the aims of production.

Christophe did not accept these ideas and defended himself every inch of the way, saying that the workers were alienated and exploited, so that not only were they not the adversaries of the anti-nuclear movement, but the latter should, in fact, assume responsibility for their problems and bring new perspectives to the union movement. 'There are a certain number of themes in the ecology movement which seem to me to be important for the workers, but I think the ecology movement, like other movements moreover, has been totally incapable of explaining to the workers and discussing with them the importance of those themes for their day-to-day problems. When you talk about the minimum guaranteed wage or social inequality, it's important after all to say that the reduction of social inequalities, the problems of hierarchy, or the problems of working conditions, are linked to a certain type of society, and that if you want to put forward another type of society, it's because you also, and as a matter of priority, want to solve those problems too.' The ecology movement should link worker demands to the critique of industrial society.

Yves Le Gall was also sorry that the ecologists had never really tried to link up with the working-class struggles and had never even wanted to convince the workers. As Georges Flamand pointed out in Paris, the ecologists were anxious above all to succeed in the middle classes from which most of them came.

Brice Lalonde was even more trenchant than Lebreton: in the society now taking shape, the working class is no longer the central historical actor; the logic of needs and communication must take priority over the logic of production. He elaborated on his theme by speaking of creativity, initiative and relationships between individuals. Whilst most of the group seemed to be won over, Christophe resisted: he 'couldn't hear very well', Brice Lalonde was speaking too fast and maybe he himself was 'a bit slow on the uptake'. Lalonde insisted. To his mind, all those, including the workers, who contributed to the imperialism of production were polluters. As for the idea that the future of humanity belonged to the working classes and the productive forces, it was a tenacious idea but one that had to be dumped. Christophe was appalled: 'I don't understand a thing.' Brice Lalonde explained that one should be suspicious of demands for equality because 'in reality equality means uniformity', which is a technocratic obsession that should be opposed by equity and perhaps open, multiple and ephemeral hierarchies. Christophe was downcast, and, what is more, 'didn't understand the half of what you were saying', and then 'I've no desire to convince Brice', but, finally, 'without being a working-class mystic, I say we can do nothing without the people who are the first to be concerned by these matters'.

Brice Lalonde retorted that the ecologists had not needed to go to the factory gates in order to have some influence on the workers. But it was to be feared 'that in the next few years, the split between ecologists and producers would grow wider than ever'. Christophe defended the central need for a link between the ecology movement and the working-class movement, but he was alone and was beaten. Everybody joined in to confirm the split. 'Not only does the message not get through', said Bourguignon, 'but it is tinged with real hostility . . . slogans like "no to nuclear power" haven't got a cat in hell's chance in a place like Pierrelatte.' Jean-Jacques Rodrigo found that some leading politicians were more willing to listen to his ideas than were some scientists. But above all he said 'I couldn't give a toss about the world of work because I have more difficulty persuading them than I do the world of non-work. I don't look on people as workers; I'm a worker myself but that's not how I see myself first and foremost. Back at the beginning, our target wasn't the workers as such, it was blokes, women, people.' Brice Lalonde and Rodrigo, and a large part of the group with them, in spite of their sympathies for the CFDT, insisted on the originality of the social frames of reference of the anti-nuclear movement and in so doing marked out the distance between themselves and the working-class movement and especially the parties of the Left.

Vacillation

If, with Christophe, the relations between the anti-nuclear militants and the trade unionists had taken on a dramatic tone, other CFDT militants tried to restore them to normal. Haggar wanted to draw the union towards the ecology problematic and sensibility; Roland Maire wanted the CFDT to play a more political role of support for the new social struggles.

As the group's work progressed, Haggar gave freer expression to his ecological sensibility and moved away from the strict union language that he had shared with Cotentin during the first meetings. Rather than bringing together the world of ecology and the world of the trade union, he wanted the cultural force of the ecologists to penetrate the world of work. Nowadays, union action can no longer cover all possible problems, and the very limits on union demands turn the union into a force for the cohesion, maintenance and reproduction of the system: 'The traditional organisations merely rearrange the existing system, and, when you come down to it, do no more than give it the occasional nudge.' Haggar adopted the critique of trade unionism developed by the ecologists: society does not exist independently of the way in which each individual organises it in his or her own existence and that is more fundamental than the workers' struggle which designates an adversary who is really an accomplice since they both belong to the same cultural universe. Each individual must challenge his or her own way of living and thinking. Haggar was swinging towards the ecology and community pole of the movement: the militants must be able, outside their work, to tear themselves away from the world of industrial values and create a more open, more community-minded life-style. Haggar spoke warmly of his life in the village and of his hope of being able one day to return to the land. His words aroused a sense of pleasure and togetherness in the group because they bridged the entire gap between trade unionism and ecology and seemed to smooth away all the obstacles.

It was Pelot, the militant from the LCR and the CGT, who opposed this illusion of a direct transition from cultural critique to the social struggle. He pointed out to the union militant identified with the fight at La Hague that the individual's self-challenging does not allow one to act on society and confront a social adversary, and that the trade union, for all its limits, was still a fundamental instrument in the struggle against capitalism and the State which is submitted to it.

But Roland Maire in his turn attacked Pelot's conception of trade unionism. It did not allow any link to be established with the anti-nuclear movement, which designates a social adversary other than capitalism and calls for new union practices. Contrary to what Pelot had said, there was not a single adversary and we should criticise the new centres of power associated with knowledge. There could be no link between ecology and trade unionism if we maintain a traditionalist conception of the latter. To link the two components, the CFDT must act as a political agent and open itself up to the new social movements; it must play the role of a political operator giving form and force to all the scattered protest movements which are the vehicle of new conflicts. The CFDT should free itself from the purely anti-capitalist frame of reference, open itself to the outside, to the new sensibilities and to the new critiques. It must help them by putting pressure on the political system.

This approach met with some resistance from inside the union. Some were afraid that it would make them lose their orientation and basis in worker demands; others imposed precise ideological and political limits on such an opening. If these resistances were to be overcome, the ecologists for their part must understand that the CFDT also had to act in concert with other unions, accept compromise and lend its name to actions whose full implications were not to its liking. This was the case in EDF with the actions that it was conducting together with the CGT against the 'denationalis-ation' of the public service.

Hannibal was against this kind of strategy, which he found somewhat 'twisted'. But, objected Roland Maire, if the ecologists wanted an alliance with the CFDT, they would need to think more politically. In particular, the ecologists had not made a clear call for people to vote for the Left in the last elections, a fact which had irritated many trade unionists. Furthermore, the ecologists often used the CFDT as a guarantee of their own seriousness, as their spokesman, without accepting its objectives, without even being interested in them. Haggar was of the same opinion: the ecologists tried to recuperate from union protest those demands which were related to their own concerns, but on the central union problems of jobs and pay, they were indifferent or hostile.

These debates demonstrated that the CFDT was not to be identified with only one position with regard to the anti-nuclear struggle; the approaches of Christophe, Maire and Haggar were profoundly different. Whereas for Haggar trade unionism could be revitalised by a new cultural climate, for Roland Maire ecologists should be prepared for the CFDT to play the role of political operator in the movement, whilst for Christophe the problem was above all to widen trade union action. The fact remained that a union's main objective is to support worker demands and labour conflicts, a pole of the action with which Cotentin, who scarcely intervened in these central debates, identified. He was first and foremost a trade unionist fighting against the deterioration in working conditions and for worker control over the productive apparatuses. His logic was essentially that of worker demands, a fact which differentiated him from both Maire and Haggar. The one most identified with working-class trade unionism, at the centre of the conflicts of industrial society, he was increasingly absent during the debates concerning the creation of an anti-nuclear movement through a link with the unions. When these debates were the sole object of the group's discussions, Cotentin left, feeling himself less and less concerned, since he was distrustful of the political action towards which Maire was tending and was less deeply involved than Haggar in the ecological way of life. This departure from the group of the one who symbolised the traditional working-class action was the clearest sign of the difficulty in linking the anti-nuclear struggle and the working-class struggle.

In Malville, it was Bourguignon who emphasised the distance between the initiatives of the confederation leaders and the feelings of the rank and file, which were similar to those of Cotentin. He too felt himself pushed somewhat onto the fringes of the group, whose preoccupations seemed to him to be far removed from those of the workers that he knew. He stayed in the group, however, but was usually silent and did not take part in its third weekend.

Thus the more specifically unionised of the CFDT militants demonstrated the distance between themselves and the ecologists, and thereby explained the complex position of the CFDT, which is not anti-nuclear, since it cannot really fight against the work tool of its members, but which is at the same time the most important ally of the anti-nuclear movement; which works with the ecologists, but forms alliances and negotiates with pro-nuclear forces such as the CGT. This complexity conferred a central role on some of the trade unionists in the intervention groups: as managers of the tensions within the action, they were more likely to bring about the conversion of the groups towards an analysis of their action in terms of a social movement.

THE TEST OF THE STRUGGLES

From local defence, the anti-nuclear action seeks to rise towards the more general objectives of a renewal of democracy and an alliance with the unions. Might it go even further and intervene in politics, either by winning the support of the voters, or by mobilising its forces to win a decisive victory against the State? It had tried both ways: the first at the local elections of 1977 and the general elections of 1978; the second on 31 July 1977, the day of the second demonstration at Malville and a turning point in the history of the struggle. We must follow this twofold rise towards political intervention and the twofold fall in which it was broken.

Towards the elections

The transition from cultural experiment to electoral intervention was at the centre of the meeting between the Grenoble–Malville group and Philippe Lebreton. Philippe had gone from a strictly ecological critique to the political struggle without the mediation of other social forces or organisations. He explained how he had passed from ecology 'in the sense of conservation' to a political commitment which was really independent because the profound causes of the destruction of nature are not specifically social. Of course, the social and political divisions which run through society are real, but they are dominated by a 'will to control, to power, to human domination over the non-human'. The Left raises real problems of social class and money, but the ecologists go much further, aiming to 'break once and for all in the history of the world the master–slave relationship between our species and its environment'.

Philippe Lebreton began with the idea of a society defined mainly by its capacity to destroy nature. From this point of view, the Left and the Right, the bosses and the workers, are alike. He constantly appealed to nature, including human nature, against social forces and conflicts. Most members of the group agreed, and each one chipped in with their own ethological illustration. In this vision, the ecology movement itself seemed to be a sort of natural mechanism or vital reflex. In the name of this 'human nature', of the individual programmed in his or her chromosomes, Philippe Lebreton could say: 'The Left is no different from the Right', and call for each individual to bring about change in themselves first of all. The will to power had to be turned against oneself: 'The classic name for it, 200, 300, 500 years ago was saintliness, quite simply. A saint was not passive, quite the opposite. He experienced a sort of upsurge of instinct, but he was able to turn it back upon himself.' This was the perfect description of exemplary action impelled by pure conviction, as opposed to political militancy, the language of the nature of things against the language of social relations.

And yet, remarked Christophe, Philippe Lebreton had stood in the elections and called on people to take part in them. How could such a non-political conception of the ecology movement have led him to take part in the general elections? Philippe Lebreton's reply was 'short and sharp'. As long as the society of the saints was not a reality, libertarian sentiments and the rejection of power were puerile. They should go for power in order not to disappear with the society of the atom. It was because time was running out for human survival and because the stake involved was so basic that they should stand as independents in the elections.

This reasoning seemed to be accepted by one part of the group, but Rodrigo, Esther, Véronique Uri, Yves Le Gall and Christophe resisted it. In their opinion, ecologists should vote for the Left. Christophe wanted to know how a political conception which jettisons social problems for the urgency of survival could accommodate the projects for self-management and the transformation of social relations that Philippe Lebreton seemed nonetheless to support. Lebreton replied that that was all part of the electoral game but that for him those themes were marginal. François Delain and Claudine approved: 'That's the only solution that offers any chance of success.' They thought the direct transition from ecology to the elections had been all the more necessary in March 1978 since the ideas of the ecologists were just beginning to come out of the ghetto of the extreme left and the fringe, and the elections would strengthen that process. They had to win the votes of all those who felt attracted by ecology: 'I'm sorry,' said Lebreton, 'but at the risk of seeming to be a moderate or a conservative, I think that people who've reached a certain stage of questioning, even if it's just about motorways or weekend cottages, are people from all backgrounds, all ages . . . Middle-aged people in pinstripe, that's a good sign, that proves that our ideas are being accepted elsewhere.' 'But in the meantime what becomes of the social dimensions of the anti-nuclear struggle?' asked Christophe, who, in 1978, had been opposed to Ecology 78 standing in the elections. He had found it centrist and had called on people to vote for the Left. Lebreton replied that ecology takes in everything, that it must tie itself down nowhere and bring pressure to bear everywhere.

In the space of a few years, the ecology ideas launched by a small number of former militants from May 68, defenders of nature and environmental experts, had attracted widespread support from public opinion. Brice Lalonde was conscious of that fact and painted a picture of victory to the Grenoble–Malville group: 'Now that the question of nuclear energy is a bit out of date, the ecology movement should continue to organise its victory.' They should try to find new battlefields because already the pro-nuclear bloc was cracking. No doubt there would be some nuclear power, but the 'all-nuclear' programme would not be achieved; the movement had only to keep up the pressure. Brice Lalonde thought there should be links with all the problems, with what he called the 'nebula'. They should go everywhere, take part in every commission, open out in order to avoid the risks of sectarian withdrawal. Why not stand in the elections? They had to get out of the ecology party and defend and popularise ideas.

Christophe did not pose the problem in those terms. It was not a question of defending the purity of a sect, but of confronting a social adversary, of linking the ecology fight to that of the workers and not only defending 'ecology interests' in public opinion and various institutions. From that point of view, the electoral terrain might not be the most suitable for the ecologists. But Brice Lalonde explained that taking part in elections did not break the dynamics of the struggle since they could go into them doing 'exactly the opposite of what people usually do . . . We should aim at total subversion of the elections.' Ecologists could use the electoral platform without becoming involved in a game which in other respects they condemned. By that, Brice Lalonde was aiming at more than a simple movement of opinion, since he thought that the ecologists could 'super-impose a new division on the existing one', because the interests they represented were more fundamental than those of the traditional parties. Impelled by its historical force, the movement could express itself everywhere.

It was this optimism that led Brice Lalonde to triumph in this meeting. In his eyes, the ecologists represented the central problems of the society now taking shape; they had gone beyond the problems and the actors of industrial society. That allowed them to be everywhere, to strike up alliances without compromising themselves, to be neither a party nor a union, which are historical categories 'in the process of disappearing'. Before a captivated group, Brice Lalonde called for initiative, creativity, the multiplication of social relations, imagination. They should free themselves from the constraints of industrial society and invent the culture of tomorrow.

It was because Christophe, as a trade unionist, was at the heart of those constraints and fighting to lift them that he resisted these ideas: he was not only fighting for a more open and relaxed society, but also against a social adversary. Yves Le Gall also became disillusioned. Since 1970, the cultural movement had been stagnating and regressing: 'Out of all the experiments there's not a thing left now.' But they were voices in the wilderness. Brice Lalonde said the movement should look for new battlegrounds after the victory over nuclear power, and Jean-Jacques agreed: the ecologists, supported by history, should go to the elections and play their own card, because 'the Left is a myth, it exists only in our minds . . . As for me, I couldn't give a damn about it, and maybe I'm even glad to have Giscard rather than the Communist Party.'

The fall

The break with the Left
The anti-nuclear movement, said Haggar, has a future only if it attracts a large number of the workers. Now, the hope of the workers lay in the Left coming to power, 'and yet the majority of the anti-nuclear movement, by

not calling on people to vote for the Left, has cut itself off from the workers'. Georges Flamand lived in the North where hope in the Left was high, and he himself had called on people to vote for them in the second round, but on the whole, in the March 1978 general elections, the movement had remained incapable of choosing because it was submerged by a political stake that was way beyond it. It had not even raised the question of the choice it should make, said Hannibal, and today the price to be paid for that indecision was enormous: it was the mistrust of the workers.

Kropo, however, thought they should not idealise the Left because it had been beaten; it also bore a heavy responsibility, and 'you can't pretend to believe that it represents the workers'. So perhaps they ought to dissociate themselves from politics. But the general feeling was that the break with the Left was not wanted. In the opinion of Haggar, they should have called on people right from the start to vote for the Left in the second round; they should have sided clearly with the workers without negotiating the alliance. The break with the Left was felt all the more deeply since the electorate of the militant ecologists, themselves mainly left-wing, was largely moderate, with the result that many militants were unable to recognise themselves in the electorate they had attracted. It was clear from this that elections were not the best battlefield for the ecologists and not a good way of measuring the movement's real influence. Many people who have an ecology sensibility, said Roland Maire and Jean-Philippe Pharisca, do not express it in political terms, so it was scarcely surprising if the militants did not recognise themselves in their electorate. Elections inevitably favour the ones closest to the big names and the libertarian and community forces are crushed by the power of the lobby. As Haggar said: 'What worries me are the people who vote for the Right in the second round and who are still ecologists.'

If the Paris group seemed to deplore the break with the Left and to attribute it to the political naivety of the movement, the Grenoble–Malville group seemed more divided. It was true, said Philippe Lebreton, that the ecologists bore some responsibility for the defeat of the Left in March 1978, because they had revealed 'its lack of ideal'. The whole strategy of the movement had been to 'blackmail the Left' and it was because the Left had not responded that the ecologists had been unable to stand down in its favour in the second round. Christophe, however, thought they ought to side with the Left because ecology was pursuing 'basically left-wing objectives'. The movement should put itself clearly in the camp of those who wanted to reduce inequalities and transform society. None of the criticisms one could make of the Left altered the fact that it was the expression of the workers. The split in the group became even wider when Jean-Jacques sided with Philippe Lebreton: the Left, the Communist Party, is no different from the Right; the Left does not exist outside of our dreams.

Moreover, recalled Claudine, when the group had met the real Left in the person of the interlocutor from the Communist Party, there had been a whole universe of difference between them, so why should they always put themselves under their wing at election time?

The movement scattered

The elections had divided the movement and driven it away from the Left. They had also revealed the absence of any control by the movement over itself, since it was divided and dispersed between the force of its utopia, the limits of its struggle and the weakness of its political thinking. In this frequently warm and community-minded space, leaders appeared, devised policies, made choices, bore the troops along with them, and tried to bring all the components of the action together on the electoral field. But when the elections came, this semblance of unity cracked.

Such was the harsh assessment delivered by Yves Le Gall. The Left, which had been the object of so much criticism, had at least had the merit of initiating internal debate after the electoral defeat; there had been nothing similar in the ecology movement. The elections had given a semblance of action and the movement had gone in search of every adventure. In this universe which refuses the constraints of organisation and democracy in favour of unanimity and togetherness, the various personalities became symbols rather than the strategists of a policy and they were given a free hand to develop their own individual policies according to their own inspiration and without control from below.

In this respect, the groups' meetings reflected the sociability of the movement, in which many things could be said without division or conflict. As Yves Le Gall said, they each had their own individual truth and nobody had to bow to a collective discipline; individual charm could flourish freely.

The elections had shown that the rejection of 'politics' left the way open to intrigue, manipulation and spectacular coups. So all that was needed was a few groups or leaders to take the whole of the movement into the elections, if only to make sure that the others did not have the field entirely to themselves.

As it approached the elections, the movement scattered. Georges Flamand realised that strategic thought was incompatible with a movement which is defined primarily by its cultural and critical sensibility. 'The election race ripped the movement apart because it did not yet have an internal democracy and a basis which allowed it to control the operation.' Solange Fernex pointed out to the Parisians that the movement in Alsace was sufficiently well established and rooted in struggles to be able to use the elections in a pragmatic way, as a convenient platform. But in Paris, where there were no social struggles and where the intellectuals and the media played an excessive part, elections became the movement's only practice, or more accurately, a substitute for the absence of struggles. In the electoral venture, many militants had felt that the movement was losing its soul, with the front of the stage being hogged by the defenders of nature and the pressure groups.

Everything pushed the movement into the elections; everything scattered it in the fight. The creative prediction had failed, the anti-nuclear movement had not been transformed into a political force by going to the elections. And now the groups were dominated by this failure. During these meetings, they lost the feeling of victory that Brice Lalonde had momentarily revived. Where could the anti-nuclear movement create its struggles, when the local fights remained narrow and defensive, when the links with the unions seemed more and more strained, and when the electoral excitement which gave a meaning to militancy went brutally cold?

Malville

Malville 76

In 1976 the demonstration at Malville and the repression which followed brought together a population directly affected by the building of Super-Phoenix and anti-nuclear militants who identified with a general critique of society. It was less a widening and elevating of local combat than the incarnation of a movement gathering together the most diverse components and making great mobilisations seem possible against everything that symbolised the 'all-nuclear' programme and its mortal dangers. For both groups, Malville 76 was the pinnacle of the struggle.

But would the mobilised population be able to go beyond the community warmth and organise the struggle? Malville 77 dealt a cruel blow to that hope: the local rank and file lost control and the repression which had briefly favoured unity was to scatter all the assembled forces.

Malville 77

TOURAINE: 'From the point of view of the movement, what was it like for those who were at Malville on 31 July 1977?'

PICCOLO: 'Terrible.'

FLAMAND: 'I cried like a baby.'

HANNIBAL: 'Terrifying.'

FLAMAND: 'Terrible.'

PICCOLO: 'It was like the First World War and Waterloo rolled into one.'

There were several tens of thousands of demonstrators; it was raining; the leaders were bickering and had no control; the police refused all contact. It was the complete opposite of the spontaneous control of the year before. Everyone felt lost in an affair that many militants had expected to be a repeat of the success of 1976. There was to be no community celebration, however, only a military operation and a lost battle. People were marching without knowing why; the local population stayed away; the police used tear gas grenades; there were several wounded and one man died. At its strongest mobilisation in France, the movement, locked in battle against the State, was breaking up. Sophia had the feeling that the demonstration had fallen into a trap set by the police and the government who had prepared public opinion to accept the repression and the death of Vital Michalon in the name of the fight against terrorism. Georges Flamand: 'It was a demo in a morgue, silence, it was extraordinary, completely blank faces, tension, tight lips . . .' 'Everybody was expecting the defeat,' said Kropo, 'everybody knew there would be a massacre . . .' Piccolo saw nothing of the battle except the defeat: 'We set out in the morning, and we marched all day, going slowly. It was raining. It took us most of the day to get there and we were the last to arrive. We stopped. There were ambulances hurtling by with sirens blaring away. One ambulance went screaming past with people in the back holding drip-feeds, and you really felt as if you were going into the front line, like cannon fodder. There was no question of grand military manoeuvres; we weren't ready. We looked ridiculous with our little goggles against the gas, we looked ridiculous. We'd bought little Chinese style straw hats and we'd stuffed the inside for protection against the truncheons; it was all ridiculous . . .' Kropo spoke of the children's crusade.

The movement stolen

The defeat came as no surprise, everybody was expecting it: the year following the 1976 demonstration had brought political defeat. After the success of 1976, the Malville Committees which had been set up almost everywhere had been invaded by various groups, and the hardest and most organised tendencies had won the day. After the success of 1976, the men of violence looking for confrontation with the State had arrived, like 'vultures', said Georges Flamand. The ecology movement, which had a base but no organisation, saw itself invaded and dispossessed of its struggle. The militants felt as if they had been a plaything for organised groups. On 31 July 1977, they had been the battalions marching for others. They saw nothing, did not know where they were going: they let their movement be stolen from them. Those who, like Hannibal and Georges Flamand, had seen the situation deteriorating after March 1977, were unable to stem the tide that was leading to disaster. In Grenoble, Yves Le Gall had been quick to see that the Malville Committees would be recuperated by the extreme left: 'The extreme left in Grenoble came piling in en masse where only a few weeks before it had shown a complete lack of interest in ecology and nuclear questions.' He saw the extreme left militancy that he had analysed and criticised in previous years grafting itself onto the movement. 'When the new militants', he said, 'tried to get their hands on the anti-nuclear movement, and succeeded to some extent, I felt that the whole movement, which had until then represented a much deeper aspiration, had lost its way, had gone off in a direction which destroyed much of its interest.' In July 1977, the movement had been contaminated.

The Grenoble–Malville group was made up of people who had taken part in the 1977 demonstration and the split in the movement was also present in the group in its first session. The real enemies of the movement, those who want to kill it off, are in this group, said Rodrigo, pointing at Valence, one of those who had supported the violent and autonomous action at Malville. Although the group was never again in danger of violent eruption and its debates were always relaxed and often cordial, Jean-Jacques threatened to leave if Valence stayed. 'He is the real enemy,' he said, 'because he killed the movement at Malville. The sort of people I saw at Malville, I tell you, I'd rather have the police against me than those people with me.' But the agitator managed to prevent his leaving and Valence attended no further meetings until the working weekends. Everything separated the two men: Jean-Jacques associated the struggle against nuclear power with the search for a different kind of life, different values, a certain ability to be available and to listen; Valence was there to make war on the State. He wounded the gentleness of Jean-Jacques who called him and his friends 'wolves and hyenas'. For Jean-Jacques, Malville 77 was the brutal and dramatic shattering of the image of an anti-nuclear front bringing together in community sociability a force for cultural break and a counter-project for society.

vvv

In search of the movement

THE CONVERSION OF THE PARIS GROUP

Setting out

The Paris group began with a question which had been raised by Sophia at the beginning of its tenth session: was the anti-nuclear struggle specific, particular, or was it set in a more general social or political action? Following this vital thread brings us across three successive answers: the anti-nuclear struggle is only one element in a more general political action directed against the State, the technocracy and high capitalism; the anti-nuclear struggle is a part of the ecology movement, its values and its refusals; the anti-nuclear struggle is a central actor on the social stage and so contains a social movement which is much wider than this specific application.

The political break

This theme was not expressed very strongly in Versailles. Pelot had already left a group in which he had been the butt of jokes which were friendly but nonetheless emphasised his isolation. It was mainly Sophia who opposed any reduction of the anti-nuclear struggle to a surge of counter-culture. Alice, who was usually silent most of the time, shared Sophia's wish to give priority to political action. These two militants from the Amis de la Terre in Paris shared a constant concern to resist both the manoeuvrings of charismatic leaders and a vaguely reformist associationism in favour of a specifically political struggle against the government's energy and social policy. Close to them on these themes were Hannibal and Emmanuel Kropo who several times denounced the dangers of the exemplary communities and recalled the need to replace the anti-nuclear action in the general political framework of the struggle against the State. But to this critique of the absolutist State Hannibal added an ecology sensibility, the pleasure of craftsmanship, the search for natural foods, and the rejection of urban life; he was even trying to unite counter-culture and political action in the anti-nuclear struggle. Kropo took the opposite way out of anti-Statism, the way of a specifically political action, based on the class struggle but directed towards self-management. Anti-Statism, the main historical root of the anti-nuclear struggle, instead of turning in upon itself or joining forces with the search for a defensive community, was transformed and enlarged in the Paris group by a desire for concrete social action and cultural change.

The protest community

If the anti-nuclear struggle was not set in a general refusal of the State, was it perhaps placed in a general movement of cultural withdrawal? Was it only one of the manifestations of an ecology *sensibility?* Communal life was rejected by Sophia, Alice and Kropo who saw it as a moralist illusion that diverts people from political action. It was accepted with some reticence by Hannibal and held no interest for Roland Maire, but it was passionately defended by Georges Flamand.

Because Georges had left home and given up his studies, because he had been on the road, had for years led a small group of anti-nuclear militants in the North and because he had experienced the strength but also the crisis of life in a commune, he defended what had never been a withdrawal for him but a breakaway and above all a place where he could live the inspiration of his struggle. He was not defending an exemplary community that protected the happiness of a simple life open to others, but a commitment which was lived and not just thought. 'Do the people round this table have their own lived experience, one which has marked them and led them to join the anti-nuclear movement, or have they no such experience which has set them apart from other people? If that were the case, then we really would be in a mere movement of ideas.' The researcher recognised in this declaration that faith without which there could be no social movement. He did not feel rejected by Georges's question since he himself knew that because he was there in an intervention that he had wanted, he was living his research and not just pontificating about actions that he knew only from his reading.

The community for Georges was first and foremost the 'reappropriation of a certain time and a certain space by means of a common project'. It was also a barrier against the 'social State' which takes responsibility for all the aspects of personal and collective life. Not only was it not on the fringe of politics, but it was actually more at the centre of it than the usual methods of collective action. Only the community movement was capable of challenging the general orientations of a society, whereas so-called political action came down in the best of cases to changing the leaders without bothering to ask about their orientations. There could be no political action without organisation, but it deteriorates rapidly if it is not supported by a community movement in which we can actually live, in resistance and fraternity, our hope for a transformed world. At a single stroke, the defence of the community and the counter-project for society had been linked through a specifically social will to struggle. This association gave Georges a central place in the group and thus in the effort of the anti-nuclear militants to find a basis for their struggle and transform it into a social movement, but his influence should not be exaggerated to the point of blinding us to the different and even opposite feelings inspiring the people who were gathered that weekend in an old building set in an almost abandoned garden.

In Haggar and Piccolo, the ecology sensibility was expressed through the fear of nuclear power, a fear which they maintained against a group which had turned away from the theme. It was the fear of catastrophe or disease so often betrayed by the employees from the Maison de la Radio whose reactions, recorded several days before, had been played back to the group. Fear, too, in the case of Haggar who worked at the reprocessing plant in La Hague, of a society at the mercy of an accident, so strict is the attention it demands to ever more precise instructions; fear finally in both men, but in Cotentin too, who also worked at La Hague, of a society of police surveillance.

Piccolo, bored with his administrative job and attracted by the circus professions, felt threatened by the world of hard technology and unwieldy apparatuses into which the society of production and consumption was taking us. He rejected artificial needs, wanting neither car nor television. Haggar was the opposite. A worker, from a rural background, and a very active trade unionist, he had believed in work as a means of personal and collective progress. Now he no longer believed in it, no longer saw his future in industry, and dreamt of returning to farming, just as Cotentin dreamt of becoming a social worker, which was another way out of an industry which is increasingly constraining and where every day the worker loses more control over his job, his working environment and the aims of his production. He listened closely to Jean-Pierre Provins, a farmer opposed to the construction of a nuclear power station in the Nogent region, when he extolled his free and responsible style of life.

As for Saint-Hilaire, he had thrown himself into the anti-nuclear struggle when he felt directly threatened by the Nogent power station, which was to be built precisely where he had hoped to live after his retirement. And finally, Jean-Philippe Pharisca was as far away from the search for an exemplary community as he was from the desire for direct confrontation with the State. He preferred to place himself at the intermediate level of the democratic institutions.

The Paris group, then, was extremely varied and not united by a common participation in a struggle. Its richness and its fragility derived from the fact that it brought together people who were trying to protect themselves or to escape from a dangerous and constraining world and people who wanted to transform this defensive withdrawal into a social and political counter-offensive.

The anti-nuclear project

The trade unionist to whom the rest of the group gave the transparent pseudonym of Roland Maire [after Edmond Maire, leader of the CFDT (Tr.)] situated himself in a different part of the struggle. He left it to his comrades from La Hague, more directly affected than he was, to talk about work and safety conditions. Very early on during the first session and more clearly still during this weekend, he linked the anti-nuclear struggle to a new form of the class struggle, one which pits the inhabitants, the citizens, against the great productive apparatuses and especially EDF, a technocratic power which was imposing an energy policy and a type of development on the whole of the nation. For him, the belief in progress was dead; it was not possible to accept the growth of the productive forces as liberating and challenge only the social forms of economic organisation. It was the very idea of a productivist society that had to be rejected, because it deceived the workers, strengthened central authority, and trapped the population in an ever tighter network of constraints. The people must wrest back the political capacity to choose its way of life and its future.

These analyses were the opposite of the anti-Statism defended by Valence in Grenoble, but also by Sophia and even by Hannibal in Paris. Roland Maire attacked EDF but did not confuse it with the State, which remained for him the political system. It was thus a social and economic adversary that he was fighting, and not a system or an absolute power. He was formulating a political project rather than transmitting a lived experience. Although very different from Georges Flamand, he joined with him in bringing the group towards the formulation of a social critique and a political project. But the distance which he invariably maintained from the ecology sensibility, his constant determination to speak in terms of union policy and also his facility with words aroused reticence in some members of the group, and especially in those who, like Sophia, adopted the most defensive position. An attitude of global protest was suspicious of what it saw as the danger of politicking compromise.

At the close of this first morning, and remembering the contents of the tenth session, it was possible to define the main characteristics of the Paris group several hours before the time chosen by the researchers to attempt its conversion. In the first place, the main tendency in the group was towards the anti-nuclear struggle rather than towards a general opposition to the State; in the second place, several of the actors were moving towards the definition of a social counter-project; and finally, the group was not very homogeneous and was thus exposed to the danger of internal dissension.

The initial phases of the analysis revealed firstly that the anti-nuclear actor sometimes challenged a social domination but sometimes the absolutism of the State, and secondly that its action was either defensive, seeking to protect a community experience, or counter-offensive, opposing present policy with a project for society. The members of the Paris group

87

NATURE OF THE CONFLICT

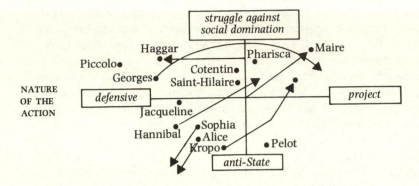

(NB: the main positions of the participants are given
here, but none of them can be reduced to a place in a typology.)

could be clearly located on the graph formed by the intersection of these two axes. Many of them were in the upper half of the graph, in other words on the side of the social struggles rather than of a break with the State, but above all they were not stationary; several of the most active amongst them were moving towards the north-east quarter of the graph, in which a political counter-project opposes a social adversary, in other words where a social movement might be formed. That is why their position is indicated by an arrow rather than a dot.

Could this impetus towards political project and social struggle transform the anti-nuclear struggle into a movement, and if so, at the cost of what sacrifices and what divisions? Surely not so easily as might be suggested by the tone of this first phase of the meeting.

Retreat

The fragility of the group at the end of this first morning came out into the open during the lunch break when Sophia gave vent to her disagreement with the tendency to devise objectives and almost a whole programme in complete abstraction and as if they were in a political party to the detriment of an effective recognition of the lived experience of the movement and, above all, of the group itself. She opposed Roland Maire's position and Alain Touraine's support for it. At the beginning of the afternoon session, Jacqueline Monceau repeated these criticisms. Sophia had spoken of blockage, whereas she herself was speaking more as a woman. At the beginning of the ecology movement, the women had played a large part, but then gradually they had withdrawn or fallen silent, whilst a specifically masculine programmatic and theoretical logic had imposed itself. 'With something big like nuclear power and all it brings with it, something which implies policing, women tend to have a more physical reaction, a gut reaction. But when there's an attempt at political recuperation, the women vanish. They systematically refuse to be subjected to yet another male logic. In 68, men and women did more or less the same thing, but then after 68, the women moved to the side.' In the Amis de la Terre she could see the renaissance of forms of militancy that everybody had rejected. The originality of the ecology movement had been its concern with 'private problems, the problems of children, with the result that the women had felt at ease, but when the ecology movement had started to reproduce precisely the one thing where women were no longer at ease, the public element, they retreated'. Jacqueline was not speaking only in the name of feminists, and Sophia, who did not consider herself one, approved what she was saying because she wanted the movement to define for what and for whom it was speaking, its raison d'être, before designating its adversary and working out a strategy. Jacqueline added that the movement must first define but also live social and human relationships.

Georges Flamand supported the protest of the two women. During the morning, he had seemed motivated above all by the will to develop a social project, but he had already stressed the importance of lived experience and community experience in setting up a movement. Now he gave priority to this grass-roots experience and was distrustful of excessively hasty political elaborations. 'Touraine is forever asking who the enemy is. You have to define a target at the top of society. That's an excessively masculine attitude. It's the attitude of the warrior who has to take on the chief. But there's another way that I would call more feminine.'

Piccolo and Saint-Hilaire, foreign to the feminist movement, took advantage of the reaction of Sophia and Jacqueline to reintroduce the theme of the defence of nature to which Hannibal gave a more scientific basis by showing that a knowledge of natural systems teaches the superiority of that which is moving and adaptable over the rigidity and inertia of many of the social and technological constructions of human beings. In this way, the protest by the women actually brought the action back towards a lived experience which had been neglected by a too directly political orientation.

Throughout most of this session, Roland Maire did not intervene and the other trade unionists, Cotentin and Haggar, also remained silent. This revealed the fragility of the movement which seemed to have no difficulty in transforming anti-Statism, the fear of catastrophe or the defence of the community into a counter-project for society. There would be no social movement in the anti-nuclear struggle if this transition did not take place, but neither would there be any if there was politicisation at the expense of lived experience and the reasons for commitment. The anti-nuclear struggle was affective rather than strategic, inspired by the search for what Jacqueline called tenderness and conviviality. It was closer to a cultural movement than a political struggle. The important thing for it was to define what it believes and what it condemns rather than its alliances and objectives. That is why the life of the intervention group took on such importance; it should itself be an exemplary place where the actors could live their participation in the refusal, the struggle and the hope rather than simply reflecting on the development of an analysis and a programme. The group, carried away in the morning by Alain Touraine's analyses, fell back upon a cultural experience of which François Dubet constantly recalled the importance, initially perhaps to resist the tensions imposed upon it by moving too rapidly towards political reflexion, but above all because its strength lay in feelings and not in a doctrine or even a militant capacity, to use a term rejected by several people in both groups.

Some struggles begin with a conflict, others are initially movements of ideas. The anti-nuclear struggle, or rather in this case the ecology movement, appeared at first as the defence of lived experience, the need for interpersonal relationships, the consciousness of belonging to a whole whose natural balances are being dangerously destroyed by productivist arrogance. The movement was initially a reaction of defence and refusal, a fact which the women in the group expressed by speaking of gut reactions, to which, they said, women were more sensitive, just as they are also better listeners and more attentive to relationships with others.

This retreat was not weakness, but rather a search for the source of strength of a struggle that everybody feared would lose itself in the world of the parties and even the unions. Desire and community on the one side, denunciation of the artifices and contradictions of growth on the other, these two elements of the movement sometimes seemed complementary and sometimes opposed. The ecologist temptation was to believe that a feeling can be translated directly into action and even into tactics without having first to define the nature of a conflict.

It was usually Roland Maire who recalled the need to define the adversary, the struggle and the forms of the action. But at the beginning of that afternoon, Roland, under attack from Sophia, remained reserved, and it was Emmanuel Kropo who attacked the appeals to nature in which he saw the risk of depoliticisation: when you talk of the laws of nature, you are surely submitting yourself to an order on which you cannot act, which is alien to social intervention. He was afraid that this ecologism might lead to what he called the alternative discourse which gives up the anti-nuclear struggle only to ask for an accelerated development of other energy sources. Encouraged by this, Roland attacked the illusion of nature lost, as if a garden did not presuppose heavy technological investment. Jean-Pierre

Provins, himself a farmer, also rejected in some irritation the ecologist illusion of a biological agriculture. 'Good mother nature doesn't give anything if you give her nothing, she's just a medium.'

The researchers, whilst stressing everything that separated the opposing positions, tried not to favour the most political approach. They acknowledged the unique strength of the women's themes and the appeal to all that the society of power has destroyed or rejected. For how could one understand and create the movement without starting from an experience which was not only the experience of deprivation but, even before that, the experience of a life which has to be defended against a death brought by the destructive proliferation of technologies and arms? A movement is not only the rejection of a domination; it is also the affirmation of a positive principle and of values from which the world can be recreated. Those who see only the positive side are submerged in utopia or in reformism, both of which are a constant threat to the ecologists. But those who reduce the action to the struggle against a domination condemn themselves to creating a militant organisation and handing power to a praetorian guard or a militarised party.

The anti-nuclear militants in the group were sufficiently politicised to protect themselves against the risks of political reformism; none of them were satisfied with the limited efforts of the societies for the protection of nature, but, precisely because they had a political past, they wanted to break with the objectivism of the parties of the Left and especially of the Communist Party. The group detested the doctrinaire language and authoritarian organisation of collective action; they preferred utopia to ideology, lived experience to theory. But their appeal to the community was joined to the search for a social project. Almost too easily in fact, since the need for struggle, for breakaway and for the organisation of the collective action was in danger of being forgotten in this impetus towards a new society. The group during these first hours had asserted the motives and the objectives of its action with equal vigour, but would it be able to link both to the denunciation of the adversary? It was difficult in the middle of that afternoon to predict the outcome of the conversion that the researchers were shortly to undertake, but the strength and warmth of the group were impressive. To use Piccolo's favourite symbol, it was living like a tree, rooted in the earth and in life-giving exchange with its environment.

The conversion

But it was divided. Not into two rival camps with one defending a great refusal and the other a project for the transformation of society, but between those who wanted to start from the bottom, from lived experience and the ability to resist the order imposed by the State, and those who sought to

91

define the struggle through the adversary that it was fighting and the stake of their confrontation rather than by the nature or the content of what was being defended. This division was not of the kind which is easily overcome. The social movements of the past had no difficulty in defining those for whom they were struggling, peasants in the service of the land owner, workers exploited in the factory, colonised peoples. But today, in a 'massified' society, although it is quite easy to denounce power, it is increasingly difficult to name those who are subjected to it. It is easy to wax indignant over the domination of information by the State or money, but in the name of whom? Newspaper readers? Radio audiences? Television viewers? But who is not one of these and, conversely, who is defined in this way outside of the moment when they are actually consuming the message transmitted from a distant centre?

The opposition formulates its refusal in the strongest of terms, but it has difficulty in naming those who are opposed to the dominations of today in the central social relationship of our society. Hence the temptation to follow Valence who was against the entire State in the name of a freedom, a work, and an individual experience which remained completely indeterminate. Hence also the ease with which analyses of the action gave way to the debating of ideas, and finally the disappointments experienced, as we have seen, each time we tried to locate the resistances to the nuclear industry in a particular place: the workers in the industry itself or the inhabitants of the communes where a nuclear power station was being built. In the intervention, this absence of an identity principle was expressed in the illusion of a direct transition from feeling to action, as if that which defends itself against technocratic domination could be directly transformed into the seed of a decentralised, self-managing world of the future. In the absence of a precise definition, the actor was apprehended only as the opposite of the adversary, and this opposite became another type of society, but one which was no more than the mask of desire.

If a social movement was to be formed, there must be an end to this lack of differentiation of the actor, the adversary and the stake of their struggle. Such was the aim of the conversion that the agitator was about to attempt. In agreement with the secretary, who now stopped supporting the grass-roots of the movement and joined his efforts more and more directly to those of the agitator, the latter attempted to escape from the utopia and the undifferentiation of the struggles and address himself to the group in the name of a movement, that is to say in the name of an analysis of a central social conflict and its cultural stake. Without fear of offending the group's susceptibilites, he declared that the anti-nuclear struggle should not be based on the refusal of modernity but on the search for a greater modernity against the false modernism of the defenders of the nuclear policy. He even went so far as to speak of the constraints of the international economic system and of the need for industrialised countries to leap forward towards new kinds of production based more on the processing of information than on the production and use of machines which consume or produce energy. At the same time, he invited the group to name its adversary, not to be content with denouncing the system, the State, or any other Everything, but to recognise the technocracy, in other words those who control the apparatuses which process information and manage a sector of social life, trying to reinforce their power and maintain their monopoly.

This intervention by the agitator was not based on any spontaneous analysis by the group of the movement contained within its struggle. On the contrary, after the lively session in the morning, the group had been dragged into crisis by the reaction of Sophia and Jacqueline and by the distance which seemed to have opened up between the politically minded Roland and the community-oriented Georges. The researchers were aware, when the group began work again towards five o'clock in the evening, of the urgent need to redress a deteriorating situation and to confront the group with a brutally drawn portrait of its action. The researcher whose responsibility it was to attempt the conversion began to speak energetically.

The attempt to get underway
Alain Touraine opened the meeting by introducing two ideas. The group was experiencing 'a sort of non-communication between two universes. One is represented by those who talk of identity, nature and culture, and the other by those whose language is more political, more social. These two levels of argument have not come together.' In his opinion, the only way to overcome this separation was to 'return to the anti-nuclear question, in other words to the definition of a certain social relationship', because 'there is a social movement when a social relationship is challenged; not an identity but a relationship of domination'. He addressed himself in particular to those who seemed to be somewhere in between the two modes of thinking, Hannibal and Georges Flamand. He was immediately supported by Emmanuel Kropo, and Hannibal also responded to his call, but with an indication of his uncertainty: 'I'm in two minds. We know the struggle has to be political, but we can't just reproduce the old models of political struggle.'

Roland Maire, on the other hand, denied the opposition set up by Alain Touraine. The ecology themes were a matter of some concern to the CFDT: 'I feel involved in this question, but I think others express it better than I do, so in the group I let them speak, although I could very well speak for myself. And in fact I did in the CFDT to groups which had an exclusively political way of thinking.' But this did not account for the conflict in which he himself had been involved in the group, in particular with Sophia.

Haggar, one of the trade unionists from La Hague, was more aware of the distance and gave it a fresh interpretation: 'We don't come from the same background, we don't mix with the same people, that's why we think differently.' Thus this trade unionist with the ecology sensibility, a worker from a rural and working-class region, charted the distance between himself and the people with managerial functions, the executives, scientists or union officials from Paris. François Dubet dwelt on this distance in order to shatter the illusion of unanimity already badly shaken by the early afternoon session. There was no small amount of confusion, and the number of private conversations increased.

At that point Alain Touraine introduced a provocative idea: instead of criticising progress, we should acknowledge that the anti-nuclear and ecology movement was, in fact, much more modernising than those who could talk only of energy, since it helps us to change our way of producing and consuming and to enter a society of information, something which also implies a struggle against the social inequalities which help to imprison our society in an imitation of the capital expenditure of the more affluent classes. 'Just as the working-class movement was born out of the rejection of machines but was able to develop only by freeing itself from that rejection, so the anti-nuclear movement, associated initially with a disgust at progress and technology, will assume importance only if it can get itself off that launching pad.' This idea sparked off a debate on modernisation in which, this time, Roland played a central part. He recognised the presence of an anti-progress mentality in the ecology movement. 'The problem is to get a proper dialogue going with the movement so that we can take charge of that something and develop a form of action which allows it to move forward and to anticipate the future.'

Georges, for his part, spoke of the two-year-old link between the Réseau des Amis de la Terre and the CFDT, whilst Hannibal was more conscious of the problems to be overcome, and Sophia and Jacqueline remained suspicious. In fact, the group had not really been drawn into its conversion. Emmanuel and Hannibal were most sensitive to the promptings of the agitator because they were constantly concerned to give the political orientations of the action priority over its cultural basis, but Roland and Georges stuck to their positions of principle whilst the rest of the group lapsed into an awkward reserve. The level of the debate plummeted sharply, firstly on the subject of the means, where Jean-Philippe Pharisca dared to say that the only way to achieve the aims of the movement was to convince the people in power, in other words to be resolutely reformist, which offended those who associated the defence of the community with the struggle against the State, and secondly on the subject of the ends themselves, where Jacqueline thought they should give up the anti-nuclear struggle and start a new action against computerisation or other techniques of manipulation, an idea rejected by the group which affirmed the central importance of the anti-nuclear struggle. But the debate foundered in confusion.

Alain Touraine intervened once more to defend the need for an alliance between the anti-nuclear social movement and a specifically political agent, which might be the CFDT rather than the parties. But the intervention was a mistake. He was, in fact, abandoning his role of mediator between the struggle and the movement in order to take on the role of expert or adviser by placing himself at the level of the struggle, its strategy and its organisation. The result was simply to lock the group into its internal conflicts and even to lead it to resist the intervention of the researchers who seemed intent on destroying its unity.

The conversion through humour
The group's resistance was revealed first by the departure of Sophia, Alice and Jacqueline at dinner time, a departure which Hannibal explained by general reasons: in conflict with the leadership of the Amis de la Terre in Paris, they were in fact withdrawing from militant action. But the departure should also be interpreted from the history of the group itself, from the resistance of these women, who always thought of themselves as a group, to a transition to political action and organisation which seemed to them to be heavy with reformism. They returned the next morning, but stayed on the fringes of the group, Sophia and Alice especially. The departure was serious since we now knew that if the anti-nuclear struggle did manage to define itself and act as a movement, it would only be at the price of deep divisions. The populist illusion, the dream of losing nothing of the past while building the future, of uniting identity and change, mysticism and politics, had been shattered yet again.

But for the time being, the other form of resistance from the group was more important and was to have unexpected consequences. After dining together, the members of the group went for a coffee in a nearby bar, taking advantage of the researchers' wish to telephone Zsuzsa Hegedus and Michel Wieviorka who were in Autrans with the Grenoble–Malville group. When the session started again, an acrimonious discussion broke out between the members of the group without the researchers being able to intervene. Ecologists and trade unionists did more than reproach one another, they hurled the most extreme accusations. The latter accused the former of irresponsibility and reminded them that the alliance with the CGT was much more important to them than support for the anti-nuclear struggle. Some of the ecologists retorted that the CFDT had only its own interests at heart. Roland, Georges, Hannibal, Haggar and Emmanuel outdid one another in polemic, in an atmosphere of high excitement, and yet of laughter too.

And then Georges asked to have another look at the last part of the discussion on the video. The tape was re-run, and at the end there appeared on the screen the words: this is a hoax. The two researchers were dumbfounded, there was a roar of laughter, and then the group, led by Roland, explained that they had set up the joke to demonstrate the group's unity against the researchers who had been trying to create opposition between its members. There were several minutes of amused comment on the researchers who were bewildered at this pretence of breakdown in the group. They were in no position to exchange impressions with one another, but Alain Touraine was quickly convinced that it was not just a hoax, the self-defence of pupils ragging the teacher, because the accusations the actors had made against one another, excessive though they were, had a basis in reality. The group had used humour in an attempt to live its unity and its conflicts both at the same time. Prevented by the fear of division from following through its self-analysis, it made light of that division in order to assert its desire to go beyond it and to seek within itself the movement which it knew could not take in all the aspects of the struggle. The joke was a catharsis rather than a hoax; it purged the group of the excessive tensions that it had imposed upon itself by trying simultaneously to separate out the components of its action and maintain its unity as a group.

In an impassioned appeal, Alain Touraine attempted to convince the group that through the joke it had embarked upon its conversion and should now forge ahead, acknowledging the distance created by the laughter between the practice and its meaning and analyse the latter. Would the group, faced with this reversal of the situation, retreat into a resistance to the researchers which might go as far as rejection, or would it take the path pointed out to it? We must follow the exchange which ensued.

Alain Touraine began: 'There is a cultural raw material which has to be transformed into political action, but there are problems and they threaten the group. Then I come along and say something unpleasant. I tell you you're divided. So the group takes its revenge by asserting its unity against me for saying it's divided. My hypothesis is that such a reaction is extremely important. It's the first positive demonstration we've had of the ability of the anti-nuclear movement to exist' (laughter). Roland was the first to reply: 'In a way, the ecology movement is the conscience of the CFDT in relationship to a certain deviationism within the confederation which consists in wanting to create an organisation like the CGT, which has its sphere of social organisation, which is powerful and which tries to give itself a structure and set up modes of intervention. The ecologists play the role that the PSU was briefly able to play for certain parties of the Left. But although there may be organisational squabbles, and different views, the two are complementary, they can live together. What the hoax proves is that there's a lot of sympathy between the two movements.'

In this view, the unity of the group was no longer a defensive reaction to the researchers but a common drive towards the search for a union between a social and cultural aspiration and a strategy for political action. And Roland pointed to the meeting place of the ecologists and the CFDT: self-management. Emmanuel Kropo went even further: 'We must distinguish the anti-nuclear movement from the ecology movement. One can understand that the anti-nuclear movement should contain a social movement. It's the driving force in relation not only to the ecology movement but also to the CFDT.' And he added a moment later: 'I'm convinced that it's by giving priority to the anti-nuclear political strategy that things will get done, and I've the feeling that we've achieved that here today. We ought to come back now to the basic problem of the relationship between science and the social use made of it. And then say on top of that: the society for which the ecologists are fighting is not only an anti-nuclear society; it must also have positive features. We need to create a project, and that's the direction I'd like to see us take.'

Georges had some reservations: 'This group is made up entirely of those ecologists who are most concerned with political critique and members of the CFDT closest to the anti-nuclear action.' But the reservation was a positive one since it provided a practical definition of the domain in which the movement could and should be created. Cotentin remarked that the CFDT's anti-nuclear and ecology orientation in La Hague had strengthened its position in the factory. Georges, Emmanuel and Hannibal added that after the electoral defeat of the Left, the initiative lay with the social forces and the political vacuum thus created increased the importance and the likelihood of a rapprochement between the Amis de la Terre and the CFDT.

The group was conscious of a success. As Georges said: 'Tonight the group has laid an egg.' Nobody thought any longer that the joke had simply been a case of the group defending itself against researchers pressing too hard upon it. The conversion had been achieved by the agitator, not so much by his attempts of the afternoon as by the way in which he had interpreted the group's joke. That joke had been set up by the most politicised members of the group. Roland Maire's part in it might have been anticipated, but nothing could have hinted at the attitude adopted by Emmanuel. If he threw himself with so much force into the search for the conditions that would enable a social movement to exist, it was because he defined himself above all as a revolutionary militant and was looking to the anti-nuclear movement for a new form of protest against social power. His role proved that the central problem of the struggle was to transform a cultural resistance into a political struggle, a fact which explained the limited part played at this decisive moment in the intervention by Georges, whose role before and after this session was invariably central but who was too attached to the community model and to the lived experience of protest to be the main agent of the conversion. This pointed to the fragility of the conversion, for no action could be developed if it did not carry along with it the awareness and the commitment of a Georges Flamand. This fragility, already visible at the end of this day and destined to increase subsequently, demonstrated how difficult it was for the ecology movement to transform itself into a social movement.

The search for a project

The progression beyond the counter-cultural withdrawal had been due mainly to Roland Maire, who was politically inclined, and to Kropo, whose attachment to the anarcho-syndicalist tradition protected him from the temptations of a purely cultural struggle. But the progress would have been artificial if it had eliminated the reason why most of the militants join the anti-nuclear struggle: the search for another kind of life. Did the departure of the three women at the end of the afternoon announce a more general division between the *politically* inclined and the *culturally* inclined, or would those who wanted to start from lived experience and its reconstruction be able to rise towards a political vision without losing the strength of their first inspiration? The long Sunday morning was given over to a heated debate around this fundamental stake: division or integration of the two main components of the movement, the cultural withdrawal and the political counter-project.

There were three phases to this debate. First, the group, carried along by its élan of the previous evening, asked if it might be possible to *construct a counter-project for society* on the basis of science, a move which would certainly lead to the imposition of a new rationalism on a cultural defence that had little connexion with science. Thanks mainly to Jean-Philippe Pharisca, himself a physicist, the group resisted the temptation of scientism. But that made it swing towards the grass-roots forces of the movement and set it off on a meditation on needs in which Georges Flamand, who had been somewhat on the fringe in the previous evening's debate, once more took a central part.

The group was advancing more rapidly now, going deeper into its conversion. Georges and Roland were now speaking the same language. Let us listen to the former, half an hour before the end of the morning: 'If we don't try to imagine the type of society we want to develop, if we just create a war machine, we risk a sort of fascism. Here's where we have to conceive a social movement, otherwise we're only building a military machine. The social movement should be constructed on positive data. The link between lived experience and theory, that's where it is. It's important for the ecology movement to live immediately, at the same time as it is fighting society. It's absolutely necessary for the two to coexist. We should try to have a type of organisation, objectives and search which correspond to the society we want to create.'

Roland summarised this in a CFDT formula which impressed the group: 'Let us live in the struggles of today the society of tomorrow.' He was critical of Hannibal for wanting to put the struggle in the foreground. 'There's a very great risk', he said, 'of organising an army to fight and thinking that with an army we'll make the State go away.' The two components of the action, the creation of new forms of social life and the political struggle, could not be separated. They were so less and less in the demands of the CFDT, a fact which was approved of by Haggar and Cotentin.

It had been at the very end of the research into the student movement, at the end of the meeting between the two groups at Marly, that some of the students had accepted the idea, introduced by Alain Touraine, that there could only be a student movement to fight against one social use of knowledge in favour of another. But in the present case, it was before the close of its first weekend that the Paris group discovered the nature of the social movement which might be present in its struggle. The theme was so central that all the participants adopted clear and stable positions in relation to it. Around Roland and Georges, Hannibal and especially Emmanuel, who had been important agents in the conversion of the previous evening, drew back a little. Their political tendencies had led them to oppose the counter-cultural withdrawal but they did not help them to bring about the transformation of a cultural protest into a social struggle. Emmanuel was afraid that they were veering away from the straight line of the working-class movement by attaching more importance to cultural problems than to the problems of work. Hannibal was also reticent but finally allowed himself to be carried away by his enthusiasm for 'the upsurge of a collective conscience of a possible future'.

Those who were closest to a defensive position, Piccolo, Saint-Hilaire and Jacqueline, took no part in the final discussion, whereas Haggar and Cotentin spoke up after a long silence. They evoked the themes of the CFDT, the importance it attached to qualitative demands and the objective of self-management. In three sessions, the life of the group had been profoundly transformed. It occasionally fell back into the state of an image-group, but for long stretches of time it acted as an analyst-group and went closely into the central problem of every social movement: how to combine the expression of new cultural needs with the fight against the society of technocratic production and market consumption in the framework of the anti-nuclear movement of today. By the middle of the day, the group's work was in fact over. Several participants left, but some, and especially those who had played the most active part, wanted to prolong the discussion.

The last, very short, session was devoted to the problem of organising the struggle. A first debate concerned whether priority should be given to the anti-nuclear action or to the ecology current. Georges Flamand, rallying to the positions of Brice Lalonde, thought priority should be given to bringing together all the anti-centralising and anti-authoritarian actions in the framework of the ecology movement. By contrast, Emmanuel remained attached to the priority of the social struggles centred on industrial relations and defended the priority of the specifically anti-nuclear action, which seemed to Roland Maire to be the only one which allowed the union of ecologists and trade unionists.

A second debate asked whether priority should be given to the national or to the local and regional level of the action. Roland gave a nuanced account of the importance of having a national coordination of the struggles, whilst Emmanuel and Georges insisted more on decentralisation and expounded the intentions of the Réseau des Amis de la Terre. François Dubet was critical of them and described the danger of diluting the anti-nuclear action in an ecology current which was itself subordinated to firmer demands such as those of women or the regional movements. The movement had a fluctuating membership, relied on voluntary workers, had almost no permanent organisation. There was an enormous distance between the grand projects for society, or the general debates on science and needs, and the reality of a struggle conducted by a small number of exemplary militants capable of attracting a considerable number of protesters for the large demonstrations but unable to hold onto them for a permanent and organised action.

This debate was marked by the twofold exhaustion of the group at the end of this meeting and of the struggle itself, aware of its weakness, its lack of organisation, and the absence of a match between its objectives and its ability to act. But the fact that the debate had taken place revealed the close link between analysis and action in the Paris group. It was impatient to act; it felt the need to break with the erring ways of the past and the disorganisation, but also with initiatives of a too personal nature and the dangers of a small managerial apparatus cut off from the grass roots. To protect the movement as much from disintegration as from the entryism of groups in search of a training ground, the Paris group wanted to build it along organisational lines in harmony with the objectives of the movement, resisting centralism, giving priority to militant participation over tactics, and opposing in particular the electoralism that almost all the ecologists had let themselves be drawn into. This concern for action indicated above all that the group had solved its central problem of integrating the cultural refusal and a social project. In spite of their differences, which had in any case become complementarities, Georges and Emmanuel, and Hannibal and Roland, were all borne along by the will to imagine and organise what they clearly saw as a social movement attacking the centres of power, speaking on behalf of basic needs, and conceiving a new, democratic way of entering into modernity.

The Paris group, impelled from the beginning towards the creation of the movement, experienced a conversion which provoked an internal crisis, formulated the terms of its problem, and struggled to find a solution to them. At the outcome of this meeting, it was not yet possible to say whether the anti-nuclear struggle was really alive and capable of developing, or whether on the contrary it was disintegrating beyond recall. But although we could not make such a historical judgement, it was already possible to advance a specifically sociological statement. We now knew the nature of the social movement potentially present in the anti-nuclear struggle, because the group had organised its work and its internal debates around the integration of the cultural withdrawal and a vision of the future, and had recognised that the anti-nuclear struggle, or rather the struggle against nuclear power was the place where ecologists and trade unionists, where those who rejected industrial values and those who were fighting against the rising technocracy, should unite and learn together to construct a new movement of democratic protest.

THE FAILURE OF GRENOBLE–MALVILLE

The exemplary community

Unlike the Paris group which was more concerned to define the conditions and the social meaning of the struggle, the Grenoble–Malville group was more turned in upon itself, towards the affirmation of its beliefs and its refusals. It was sustained by a utopia, in other words by the conviction that the realm of the desirable directly coincides with the realm of the necessary, that it is both inevitable and good to change life. To use the language of Max Weber, it placed itself in an ethic of conviction rather than an ethic of responsibility.

The group's work began, at the start of the weekend, with an intervention by Marie-Jeanne Vercors, a leader of the anti-nuclear struggle in the Malville region. She was very much listened to because of the part she had played and because she lived in a working-class environment – she could not be accused of being one of the affluent classes defending their privileges. Against the dominant tendencies, which she rejected, she set exemplary refusal and withdrawal. Marie-Jeanne was happy because, together with her own folk, with her own 'tribe', she had created a group which had freed itself from false needs and useless expenditure, which ate wholesome food, and had set up a mutualist aid system much more efficient than the monstrous bureaucracy of the Social Security. She refused to be taken as a political militant but knew the limits of her exemplary action. She was guided by religious beliefs which freed her from the bourgeois ideal of possession and did not believe in social and political transformations which were not based on the effort of each individual to assume responsibility for themselves.

101

Esther, a teacher, and Claudine often expressed similar reactions. Both wanted to live differently and help others through their own personal experience to free themselves from the dominant values which imprison them in the 'bourgeois mentality' of wanting to possess more than others. When the group tried to designate the people mainly responsible for the nuclear policy, Esther and Claudine said: we are the ones who consume too much. If we cut down on our own consumption, the EDF policy will crumble. Their confidence in personal reduction was shared by Jean-Jacques Rodrigo who had for a long time been one of the main leaders of the Malville Committee. One should 'do things that gradually replace existing institutions', and Claudine even wanted 'to ask the government to give us our own territory where we could organise ourselves like a free commune with a plan for self-management'. In this way, it might be possible to begin to achieve a human society which would at long last be fit to live in.

The action was here defined almost entirely in terms of initiative, conviction and example, and not of a programme or a detailed analysis of a situation. It was founded on a belief which sought to transform itself into community experience, to make its achievements known, and to obtain reforms. Marie-Jeanne acknowledged the progress made in one generation and accused the nuclear policy of threatening the achievements of the May movement and the women's action. Thus was defined a first phase of the action, most certainly an important component of a possible social movement, for the themes introduced by Marie-Jeanne, Esther, Claudine and Jean-Jacques were defined both by their objectives and by their adversary, who was more cultural than specifically political.

The war against the State

Marie-Jeanne maintained a global refusal, countered it with lived experience, and was suspicious of political organisations. She was by no means tied up in positions of principle and had for long been responsible for the most concrete tasks of organisation in the service of the anti-nuclear struggle, but it was difficult to define her action as specifically anti-nuclear, since she was fighting values, a civilisation, of which the nuclear policy was only one manifestation. It was easier to define her moral protest than to predict her political choices. A social movement could certainly not exist without the force of conviction she represented, but it can be formed only if it emerges from the exemplary community to confront its adversary more directly and more offensively.

It was Valence and Leforestier who breached the defensive position of Marie-Jeanne, although without attacking her personally. Valence, bolstered by his anarchist passion, told her: 'I'm convinced that the concept of individual freedom is a bourgeois concept. There's no end of executives, people like that, who are able to have a full sex life, whereas from the point of view of the liberation of the masses, it's often in the working classes that you get problems. What I recognise from my experience, in my background, is that it's in the bourgeoisie that individual freedom is perfectly possible. And as long as there's no collective challenge, there's no danger.' Valence was not criticising the 'illusion of liberation' in the name of a collective political project – he was even suspicious of the notion of project which he found reformist – but in the name of the necessary struggle against the State. He was against all limited reforms, all the plans for citizen participation in decision-making. Nothing should divert attention from the struggle against the State, its centralism, its army and its police. Democracy was no more than an illusion. The sole aim of the action should be to 'destroy a world'. He was even distrustful of the anti-fascist theme because that project, like all the others, was just a stepping stone to the formation of a new power and the liquidation of the popular struggle, as had been shown by the example of Catalonia during the Civil War to which he referred several times. He was not fighting a kind of life, a social organisation, and he did not want to change the institutions; he was fighting the naked power of the State and its violence. It was really on this score that he was opposed to Marie-Jeanne: his definition of the adversary was different. On the other hand, his conception of the action called for the defence of existence and of an authentic community. He was an anarcho-syndicalist, believed only in direct productive work, and wanted to suppress all that was abstract, all that was 'sublime', the artists and the intellectuals as much as the power of the State. He placed himself under the sign of the violent Italian autumn and May 68 in France, in which he was too young to have taken part.

Esther and Claudine came somewhere between Marie-Jeanne and Valence. Like the latter, they did not believe in the institutions and approved the call to the General Council of the Isère only to bring out its impotence and turn the political institutions into derision. On the other hand, they diverged from him during a debate on rape. Women, they said, should take responsibility for themselves, learn to defend themselves, and above all wage a campaign to denounce crimes against women. Valence, on the other hand, condemned women who appealed to the courts when it was the dominant order itself which had created the subjection of women. Nothing could withstand his will to destroy the social order imposed by the 'Areopagus of rulers and capitalist interests'. He was as suspicious of moral protests and the appeal to rights as he was of political propaganda and commercial advertising. He believed only in the direct confrontation of the productive workers and the State. Everywhere the mechanisms of assimilation were at work, in moralism as much as in reformism, in sociology as much as in the Communist Party. The fire of his protest consumed everything.

Although Esther and Claudine did not adopt his extreme positions, they did not reject them either, and Marie-Jeanne would later have the opportunity of displaying her solidarity with him in the most spectacular way. What all three had in common with him was a definition of their action as defensive rather than as counter-offensive, through a refusal rather than a project. And even if Marie-Jeanne or Esther were more concerned with using the possibilities for pressure that the institutions might offer, they never opposed Valence's repudiation of an order which is more political and State-controlled than social, an absolute power more than a social relationship of domination. Claudine called for civil disobedience and Esther also gave priority to the struggle against the State.

During this first weekend, Valence, even though he had missed most of the previous sessions, occupied an important place, almost central in the sense that his positions were asserted so strongly and so often that many of the participants situated themselves in relation to him. Now, we knew that on the Malville Committee he and Leforestier had represented the diversified tendency, the one which accepted violence. Thus the central figure in the group was the one who had taken least part in its discussions, who defended the most extreme positions, and was seen by the others, and especially by Jean-Jacques and Yves, as the main agent in the break-up of the Malville Committee. This situation brought out clearly the importance of the combination of anti-Statism and the call for authenticity in the general tendencies of the anti-nuclear struggle in Grenoble.

The political struggle

Véronique Uri, a scientist and a militant from the LCR, was alien or hostile to the theme of the exemplary community. She did not live in a circle of friends, like Marie-Jeanne, but in a scientific environment which reacted badly to her criticisms and shut itself off in a blindly conservative professionalism. As a result, she was above all politically inclined; she declared that it was absolutely necessary to have the support of the working-class movement for the anti-nuclear struggle to triumph. She shared Valence's determination to fight the State, as well as his hostility towards the Communist Party whose action contained the seed of a new authoritarian State and which defended the nuclear industry, but she was also the bearer of a project for society: she was alive to the movements for cultural liberation, especially the women's movement, and to the spirit of May. Esther defined the differences between herself and Véronique accurately: 'It's the choice between living one's ideas and militating.' Véronique was above all a militant, a political, union and anti-nuclear militant, preoccupied with objectives and strategies, with organisation and alliances. And she was all the less inclined to defend the scientific milieu, which might nonetheless be seen as a bulwark against the technocracy, since she was keenly conscious of the scientists' loss of control over their own work, a feeling shared by Christophe, an engineer at the CEA. Even in her professional life she came up against the sway of a power that she defined politically rather than socially. She rejected the notion of technocracy. It was not the directors of EDF who were responsible for the nuclear policy but the *political leaders* directly, who, she frequently recalled, were not separable from the multinationals. And were not the latter associated with America, that is to say yet again with a political power? Hostile to all reformism, convinced of the need for a complete break with existing institutions, she was fighting nuclear power as the symbol of the authorities' grip on the whole of social life, including science. Véronique was the only one to combine the struggle against the State with the reference to a political project which, in her case, was also cultural. Hence her isolation. She was a long way from the positions of Marie-Jeanne and almost as much from Esther and Claudine, but she was just as suspicious of the scissionist tendencies displayed by Valence, since for her they contained a political weakness, the inability to involve the great forces of the organised working-class movement in the struggle.

The liberal ecologists

'You'll never destroy the State; but, for myself, I couldn't give a toss about destroying it; what I want is to live differently and now; and what I claim is that if you manage to do that, the State will just quietly die the death.'

This answer to Véronique came not from Marie-Jeanne Vercors but Jean-Jacques Rodrigo, whose position was not to be confused with Marie-Jeanne's. Like her, he thought there was 'a whole load of things we can do' and that it was possible to use the existing institutions to change society, but, more than her, he was concerned to develop a counter-project to replace modern society. 'The most important thing is why we're fighting.' If he was fighting nuclear power, it was because the present policy was designed to create an irreversible situation, and thus dispossess us of our future. But it was not a case of opposing one preference to another, one project to another. Our society has crossed the threshold beyond which the negative effects of growth are greater than the positive effects. Frequently quoting Illich and the Club of Rome, he pointed out various aspects of the regressive development that was carrying us along with it, in health, education and the economy. We must fight for collective survival, relying confidently on the scientists and the experts and especially by becoming involved in specifically social struggles which were much more realistic than a fight to the death against the State, a fight which was lost in advance or perhaps devoid of meaning. According to Jean-Jacques, it was not the

State which was repressing us, but 'the rest of the French', the majority who served the technocracy. What he was fighting was not only nuclear power but all that came with it, a technocratic spirit which appeared in many areas of life. He introduced into the group the language of social struggle rather than the language of rejection of the State. He said in so many words that he did not feel the oppression of the State; on the other hand, he was trying to designate precise social adversaries; he was fighting against the imposition of decisions and against waste. He defined himself as an ecologist fighting the great apparatuses of production and management of the social organisation. His transition from a break with the State to a social conflict explained his insistence on the need to open up society and the possibility of achieving social change.

All this set him violently and repeatedly, as we had known from the beginning, against Valence, who attacked Jean-Jacques's reformism, his moralising illusions, his 'Catholic' tendency. In fact, everything opposed these two men, who clashed during the research as they had fought one another in the Malville Committee. Yves Le Gall's attitudes were close to Jean-Jacques but he was more concerned than the latter with defining the political strategy corresponding to their social project, a strategy for a break with those who called irresponsibly for violence and for an alliance between the ecologists and the CFDT.

The opposition was complete between the tendency to withdrawal and breakaway which dominated in the group, and the attempt by some to become involved in action for social change, whether it be more reformist, as Jean-Jacques wished, or more revolutionary, in the spirit of Véronique. During that weekend, Jean-Jacques, profoundly hostile to Valence, said very little, and then more to contradict his adversary than to develop his own ideas. It was this isolation which pushed him to insist on the rights of moral conviction, which should not be submitted to the decisions of the majority. His reforming spirit, wounded by the failures of the action and threatened by the dangers that Valence represented in his eyes, was reduced to moral protest.

The field of the action

Such were the four main orientations of the anti-nuclear action in the Grenoble–Malville group. They were the same as in Paris, and could be located on a graph formed by the intersection of two axes: defensive action or counter-project and struggle against the State or will to transform social relations.

The anti-nuclear struggle began with a utopia, the ideal image of an anti-society of consumption and merchandise. If this utopia was to be transformed into a social movement, it must open up, let itself be penetrated

NATURE OF THE CONFLICT

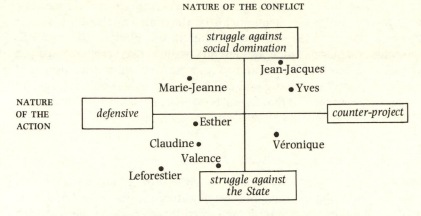

(In this graph, the members of the group are all shown by
dots and not by arrows, as was the case for several members of
the Paris group who were defined by a movement rather than a
position.)

both by the presence of a specific and no longer generalised adversary and
by the recognition of a possible field of action. The juxtaposition of good and
evil, of life and death, must give way, if a social movement were to be
formed, to the thought of a conflict between particular actors disputing a
general stake. The creation of a social movement is necessarily associated
with the reinforcement of a political project linked to the awareness of a
specifically social conflict. It becomes possible only if this tendency is
reinforced whilst its opposite is emptied. Now, during this weekend the
converse had happened. The combination of the withdrawal into an
exemplary community and the rejection of the State was reinforced, whilst
a political and social counter-project was so difficult to introduce that it had
to come down to a moral protest. Thus we could now formulate the problem
facing the group. How could it pass from its present state, in which the
refusal of contradictions was stronger than the conflict and the social
movement, to the opposite state in which the whole of the struggle would be
directed towards the social movement? In other words, how could it get
from the south-west to the north-east of the graph?

In the present situation, it was the great refusal which won the day.
Véronique was drawn towards anti-Statism rather than towards the
cultural and political counter-project, and the call for the exemplary
community was linked with the struggle against the State rather than the
development of a social counter-project, as was shown by the example of
Esther and Claudine. Jean-Jacques was isolated, in painful awareness of the
ruin of his hopes and the treason that had killed the incipient movement.
Could this tendency be reversed? Such was the question that was to control

all our analyses, just as, in the register of lived experience, it had controlled the history of the group, dominated from the outset by the open conflict between Valence and Jean-Jacques. During the first weekend, Valence was victorious, and Marie-Jeanne, Esther and Claudine, like Véronique, seemed more attracted to his position and to Leforestier's than to the position of Jean-Jacques or Yves. The strength of this tendency suggested that it would be difficult to reverse, and that the reversal could be achieved, if at all, only at the cost of a serious crisis, of a rift in the group.

Search for unity

Besides François Delain, who said very little during this weekend, two participants have hardly been mentioned until now: they were Christophe and Bourguignon, the two trade unionists. It was because the part they played could only be defined from the viewpoint of the forms of the struggle as a whole. The trade unionists, in this field, which was more one of ideological conflict than of organised action, were the only ones who, as comparative outsiders perhaps, might find a way to integrate such diverse and even antithetical components.

Christophe never took part in the debate whose terms have just been defined. Because he was a trade unionist, he asked himself the question: how could one link the anti-nuclear struggle with the working-class movement? How could one unite demands fought for in the workplace and a protest concerned with the style of life, and thus with existence outside work? In doing this, he was the one who placed himself most explicitly at the level of the conditions that would enable the anti-nuclear struggle to exist and succeed: 'if the anti-nuclear struggle is not taken up by a majority, it will fall flat on its face'. But his central position in the debate came from the fact that he was not speaking entirely as an outsider. His point of view was that of an organised movement, of which everybody, in some form or other, recognised the central importance, but he wanted to let himself be questioned and challenged as a trade unionist by the anti-nuclear militants, firstly because he recognised the depth of their convictions and because he knew that a social movement was not only a machine for political intervention and must first be a protest and a commitment – 'getting a movement to advance only by having a majority take charge of it is to wipe out basic aspirations' – and secondly because he thought that the great social movement that our type of society calls for could not be restricted to problems of work. He wanted to fight against all forms of power: 'The power of one class over another, hierarchy, the division of labour . . . the power of the intellectuals over the manual workers, the power of men over women', because 'it is true that all these forms of power are sustained by capitalism, but they could also be sustained by any other form of power'. Being a trade unionist, he had no synthesising solution to offer to a debate whose main terrain was not that of work. He stood back from the ecologists and held up to their view the image of a working-class movement which had been able, in different circumstances, to transcend the opposition between defensive withdrawal and counter-project, between social struggle and resistance to the State. Above all, he was in search of a synthesis between this working-class movement which was firmly established but already too imprisoned in the constraints of institutionalisation and mass organisation and the ecology or anti-nuclear current, bubbling with energy and ideas but divided and incapable of controlling its course.

Bourguignon, a trade unionist from the CEA, said: 'The CFDT tries, in its struggles, not to separate the life of the firm from life as a whole, and that goes back to the concept of popular unity, to the struggle of women, of immigrant workers and to neighbourhood struggles. All that has got to have some sort of coherence at the level of the project but also at the level of the struggles.' This search, at the central point of the weekend, took on a dramatic form because Christophe was reluctant to reformulate the principal objective of the struggles in terms other than those around which trade unionism had been organised. He first declared what was driving him on: the search for the unity of individuals, workers and consumers, whom the dominant power slices up into separate roles: 'If we do nothing against the division of labour, we have the same hierarchy, and from that it's obvious that if you want to ensure a minimum of social peace, you've got to give people substitutes for personal fulfilment, like consumption for example. If another type of society reproduces the same types of oppression, it'll have the same needs for consumption as the capitalist society and it'll need the same type of development. And in that case, we'll have the same fight on our hands against a socialist regime reproducing the same type of problems.'

A few days before, Christophe had been seriously injured in a bicycle accident, and so was lying down in the middle of the group and could only speak with difficulty. This added to the effort he was visibly making to say the sentence which followed and which took the group's work to its highest point: 'I'll go even further, but here I'm really doing violence to myself. I wonder if the capitalist system and the pressure groups Véronique was speaking about and which are the things we have to fight against nowadays, have not effectively installed in the State apparatus top civil servants and high-ranking technocrats who are in the process of setting up a policy which, whatever system we have in ten, twenty or thirty years time, will have made things irreversible.' A few minutes later, he repeated how much effort the idea had cost him. He was conscious of being at the crossroads of trade unionism and a new social movement which would continue the latter whilst being different from it. Christophe saw capitalism at the origin of the technocracy, but the essential point of his declaration was that the latter could henceforth make itself independent of that which had given it birth and become the main agent of a new type of power, more extensive than the specifically economic power of the capitalists. Jean-Jacques Rodrigo's summary showed that he had clearly understood Christophe: 'That really does demonstrate that the ones we have to fight are not the capitalists, but precisely the blokes in power.' The expression was vague but the commentary brought out clearly Christophe's central idea: it was possible to name a new adversary and consequently to define a new social movement, and so come out from behind the protective barricades of the exemplary community and the rejection of the State.

Bourguignon's thinking was less tense, but he combined within himself the dominant perceptions of the anti-nuclear militants and the spirit of trade unionism. More libertarian than Christophe, to the point of evoking the Ukrainian and Catalonian anarchists, this man, who had grown up, studied and worked in the most adverse material conditions, had retained a profound sense of revolt against the social order and fought against the increasingly heavy constraints weighing on the workers and all those who are manipulated by the State, capitalism and all forms of power. The two trade unionists were equally aware of the tension between the raison d'être of a movement and the conditions for its victory. Christophe said: 'I think the desire for worker autonomy, where it exists, is somehow incompatible with the delegation of power through the representative system.' And those were the words of a union militant, a shop steward. The strength of the trade unionists came, then, from the fact that they were close to the general directions of the majority of the group but also spoke from outside, and were thus not involved in its divisions, and finally that they were representatives of the working-class movement. Their weakness was that they were more an example and a question than a force for integrating the elements of the action.

The whole of the group could now be located in the field of the anti-nuclear struggle. The trade unionists were in the centre of the graph, although on a parallel plane, in fact. They belonged in the south-west quarter, where Bourguignon was close to Esther, and in the north-west quarter, where they were not far away from Marie-Jeanne. They were remote from both Véronique and Jean-Jacques, even though the last two were members of the CFDT. The arrow indicates the strongest tendency within the field during that weekend.

The question now was whether the group would use the trade unionists' intervention to create its movement and formulate the conditions for transforming the struggle into a movement.

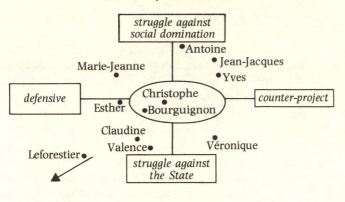

The separation

The trade unionists did not succeed in carrying the group along with them. This was primarily because several of its members, including Christophe and Bourguignon themselves, recognised the distance between the workers and the ecologists. The clash between Brice Lalonde and Christophe during the penultimate open session of the group had already revealed that. The ecologists were more often than not unacquainted with the problems of work and did not understand the importance of the unions, whilst the workers themselves were not very sensitive to the themes of the ecologists – in the CFDT itself, the national leadership was very much in advance of the majority of the unions on this question. Bourguignon, who had tried to introduce the anti-nuclear struggle to union militants in the Rhône valley, described how his attempts had failed. Véronique also recognised that the CFDT leaders had gone as far as they could. They all spoke of the CGT's extreme opposition to the anti-nuclear action and the impossibility of mobilising the workers in the nuclear industry against their own jobs, especially at a time of unemployment. Claudine went even further: the unions, preoccupied with wages, working conditions and employment, could not play a central part in a struggle whose stake, the death or survival of the human race, was much more fundamental. Véronique, herself an active union militant, did not believe that the problems of work could be the rallying point of all the new demands. She believed rather that all the struggles, union and ecologist alike, should come together in a general political action for the long term, whilst preserving in the short term the autonomy of each individual struggle. This opposition was all the more striking because it came from anti-nuclear militants who were for the most part members of the CFDT and who all recognised the central importance of the working-class movement. It did not affect the search for a privileged alliance between the anti-nuclear militants and the CFDT, but it brought out the distance between this policy of alliance and the desire present in the

CFDT to extend its action to new domains, to every aspect of collective life and social change.

After the effort made by Christophe, the group fell back. His central intervention had occurred at the end of the Saturday. On Sunday morning, very rapidly, we witnessed the return of the utopia in terms almost identical to the ones we had heard on the first morning. There was fresh talk of the Club of Rome and Illich. It was then that Jean-Jacques recalled most forcibly the finite nature of resources and the ineluctable catastrophe that would be caused by their depletion or insufficiency if our societies did not change quickly and profoundly. Esther reverted to the idea that the main thing was the work one accomplished on oneself. Valence denounced the rule of the market place and of the value of trade over the value of use. Claudine wanted to do away with money, that 'abstraction which rules over us'.

This return to the beginning was accompanied by a keen sense of failure. Bourguignon: 'In a way, we're each of us exploring the problem individually, following our own feelings, but I don't see any global project emerging. We're setting individual change against social change, we're separating the technocracy from the whole set of social relations.' Christophe echoed him: 'Bringing together in one global project all the dissatisfactions expressed in terms of a project for society doesn't seem at all easy to me.' His main action remained trade unionist in nature, located in the firm, and he could see everything that was against a real union between the workers' action and the anti-nuclear struggle. Jean-Jacques Rodrigo, who had suffered more than anybody from the break-up of the Malville Committee, recognised that there was no profound unity between all those who had taken part in the action against the fast-breeder and that consequently there could be no such thing as an anti-nuclear movement. At the end of the meeting, he addressed himself directly to Valence, his adversary: 'You and me have got sweet bugger all to do with one another, and if the pair of us can't agree, we'll never get anywhere.' Valence was of the same opinion: 'We have to realise that we're on the run. I didn't come here to rebuild the anti-nuclear movement. It's dead.' Yves Le Gall acknowledged a failure that he had foreseen when he saw the leftists take control of the anti-nuclear struggle. He wanted to advance as far as possible beyond this phase of the movement and attempt the rapprochement of the Amis de la Terre and the CFDT, an alliance resisted by Valence who denounced the confederation's 'incredible purge' of revolutionary militants.

This feeling of failure became even more oppressive during the last few minutes of the meeting. For Claudine, the militants were gathered there 'like vultures round carrion'. When the researchers asked each one in turn to sum up in a few words the conclusion they drew from these two days, Bourguignon said: 'I don't know if we can go any further.' Jean-Jacques said: 'I've got a better understanding of the things dividing us.' Christophe and Véronique gave the same answer: nothing to say. But Christophe changed his mind: 'We can start over again with something other than energy, the fight against hierarchy, the women's struggles, they still mean something after all.'

The Grenoble–Malville group had not achieved its conversion. Christophe was in fact the only one who had made the attempt, and he realised his failure as much as the others did. Even the utopia seemed to have disintegrated just as much as the impossible movement in the realisation of a failure which was not only that of the struggle against the Super-Phoenix under construction at Malville but of the whole anti-nuclear struggle. Such a point had the group reached. But was that result to be explained by the real state of the group or might it not rather depend on the researchers whose role, as we said at the very beginning, was decisive in this central phase of the intervention if the group was to succeed in its conversion?

The inversion of the movement

It is not possible to separate out the groups' influence on the researchers from the action of the researchers on the groups. Nor would a comparison of the two groups be of much use in this respect, since they were always and in many ways different in composition and situation as much as in the personality and the role of their respective researchers. It would even be contrary to the spirit of the intervention to try to divide out two such inseparable factors, since the work of the groups consisted simultaneously in self-analysis and intervention. So rather than trying to isolate the effect produced by the researchers, we should try to discover how the differences between the groups, related to the behaviour of both the actors and the researchers, showed up the same potential social movement in different ways, now flooding it in light, now throwing up shadows.

If the struggle really was the vehicle of a social movement, then either the attempted and successful conversion would bring it out, or a non-attempted or failed conversion would bring about the disintegration of a struggle which would not be able to find stability at a lower level and would thus fall into a state of crisis, destroyed by its inability to discover its true nature. Thus the presence of a social movement, which would be revealed directly in the case of a successful conversion, would also be revealed, but indirectly, if the conversion failed or was not attempted, if the struggle, instead of crystallising into a movement, was to be inverted into an awareness of the impotence or the impossibility of the movement.

Having already, with the Paris group, obtained a print of the movement, we were able to see its negative in the Grenoble–Malville group. The point reached by the latter provided a fairly clear image of the reverse side of the

113

movement, revealed in the absence of conversion. Firstly, the principle of Identity, the definition of the actor of the movement, was replaced by an *anti-I*, by the idea that the action was impossible. The victims of the nuclear industry and of the whole social system whose pernicious effects it embodies are alienated, deprived of awareness, prisoners of the constraints of daily life and the dominant ideology.

The principle of Opposition, the definition of the adversary, was also inverted into an *anti-O*: instead of analysing nuclear energy as the effect of a social power, it is considered as the prime cause of pernicious social facts. Nuclear energy, it is then said, creates a centralised, not to say a police, or even a totalitarian, society. There is even talk of a nuclear society, a formula which introduces a technological determinism of social organisation completely at odds with the analysis of society in terms of social relations and movements.

Finally, the principle of Totality, the stake of the struggle, was replaced by an *anti-T*, by the idea of anti-progress, of regressive evolution, or in a more limited way by the idea of a *natural limit* to growth. These three elements do not combine to form a struggle which is of a different kind from a social movement but rather to render a social movement impossible: the alienated actor comes up against a technological logic which carries him naturally, scientifically, towards catastrophe. There is then no alternative but to cry in the wilderness, denounce the lie and the blindness, set certainties against the destructive machine and blind productivity. Thus the absence of conversion, whilst seriously weakening the intervention, still allowed us to recognise that the anti-nuclear struggle is well defined in relationship to a potential social movement. The results of the Grenoble–Malville group cannot be explained without the hypothesis of a hidden movement, in the absence of which the struggle decomposes, reverses and auto-destructs.

6

The collapse

We are approaching the central point in the intervention, where, more than ever, the analysis of the struggles has to merge with the history of the group, beginning with the development of the meeting which brought the two groups together at Autrans in the Vercors. A few participants were absent: Emmanuel Kropo, kept away by business; Sophia and Alice, whose absence was probably due to a train strike; and Jacqueline, who had to look after her baby. The meeting as such lasted some fifteen hours.

THE DISINTEGRATION

Hope

The morning of the first day began with a discussion about the organisation of the action, initiated by Roland Maire. His own, highly unionist, position won the support of several members of the group: the movement should stop making general pronouncements and get itself organised, set itself precise objectives and learn to negotiate. Christophe, although more aware of the obstacles to be overcome, was no less convinced than Roland of the urgent need to bring feelings and ideas together in concrete actions, similar to union demands in the workplace. Esther and Marie-Jeanne rejected this position, returning with insistence to the importance of lived participation, and therefore of local action, but the farmers in the group, François Delain and Jean-Pierre Provins, were sceptical of the peasants' ability to mobilise for the anti-nuclear struggle, an attitude which strengthened the tendency led by Roland.

At the opposite extreme, Valence and Véronique Uri stressed the primacy of general political problems, the need for a general and not just local action. Georges Flamand won general support for his reminder that the action should be close to lived experience and should be set in the 'neighbour-hood', which might, depending on the specific problem, be the street, the region or the planet. The nature of the actor-group depends on the nature of the adversary. Thus the concern for organisation seemed to be closely

115

linked to a will to create a social movement. The group members who had come closest to the image of such a movement, Roland, Georges and Christophe, were the leaders of a discussion which seemed to be moving quickly towards actual proposals.

But in the second half of the morning, the wind changed as doubts were voiced over the possibility of engaging in anti-nuclear actions as concrete as those of trade unionism. The group hesitated for a moment, but then retreated rapidly towards the defence of examplary action or witness. Haggar described his own kind of life which seemed to him to be richer in human terms and happier than that of his neighbours; Marie-Jeanne Vercors, supported by Esther, spoke in the same vein and added the importance for her of a life illuminated by spirituality and not by the scramble for material goods. The fear of a takeover by the leftists, the awareness of hostility from the CGT and of general indifference amongst the workers towards the anti-nuclear action brought the group back towards moral witness, far from the preoccupations of Roland. It was a very clear retreat, which appeared to the researchers as an inability to define the potential action, its basis, its adversary and its stake. At the end of this first morning, the spirit of Grenoble–Malville seemed to be stronger than the projects of the Parisians, and the plans for organisation, attractive as they were in theory, could not be brought to any clear definition, and so provoked a withdrawal into exemplarity.

This retreat was halted at the beginning of the afternoon by Roland Maire and Georges Flamand, who asked Alain Touraine to define as a sociologist what a social movement is. Their aim was to turn the group in that direction. Alain Touraine spoke at length. Our hypothesis, he said, is that the anti-nuclear struggle contains a social movement which might in future play as important a role as that once played by the working-class movement. It is in that struggle, more than anywhere else, that the new social movement can take shape, and it is in this group, at this very time, that it can best become aware of itself. But only if the group takes on the self-analysis of its action.

It was a direct call for the group's conversion. The researchers could not expect it to succeed immediately: what some people had achieved with difficulty at Versailles could not be obtained in a moment from those who had much more ground to cover. But the call had the effect of strengthening the intervention by Roland and Georges and bringing out the real resistances to the formation of a social movement. For it was indeed the voice of the social movement that was making itself heard that afternoon, and more and more loudly. Georges Flamand supported Alain Touraine by declaring that the movement should reappropriate the work of the researchers, especially at a time when important negotiations were underway between the Amis de la Terre and the CFDT. Almost at once, however, came the most frequent objection to Alain Touraine's hypothesis. It was dangerous, said Véronique, who belonged to the LCR, to set up a new social movement in place of the working-class movement as if the latter had outlived its usefulness. The truth was that the anti-nuclear action would have no force if it was not taken up by the working-class movement. Whereupon Hannibal reiterated his main theme: the central adversary is not a new social class but the power of the State, for it is the State alone which takes the important decisions in nuclear matters. However, these objections were rejected by the group leading the discussion. Christophe reminded Véronique that it was not enough to call upon the workers if you believed in the importance of the anti-nuclear struggle, since the workers do not easily associate themselves with it and play only a marginal part in it. Haggar, the working-class trade unionist, said more forcibly that the ecologists had restored strength and breadth to union action in La Hague, and finally Roland Maire pushed the counter-attack onto the ideological level by speaking of the crisis of Marxism as one of the important aspects of the crisis in industrial values.

François Dubet was in charge of the discussion at that moment. He intervened forcefully on several occasions, abandoning his role as an advocate of cultural withdrawal. He asked: 'Who are we fighting?' And Georges Flamand wanted each one to answer in turn. The group went through a period of elation. Roland Maire was the one who most clearly defined the adversary of the struggle: the technocracy, meaning power exercised in the name of knowledge. It was true that capitalism could use the technocracy, but the latter had nonetheless an existence of its own, and one which was increasingly important. It was also true that the technocracy was most usually connected with the State but it was the technocracy, at the centre of public administration, which was the true holder of power.

Such a declaration was not enough, however, to define a social movement, just as the conversion of Kropo and Hannibal, the most political of the Paris group, had not been enough to carry that group along with it and it had needed Georges Flamand on the Sunday morning to raise his attachment to community life to the level of its political meaning for the conversion really to succeed. Hence the importance of Haggar at this moment. He said: 'Power is those who can create needs which keep us in shackles for the whole of our lives.' Although a working-class trade unionist, he was speaking on behalf of a way of life and not just of working conditions. Had he not just said of the ecologists: 'What they are challenging is the social value of work, the social content of work. People are questioning the value of work.' With this attitude he was consciously putting himself outside the usual realm of union action. Georges Flamand, after repeating Roland Maire's definition of the technocracy, added: 'In

1977 people realised that nuclear power was a type of development and also a type of supervision', thus responding to François Dubet's pressing demand for the union of cultural defence and political project. Yves Le Gall, an ecologist, reinforced this tendency within the group by declaring that the anti-nuclear struggle was dead, that it would not become a social movement because it had been corrupted by the leftists, and that out of its ashes should rise the alliance of the Amis de la Terre and the CFDT which would be the alliance of workers and inhabitants, of demands against the system of production and the refusal of a system of consumption.

The question now was whether this success would be enlarged upon, whether the group would add to the definition of its adversary a definition of itself and of the stake of its combat, and whether the conversion would be extended to other members of the group. Yves Le Gall had just gone over to Roland, Georges and Haggar, but Hannibal and, for very different reasons, Véronique were still a long way from the image which had been given of the possible social movement. Valence was openly hostile; Bourguignon and Christophe were following Georges and Roland but with some hesitation; Esther, Marie-Jeanne and Piccolo remained attached to a defensive position which the latter summed up simply: 'Before we can build, we've got to stop.' It was now the middle of the afternoon. When the session began again, everybody present was aware that they were approaching the central point in the research.

Decomposition

(a) The group tried first of all to define the social basis of its struggle. It thought first of the farmers directly affected by the building of a reactor, then of the people who work in the nuclear power stations and reprocessing plants. Were they not directly affected? But those who were in a position to speak on behalf of the farmers, François Delain and Jean-Pierre Provins, rejected the idea that the peasants are anti-nuclear. They defend their land, are worried when they see high voltage cables being strung across it, and try to get the best price for it, but, as Saint-Hilaire pointed out, they are opposed in exactly the same way to the building of a dam. François Delain and Esther added that agriculture and forestry are not natural but man-made, and Jean-Pierre Provins vehemently reminded the group that everybody had asked the farmers to increase production as much as possible and that the farmers themselves wanted to live the same kind of life as other people at long last. As for organic farming, he thought it marginal or dishonest. These extremely strong and sometimes even brutal interventions provoked little reaction from the group which could not really dispute what peasants said about peasants.

Consequently, attention was turned to the workers in the nuclear in-

118

dustry. Haggar's attitude was the opposite of the farmers'; he was afraid because nuclear power allows no mistakes and because a mistake is always possible. Bourguignon added that in the nuclear industry working conditions were increasingly difficult, safety increasingly neglected, and the rules of discipline increasingly stringent. Here then, it seemed, was an anti-nuclear focus. But were the workers really anti-nuclear or were they just defending their working conditions? Christophe maintained that the problems of work should be linked to the problems of life style, which brought criticism from Piccolo and Hannibal: the workers and the unions were trying to organise the nuclear industry not fight it. The workers were defending their jobs and so defending what the anti-nuclear movement was fighting. Every one during this discussion was aware of the poor participation of the workers in the anti-nuclear struggle and of the problems encountered by the CFDT leadership in winning acceptance for its general tendencies.

The failure was twofold, and the group could not escape it. There was no further attempt to define a different social basis, to ask who the ecologists are, who are the ones who listen to them, and in whose name they speak. But did their inability to answer this question betoken the absence of a social movement? It is hard to imagine a working-class movement having the slightest doubt as to its social basis, but the anti-nuclear and ecology movement, as the double name suggests, is defined better by what it opposes and by the model of society it defends than by the identity of those for whom it speaks. The inability to define the actor of the struggles does not, then, indicate the impossibility of creating a social movement. But at the outcome of this part of its reflexion, the group was a long way from the lively warmth of the beginning of the afternoon.

(b) A new debate was begun whose outcome was to prove decisive: is the anti-nuclear and ecology movement inspired by the rejection of the industrial and technological world to the point even of mistrusting science and rationality, or does it define another model of development which would not only be more democratic but would have science and modernity on its side, criticising present irrationality or waste, recalling the need for economic survival and seeking a transition to a kind of consumption and production based more on information than energy? An entirely defensive orientation leads to a withdrawal from present society, but the search for another type of development constitutes the stake of a social conflict, since in the latter case the adversaries involved accept the same cultural values of science and rationality, but give them antithetical social expressions.

The researchers were ready to make do with even a limited attempt by the group to go beyond an attitude of withdrawal and the utopian phase, to give some idea of what might be the management of a society transformed by the victory of the anti-nuclear forces. Which way would the group turn? Would

119

it reject science, technology and industrial society, or would it challenge the social use which is made of them in the name of a more open science, a more rational evolution of technology, and a better consideration of the social and political factors involved in overcoming the crisis? The answer was not slow in coming.

Jean-Jacques Rodrigo, kept on the fringe of the Grenoble–Malville group during the first weekend at Autrans which had been dominated by anti-Statism and the search for the exemplary community, demanded the reappropriation by each individual of the technologies they use. We use machines without knowing how they work, just as allopathic medicine dispossesses us of our body. Véronique Uri, the physicist, also wanted researchers not to be permanent and thought that a liberated society should use 'not too complicated technologies'. Similarly, Hannibal thought 'that another vision of people gives another kind of medicine', and Piccolo extolled the virtues of homoeopathy and acupuncture against the pomposity and the sterility of orthodox medicine.

They all, in various ways, expressed the conviction that a different kind of political and social orientation would create different forms of knowledge and organisation. In such conditions, there could no longer be a social conflict over a common stake, but only two general conceptions in direct confrontation. Some added that we must choose between nuclear power, which is the instrument of authoritarian centralism, and solar energy, which brings the promise of a new democracy. It was a vision all in black and white. The protesters did not claim to be the true defenders of science, rationality or modernity; they mistrusted science, rationality and modernity. The principal tendency in the group was not so much to define a new conception of science and a new society as to defend itself against a whole industrial and technicist culture that it rejected in the name of lived experience, balance and community.

Not everybody followed this dominant feeling. Roland Maire tried to go behind the rejection of technologies to rediscover a will to struggle against a certain social appropriation of knowledge and against the concentration of technical knowledge, whilst Yves Le Gall rejected the technological determinism which he saw in the preferences expressed and Georges asked the group to go beyond withdrawal and define an 'intermediate political strategy'. But they were unable to divert the current that was carrying the group along.

Alain Touraine then intervened with some passion. He wanted to set before the group the image of the possible stake of its struggle. He saw in the anti-nuclear movement a fight against a false technocratic modernisation and a way out of the crisis through the struggle against inequality and waste and the transition from a society of capital to a society of information. He also dismissed the condemnation of existing medicine in the name of alternative medicines whose value seemed to him to be derisory or feeble, and he was suspicious of anything that suggested the existence of several opposing sciences. He added, however, that this assertion of the modernism of the anti-nuclear struggle might favour the action of a new managing elite and for that reason should not be divorced from the struggle against the holders of technocratic power. Piccolo and Esther protested against these ideas and, although Le Gall and Flamand gave him their support, he was isolated. The group was in crisis. Jean-Jacques Rodrigo murmured: 'It's so embarrassing.' The afternoon was over. The group had shut itself off in its refusal.

The first intervention by Alain Touraine at the beginning of the afternoon, supported by François Dubet, had spurred the group on towards the definition of its adversary. His second intervention did not stop it in its search for an entirely different society. Now, a social movement is not defined purely by difference, especially if it is a popular movement. Only the ruling classes naturally develop an ideology which glorifies freedom and difference; those who are subjected to a domination strive to reappropriate for themselves the productive forces of society by wresting them from the power of the dominant classes. During that long afternoon, we saw that a utopian movement, which sets one model of society against another, is incapable of going beyond a declaration of intent and unable to invent a new politics. The group was experiencing its own impotence. Those who had been most successful in defining the adversary were reduced to silence or pushed onto the fringes. That which had already happened at the end of the morning, before the massive intervention by the researchers, took on a much stronger meaning after so many hours of discussion and repeated and vigorous intervention by the researchers. The group had seemed to be edging towards the social movement, but had then suddenly drawn back. It had not been able to define the actor of the struggle, and it had defined its own tendencies in a way which left no room for a cultural stake accepted by both actor and adversary. Those who wanted to break violently with the State and those who believed more in the force of personal example than in politics were closer to the heart of the anti-nuclear struggle at that moment than those who, like Roland, Georges and Yves, wanted to make it the starting point of an anti-technocratic struggle.

Division

The absence of an established social movement left in direct confrontation a global refusal, made up equally of a break with the State and personal withdrawal, and a political tactic which, in the absence of an established movement, tended to become reformist, to dilute into putting pressure on important agents in the political decision-making process.

How should the action be organised? Jean-Jacques Rodrigo, opposing Alain Touraine's intervention before dinner, refused to define the anti-nuclear struggle as a movement against the State technocracy, since 'to fight such a big thing as that we'd need to give ourselves a technocratic form of organisation. If that's what we have to do to achieve our aims, then I say no. I'd try anything else, but I don't accept that.' The former leader of the Malville Committee in Grenoble no longer thought it was possible to create a movement.

This acknowledgement of failure led Véronique, Valence, Leforestier and also Esther to define the anti-nuclear movement as a mass movement, a great gathering of all those opposed to nuclear power. For Valence, the anti-nuclear action was a struggle like any other, and was already dead. It was the trade union that was the pivot for all the mass movements. The idea was shared by Véronique for whom the working-class movement was the only central actor in the social struggles. Jean-Jacques reacted violently. He broke openly with Valence and Véronique: he could not, he would not, work with them any longer, and Roland Maire rejected Leforestier just as clearly: 'I won't work with you because it's not possible to share a platform with you.'

The strength with which Véronique, Valence and Leforestier defended what had been the practice in the struggle against Super-Phoenix led other members of the group to declare their reformist tendencies much more clearly than before. Jean-Philippe Pharisca maintained 'that you should know when to put your flags away and that the small leftist groups who trumpet their revolutionary faith are destroying the movement by spreading fear. What we should really do is try to convince the parties, introduce ideas into the political system.' Saint-Hilaire recalled how a demonstration in the Nogent region had been a success because there had been no red flags. Jean-Jacques thought it was absurd to have a revolutionary attitude in France, a country where it was much easier to live and protest than in Argentina or the Soviet Union. Roland Maire wanted to go beyond this reformism and work out a union strategy and an agreed platform between trade unionists and ecologists. Thus, to overcome the contradiction between reformism and the support for a mass movement led by revolutionary groups, a pragmatic attitude of seeking alliances was developed. Georges Flamand handed round the text of a planned agreement between the Amis de la Terre and the CFDT, wanting the group to discuss it and give it their support. Alain Touraine objected on the grounds that they should not confuse the sociological intervention with a place to organise the anti-nuclear struggle.

At the end of the evening, during a final tour of the table, the divisions thus revealed became even deeper. Esther and Marie-Jeanne sided clearly with Valence and Leforestier in defending a universal gathering against a common adversary. Pharisca himself was opposed to the LCR being excluded. And yet it was at that moment that Yves Le Gall gave the most coherent and detailed analysis of the potential movement. He defined the adversary of the struggle, which was the nucleocrats and not the State as a whole; its form of action, based on a decentralised network and not on a revolutionary mobilisation; and its objectives, which were to be a broadly political movement, the master of its own tendencies and not a mass movement, nor a training ground for agitating minorites. He was listened to, but although he represented the movement in the group at that moment, he was unable to carry the others along with him.

It had been a central day in the intervention, and its results were so negative that after the end of the meeting the researchers gave way to discouragement as they analysed the results during the night. Because he had several times presented the image of the movement to the group, because he had tried several times to convert it, and, in Versailles, had partially succeeded, Alain Touraine was the most pessimistic. He felt in a very personal way the distance which seemed to him to be virtually insurmountable between the movement and the struggle.

The researchers in this sociological intervention had constantly os-cillated between two opposed attitudes: sometimes, speaking in the name of the movement, they had exalted the group which seemed to them to be the bearer of that movement, whilst at other times they had felt the distance between the real struggle and the potential movement as their own isolation or personal failure. That is why the leader of the research was critical of the agitator of the other group who had not attempted its conversion because she was too closely identified with the group to be able to adopt the detached attitude needed for analytical work. This reaction on the part of the research leader should be analysed like the behaviour of the group members as a source of information on the state of the struggle. The dejection or the resentment of the researchers who had led the attempt to convert the group indicated more clearly than any amount of declarations the absence of a social movement.

But this awareness of failure was not specific to one or two of the researchers. It was also present in the group, some of whose members felt ill at ease, took no further part in the discussion, or confined themselves to asides, whilst others, like Jean-Jacques and Valence or Roland and Leforestier, clashed violently. That evening the whole group felt that its raison d'être was disappearing, that great hopes and general ideas were no longer enough, that the impotence of the anti-nuclear struggle was there for all to see.

Return to the grass roots

The search for a movement, thrown off balance, defeated, strove to touch land again, to rediscover its first aspiration, the refusal of the apparatuses, the specialists and the parties. Almost all the participants were one in the desire to return to the grass roots. Hannibal, who so often played the role of expert in the movement, denounced the excessive influence that scientists can acquire. Roland, one of the chief editors of the *Gazette nucléaire*, produced a self-criticism of the GSIEN. Yves Le Gall, an ecologist, criticised the recourse to a generalised ecological model. Esther went so far as to condemn, as Jacqueline Monceau had done in Paris, the scientists' participation in the meetings organised by the movement. Bourguignon, a trade unionist, was suspicious of the role of the apparatuses in the CFDT itself, and Véronique thought, like Pharisca, that one should know when to leave the flags at home in order to preserve unity amongst the rank and file.

Such was the tone of the morning: *populist*. The anti-nuclear movement no longer defined a conflict between two opposed conceptions of social change, but set sentiment against theory, and the grass roots against the intellectuals of all kinds and the power they acquire through words and expertise. It had become a defensive attitude, a search for autonomy from the organised political bodies, the parties and sometimes even the trade union organisations. Somebody said: 'There's only intellectuals here. We could do with ten or twenty workers and peasants', forgetting on the one hand that the group included several farmers and workers, and on the other hand that it had already admitted several times that workers and peasants in the country as a whole took very little part in anti-nuclear action. This populist tendency demanded new forms of leadership and participation, protested with Georges Flamand against the parties which behave towards the workers like 'the owners of the means of production', and wanted new forms of social democracy. It reached its extreme point when the anti-intellectualism was turned against the sociologists themselves.

Christophe was the first to protest against the pressure they were putting on the group to accept a particular image of the action which corresponded to the positions of Roland, Georges or Hannibal but not to those of the majority. Piccolo joined in, but their criticisms were much more moderate than those of François Delain and Marie-Jeanne Vercors who found the research demobilising and understood her husband's distrust of such 'intellectual masturbation'. For her, the actor's participation was a 'matter of gut feeling', a point made even more violently by Valence: 'What you just can't understand is all that's instinctive in the working class, and just how completely fed up they are with politics.' Saint-Hilaire contrasted the rather pointless lucubrations of the group with the concrete actions in which too few militants took part. Hannibal, Georges and Roland were the only ones prepared to say how important the research had been for them.

At the end of that morning, the tendency which prevailed was the alliance between Valence's anti-Statism and Marie-Jeanne's appeal to the exemplary community. The local militants, those who still called for universal participation in a spontaneous mass action against Super-

Phoenix, rejected the remote, intellectual and, to their mind, almost technocratic projects for the creation of a political action. But they were not triumphant; they were eager to regain their freedom and return to the natural environment of their action. They were suspicious of both the researchers and the members of the group who seemed to them most inclined to behave like leaders, like politicians.

At the outcome of this second weekend, and thus shortly before the researchers were due to present their initial hypotheses to the groups, there could be no doubt whatsoever. The attempt by the researchers and some members of the group to create a social movement had failed, had provoked a rejection and the break-up of the struggle. The attempt to define the actor, the adversary, and the stake of their struggle gave way to a great refusal, a global appeal to a grass roots that was never defined, a sentiment that was supposed to be obvious, and a unanimity which scarcely concealed the inability to choose and to act. We had known what an anti-nuclear movement might be, and now we knew that the anti-nuclear movement was unable to create itself, but flowed back instead towards a defensive and utopian populism.

This judgement of a historical nature on the state of the struggle in the spring of 1978 was not of the same kind as the sociological judgement on the nature of the potential movement. There was nothing to prevent us from thinking that this ebbing of the struggle was temporary, that it could be explained by the defeat and the divisions of the Left. But our speculations and our attempts to reconstruct the struggle would have to begin with this historical acknowledgement of its break-up between opposing tendencies and of the size of the obstacles separating the struggle from the movement within it.

THE WILL TO ACT

Paralysis

What was the situation in the Paris group at the beginning of the third meeting, which took place, like the first, in Versailles? It had arrived in Autrans after succeeding to quite a large extent in its conversion, but it had come back with the feeling of a failure which it blamed mainly on the people from Grenoble, intractably hostile to the Parisians, but also on the researchers. The most active members of the group, Roland and Georges, were also the most vigorous in this attack. The researchers had held themselves aloof from the group and, perhaps because they were not managing to draw the participants from Grenoble–Malville in the direction they wanted, had turned against one another. These words could be interpreted as the response of Roland and Georges to Alain Touraine's opposition to their attempt to transform the intervention group into a meeting place for militants organising the collaboration between the Réseau des Amis de la Terre and the CFDT.

Their discontent was understandable but ambiguous. For them, the transition to concrete action was the only way to escape from the confusion and the despondency and thus represented a kind of progress on the previous state of the group and the anti-nuclear action. For Alain Touraine, on the other hand, this too rapid search for alliances masked the inability of the struggle to transform itself into a social movement, and without a strong anti-nuclear action the negotiations ran the risk of becoming no more than what Hannibal called cosy little chats between the top brass. He had also wanted to try everything possible in Autrans to obtain at least a partial conversion of the Grenoble–Malville group. The 'frustration' that Georges said he had felt during the second weekend was thus a sign of the researchers' failure to bring about the conversion of the Grenoble–Malville group with the help of the Paris group. Could the latter, after this failure, resume its upward progress and give practical form to a social movement after defining it theoretically, or did its search for immediate objectives represent a position of withdrawal, the abandoning of the unattainable social movement in favour of what we called an institutional pressure, of action in favour of alliance?

A first, very important, indication of the state of the group came in the first part of the meeting devoted to Alain Touraine's exposés on the problem of the anti-nuclear struggle and François Dubet's exposé on the history of the group, exposés which it would be pointless to summarise since they aroused no reaction. The disenchantment caused by the meeting at Autrans was expressed through the paralysing of the group's attempts at self-interpretation which were never taken up again during the weekend. The group behaved hardly at all like an analyst-group and reverted more and more to the state of an image-group or even of a witness-group. It is in this context that we need to see the central importance that was invariably attached to organisational problems. The refusal of self-interpretation indicated the defeat of the Paris group by the Grenoble–Malville group and the liquidation of its conversion. The group tried to fill the vacuum thus created with limited tactical preoccupations. It was keenly aware of its setback and made an attempt to recreate the image of a social movement, but was no longer in a position to do so theoretically by responding to the promptings of the researchers, and so preferred to begin with more practical objectives. Would this enable it to rediscover the social movement, or would it deflect the group from the search by tying it up in tactical problems?

A fresh start

The gravity of the failure at Autrans explained why Roland Maire and Georges Flamand began by setting themselves limited objectives. Their caution was justified both by an awareness of the setback to the anti-nuclear action and by a deep distrust of political parties and electoral intervention. Both men had been opposed to ecology candidates standing in the general elections. Roland recalled the Communist Party's hostility to the anti-nuclear movement and the paralysis of the Socialist Party where Jacobin forces remained powerful. Both men were deeply suspicious of the entryism of the leftist militants who were transforming the anti-nuclear action into a training ground for a doctrinaire politics. Weak, divided, demoralised, abandoned by the main parties, the anti-nuclear action had to reorganise and above all seek reinforcement in alliances, firstly with other anti-technocratic defence movements but above all with the CFDT. Georges Flamand had been amazed to see how much importance the confederation attached to the anti-nuclear action, and Saint-Hilaire, judging from the struggle in the Nogent region, maintained that only the CFDT was capable of leading a serious mass action nowadays.

But this priority given to the search for alliances worried some of the ecologists: Hannibal wanted an independent ecology movement to be formed, allied to the CFDT by all means, but more concerned with asserting its own identity and mobilising its own forces. He was afraid of agreements at the top and asked at least for a 'transparent diplomacy', by which he meant keeping the rank and file militants permanently informed of the discussions in progress. Emmanuel Kropo wanted the search for alliances to take second place to the widening of the anti-nuclear struggle towards other objectives. These criticisms by Emmanuel and especially by Hannibal led Roland and Georges to formulate their plans more ambitiously. They refused to choose between mobilisation and organisation, and Georges answered his critics by saying: 'You can call my method political if you want, but at least it's aimed at strengthening the social movement.' Roland, defending the point of view of the CFDT, defined it ambitiously as 'the creation of a political movement whose prime aim would be not to seize power but to reorganise social life through struggles for which nuclear power is a choice target'. Haggar, a trade unionist usually concerned mainly with voicing his ecology attitudes, emphasised this recovery by demanding the transformation not only of the forms of political action but of its content too, which should go beyond the party manifestos.

From the anti-nuclear to the anti-technocratic

By the middle of the meeting, the tone of the group had clearly changed, bringing renewed optimism to the researchers, who had initially been critical of the concern, which they thought premature, with the practical organisation of the struggle and its alliances. The agitator reminded the group of the hopes that had been placed in the anti-nuclear struggle and of the need to define it by its own raisons d'être and its own objectives. The reminder produced further progress from the group, or at least from its most active members, who now acknowledged the crisis in the movement and tried to overcome it by setting against the counter-cultural movement and the great refusal, now exhausted, the need to build a true social movement. They should no longer fight nuclear power as such – 'We can live with nuclear power', said Roland – but the technocratic power which used its whole weight to impose on society a certain energy policy, centred on nuclear power, a certain kind of development and so a certain kind of life. The novelty in this was the group's acceptance that the anti-nuclear movement was exhausted. Sophia said: 'There was often despair over what we were experiencing', and Piccolo admitted the demise of his Anti-Nuclear Committee of the 14th Arrondissement.

These themes were taken up by Georges Flamand himself: the movement had lived on the 'floating' generation of post-68, but now the climate of crisis was causing people to withdraw into individual and family life. Some ecology themes had passed over into public opinion but their action was decomposing because their specific social basis was disappearing: 'The fringe is dead. We've got to start from that fact.' He described his own experience: 'The fear of nuclear power worked at Gravelines from 1972 to 1975; there was a fantastic demo in 1975, and then the whole thing went downhill. All the people who'd been motivated by fear left.' Haggar: 'Well I tell you that people have stayed and they're still afraid.' Georges: 'Maybe, but they don't militate any more.' He was convinced that the specifically anti-nuclear action would die out of its own accord when reactors had been built in every region. To his mind, what was happening in France confirmed the American experience where the counter-cultural rejection of nuclear power had rapidly collapsed and a new movement was now trying to find its way, as in France.

This need to advance beyond the anti-nuclear action was also demonstrated by the increasing lack of interest in the technical or economic protest against official projects. Jean-Philippe Pharisca, a physicist, agreed that the militants were no longer interested in the technical files, which were well known by now. Hannibal's progress on this score was truly remarkable. Although he still played the role of counter-expert in the anti-nuclear struggle and gave numerous lectures on the technical obscurities or flaws in the programme for the construction of nuclear power stations and especially fast-breeders, he now admitted that the struggle should no longer be conducted on this ground but against the technocracy. Emmanuel Kropo followed the same development but more dramatically. His recent reading of the report drawn up by Genestoux for the ecologists on the government's nuclear policy had opened his eyes to the full scope of the official projects, and consequently to the difficulty of fighting at a purely technical level and the need to oppose a global policy with another political project. Roland Maire, just before the close of the meeting, went so far as to say: 'Our files are good, but theirs are also credible in the present system. In reality, we're turning around the questions: what kind of life, what development, what future? But both projects have their logic.'

How far from the spirit of the first anti-nuclear campaigns and even from so many recent pronouncements by the Amis de la Terre or the anti-nuclear committees! Alain Touraine encouraged this reversal of perspective which he thought necessary for the creation of a broadly based and durable social movement which would take over from a cultural refusal that was both too generalised and necessarily transitory.

The group had become acutely aware of the importance of its work at the same time as it had realised the urgent need for a change of perspective. It was a long way from the tactical preoccupations of the beginning of the meeting and was no longer divorcing the search for alliances and forms of action from a fundamental reorientation of a struggle which had to become the pivot of a much vaster movement directed against the technocracy in every domain of social life, especially computerisation, and not just energy policy. At no other time in the research had there been such a profound realisation that the group's work should lead to decisive conclusions for the future of the struggle. Some of the participants at that moment were very close to the sociologists, including Roland Maire who adopted their vocabulary to show his awareness of the proximity and also to persuade the group to accept the ideas which had first been introduced by the agitator. After several hours of experiencing the destructive effects of the failure at Autrans, the group had first set itself limited aims and then, by criticising them itself, had rediscovered together with the researchers the meaning of the distance which separated the real struggle from the potential movement, adding to that the awareness, never before expressed, of the exhaustion of the anti-nuclear struggle. It abandoned the appeal to fear and the recourse to technical or economic arguments in its struggle against nuclear energy and concentrated on a directly social and political position. There was no longer any question of saying that nuclear energy leads to the technocracy; it was recognised that the central and indeed almost exclusive role of nuclear power in the energy policy had been imposed by a technocratic power which was using it to create a type of society, as much at the level of production as of consumption.

But did the group as a whole accept this new direction? Was it rising towards this global conception, or was the latter just the idea of the few and incapable of winning over the rest of the group and, *a fortiori*, the anti-nuclear militants?

Falling back

In fact, the upward progress of the analysis had been the increasingly solitary feat of Roland Maire who was for a long stretch of time the only one to speak, supported by brief interventions from Georges Flamand and Hannibal. His isolation was quickly realised. Haggar, a trade unionist and ecologist, who was nonetheless sympathetic to anti-technocratic ideas, was the first to show signs of anxiety: 'You won't get the people at the bottom to budge if all you're fighting is the technocracy', and he reminded them that the raison d'être of the mass anti-nuclear movement was the fear of the lethal dangers that nuclear energy created for the population and especially the workers. He added shortly afterwards: 'I've been aware from the beginning of a manipulation of language. If I'd come here to be persuaded to join the anti-nuclear movement, you wouldn't have done it with all those refined intellectual speeches of yours.' He was worried by an 'anti-nuclear technocratic language' whilst at the same time refusing to play the workers off against the intellectuals for the greater pleasure of high society ecologists who thought how terribly jolly it was to applaud a worker.

Saint-Hilaire did not criticise Roland Maire but reminded him of his own reasons for opposing the nuclear industry, his fear, when he came to retire in the Nogentais, of seeing the projected reactor make life there too dangerous. And it was this same distance between an anti-technocratic political project and the motivations of the anti-nuclear struggle which was felt by Sophia, who confessed to feeling less involved in the struggle, and by Jean-Philippe Pharisca who, with his usual mild language, admitted that at the end of this work by the group he felt 'a bit tired'. Emmanuel Kropo recognised that the discussion had been led by only a few people and had not turned up anything new; he too felt relegated to the fringe. Finally, Piccolo, shortly before the end of the debate, gave his pessimistic conclusion: 'Fighting against a will to power is even more woolly-minded and abstract than fighting nuclear energy, which is already woolly and abstract for the average kind of person in the 14th arrondissement.' His anxiety was all the greater since the anti-nuclear struggle should not be reduced to small ideological groups but should rather, in his opinion, outflank the action of the parties from the bottom and galvanise people who had until then steered well clear of political activity. Roland Maire, Georges Flamand, and even Hannibal, remained isolated.

We had returned full circle to the starting point of this final meeting, to a project for an alliance between the Amis de la Terre and the CFDT. This was not a diplomatic operation for the anti-nuclear militants, but both more and less at the same time. Less because the most active militants in the struggle were also the most aware of its disorganisation and thought the alliance with the CFDT would enable the two movements to define not general principles but concrete objectives and so lead to a new mobilisation. More because the intention of the protagonists in this alliance really was to create a social movement, above and beyond the political parties. But the overwhelming fact was the failure of the transition from anti-nuclear sentiment to anti-technocratic action, the still insurmountable distance between the fear and the refusal of the nuclear industry on the one side and a counter-project for economic and social development on the other, based on preferences other than the choices of the government and the large firms. The life of the anti-nuclear struggle could only be dominated in the period following the intervention by a constant misunderstanding between a great refusal which its adversaries accused of being a retreat into a sect and strategic initiatives which many would oppose as political wheeler-dealing.

The group broke up, at the end of the Saturday evening, powerless to react against the forces that were destroying its struggle.

THE END OF A UTOPIA

Return to the conversion

During its last weekend, the Grenoble–Malville group was in no better state than the Paris group to discuss the researchers' analyses, but in its case it had still made no attempt at conversion. Perhaps it was too late and the weight of two failures in a row too heavy? At least the researchers were convinced that they should tackle something which had been neither achieved nor attempted during the first weekend and commit themselves entirely to the attempt at conversion, accepting all the risks involved, including the risk of a break-up of the group. During the whole weekend, they worked at length, with a sense of urgency, and sometimes even aggressively, on those tendencies which seemed at variance with the research team's image of the movement. Their work was made easier by the absence of Valence who had vanished yet again, as he had during most of the first part of the intervention. Bourguignon was also absent, because of a feeling of discouragement that he had already expressed several times.

The agitator opened the session by showing the weakness of an anti-nuclear current of opinion incapable of defining the We it spoke for, the adversary it was fighting and the stake of the struggle. He recounted the partial attempts to create a social movement and called on the group to turn its back on an attitude of refusal in order to define a counter-project for society and from that the conditions of a specifically social struggle. The ensuing discussion lasted almost four hours until, at five o'clock in the afternoon, the group came to a halt, aware of having achieved something important and in a state of collective jubilation, before listening to Michel Wieviorka's interpretation of the history of the intervention. These hours were one of the high points of that intervention. The two researchers, whose action had never until then been coordinated, constantly supported

131

one another, and although it was true that not all the members of the group took part in the discussion, neither was it monopolised by a specific tendency: Leforestier, Esther and Claudine intervened as much as Yves Le Gall, Jean-Jacques Rodrigo and Christophe, who constantly gave the impression of making a tremendous effort to search for and discover himself and the aims of his action. The Grenoble–Malville group, in spite of its failures and the heavy memory of the Malville demonstration, retained an impressive strength. It no longer took refuge in discussions on the situation or lived experience but placed itself squarely before the question put by the sociologists: in what conditions could the anti-nuclear wave be the bearer of a true anti-technocratic social movement going beyond the illusion of the utopian withdrawal into the warmth of community experience?

The project, the struggle and lived experience

The elaboration of a project is only another name for the search for a social movement. Véronique Uri made no mistake about it: defining the anti-nuclear action as a social movement and recognising the originality of its project was to separate it from the working-class movement, or at least to make it independent of it. Because she rejected such a separation, she logically rejected the distinction between capitalism and technocracy and saw in the anti-nuclear action only a mass movement, in other words a particular struggle whose general meaning could be seen only by those who locate themselves in the working-class movement.

She was attacked by Leforestier who rejected the parties of the Left together with the whole apparatus of social domination. But the interest of the discussion lay rather in the attempts by Christophe, a trade union militant, to defend the anti-nuclear project without breaking with the working-class movement. He said: 'The capitalist system has set up this technocracy as a kind of comprehensive insurance policy against any form of power for the people', but he added immediately: 'Even if the 1978 elections had brought a change of power that might have seemed to challenge the capitalist system, the fact is that that system has set up a system of control that we wouldn't have been able to fight.' And then: 'I think the system could perpetuate itself whatever social means are set up.'

The important point here was not so much the capitalist affiliation of the technocracy as its autonomy. In clear terms, the energy policy was indeed created by the capitalist regime, but it was EDF and the CEA who were effectively in control of it, and a victory of the Left would not have made them change direction. This led Christophe to the conclusion: 'One way we have of tossing out the capitalist system is by tossing out the technocratic apparatus.' François Delain was more precise: 'The enemy is technocratic power. If that falls, all the rest falls.'

The collapse

Christophe was strongly supported by Claudine who located the root of power not in the capitalist system but in individual psychology. She was no happier than Leforestier with the identification of power with capitalist domination and provided a much more general but also much vaguer definition. Christophe was discovering that not only did the anti-nuclear struggle have a specific adversary but also contained a general project for society, to the extent of being able to give new depth and conviction to working-class trade unionism.

Véronique was conscious of her isolation. One of the first to speak after the agitator's exposé, she then remained almost silent, intervening only to indicate everything that separated her from the group as a whole, which was allowing itself to be carried along by the utopia, since, according to her, projects for social experimentation presupposed that capitalism had already been eliminated, a task which only the working-class movement could accomplish. There was an ambiguity in this relegation of Véronique to the fringe. It showed in some that the group was prepared to speculate on the anti-nuclear project, whereas the contribution of others consisted in opposing the nuclear policy with the defensive force of community experience rather than a political strategy. Hence the length and the warmth of a debate in which the defence of lived experience was opposed to the search for a project.

It was mainly Esther who defended the values of the community, but she was also the one least inclined to set the concept of community against the political project in any strong way. Leforestier, Marie-Jeanne and Claudine were more clearly hostile to the ideas defended by Zsuzsa Hegedus. The first said: 'It's the affective dimension that attracted people into the movement, and I don't see in the name of what theory we're going to ditch that', to which Christophe replied: 'That excludes the conflictual relationship we have with the outside world.' But Leforestier was afraid that this insistence on the struggle might lead to the setting up of a new party, a new apparatus, a new mobilisation, and thus to the reinforcement of what they were fighting or even to the reduction of a vast movement to just one more doctrinaire little group. Jean-Jacques, strongly attached to the community model, tried to find a compromise by criticising the tendency of the anti-nuclear struggle to turn in on itself and make its own internal warmth the aim of its action until the shock of events showed up its impotence. But the problem summarised in the exchange just quoted was too fundamental to yield to any attempt at compromise. Against the transformation of the political, trade union and working-class movement into an apparatus of social management, Leforestier, like Claudine and Esther, appealed to the exemplary community and demanded the return to an ethic of conviction.

Faced with these three and their resistance, what were Christophe, Jean-Jacques or Yves defending? Was it really a social movement capable of

133

developing a policy, or was it, as Leforestier feared, a mere political strategy? Yves Le Gall, who was better able than anyone to formulate the orientations of a social movement, followed the statement of his general ideas with propositions that were much more limited and even, in fact, closer to the idea of social experimentation than to a political project. He criticised the survival of 68-style illusions and was afraid that a utopian vision of society would lead to totalitarian solutions. Those who talked of real needs and real science were not far from wanting to impose them by force. He, on the other hand, wanted a democratic action totally divorced from prophetic utopias and capable of casting a critical eye on its own practices, but also of protecting itself from the temptations of the politics of wheeler-dealing.

Michel Wieviorka pointed out to him that his concrete propositions fell far short of his analyses. It was Christophe who answered by trying to overcome the opposite objections of Véronique and Esther. He quoted the case of Denmark where there had been attempts to set up communes which the authorities had accepted and turned to their own advantage as long as they had not challenged the regime itself. When they had attacked it, they had been repressed. So they themselves should try in their social and cultural experiments to develop this dimension of a general challenging of power. Yves Le Gall rallied to this position: if 150 people got together to take over a block of flats and manage it collectively, that would already represent a considerable advance on the present struggles.

At the outcome of this first discussion, the agitator was able to form a positive judgement: 'For the first time, you have analysed the movement and the conditions for its creation; you have adopted an analytical position. Now each one of you should explain his or her positions so as to transform them into political actions.' As in Versailles during the first weekend of the Paris group, the Grenoble–Malville group had begun its conversion on the initiative of the researchers and had at the same time become differentiated. Christophe, Le Gall and Jean-Jacques, in accord with the agitator, had produced an analysis which had managed to impose itself in spite of the reticence of Véronique, and which had grown constantly stronger in spite of opposition from a part of the group.

Nothing enabled us to say that the group could be brought towards the movement which had just been outlined, but it was undeniable that the intervention had reached its main point, where the group, which symbolised the real struggle, would react to the image of the movement it contained within itself and which the researchers had helped it to bring out.

Science and society

The debate on science which followed this long discussion of the community spirit ought to show whether the group was capable of recognising the existence of a cultural stake and defining a policy of democratic control of scientific and technological production, or whether, on the contrary, it would yet again give in to the dream of a science oriented by community needs in opposition to a science guided by the technocrats.

Esther defended the second position: let each community, she said, have its own scientists. She even saw computer technology putting itself naturally at the service of grass-roots democracy. Yves Le Gall was on the opposite side: he believed in the separation of scientific production and needs and wanted to set up an intermediate, political, body, between scientific organisation and the democratic expression of needs. As so often, Christophe was at the centre of the group. He recognised the autonomy of scientific development and did not believe one could avoid conflicts between science and democracy, but he also thought we should develop counter-research corresponding to other needs, against the official science serving the great apparatuses of domination. But he could give only very limited examples to support his idea and soon let himself be persuaded by Zsuzsa Hegedus that 'the movement is the place where knowledge and the creation of needs finally come together'. This immediately obtained the agreement of Esther who declared: 'If a scientist has discovered his bomb, one ought to be able to say to him: burn all your work, we don't want it.' Christophe also declared: 'There are technical objects that you want or you don't want, according to the control you're going to have over them.' From which Zsuzsa Hegedus drew the conclusion of this debate: 'We should question scientific choices in order to refuse what is uncontrollable.'

But all of this, in fact, led to the suppression of science as a stake, its transformation into a sign of cultural choice, hence its total submission to a collective will. It was the utopia of a counter-culture and a science in the service of the people, not to say popular itself, and which did not bring us any closer to a social movement, which is, on the contrary, always a social conflict for the appropriation of productive forces in society which cannot be reduced to the ideology and the interests of one of the two adversaries. One could understand the irritation of Véronique who thought the group was counting its chickens before they were hatched. In fact, this difficult debate had caused the group to lapse back into the illusion of the exemplary community and counter-culture at precisely the moment when it thought it was struggling free of it.

Retreat

Was it because Michel Wieviorka, who then presented his interpretation of the history of the group, had stressed the conflict between Valence and Jean-Jacques and the rapprochement between the 'locals' and the former? No sooner had he finished than the discussion focused on the internal dissensions of the group. And yet he had referred in much greater detail to the discussions with the interlocutors and the weekend when the two groups had met. The reason could only be, then, that, after the long debate led by Christophe and Yves Le Gall, the other participants were reacting by attaching themselves to that which divided the group. The reversal was rapid. Esther led the discussion and defended Valence because he was a proletarian, the representative of 'those who aren't allowed to speak, of those who have no power'. Marie-Jeanne joined her because Valence represented the younger generation that she was so fond of. Leforestier maintained his support for Valence in spite of Michel Wieviorka's attacks on him, and Jean-Jacques repeated his accusations against the one who 'had chosen his own exclusion' and had been responsible for the events in Malville.

The group was instantly divided. On the one side, Yves Le Gall attacked the ecumenicism which had led to impotence and accused the local militants: 'You are responsible for this situation because you're the ones at the centre of the struggle and it's the choices you've made from the beginning which have reduced us to impotence, because you've prevented the necessary clarification, because you refuse to choose. In my opinion, you're the ones responsible for the shitpile we've got ourselves into in this region.'

On the other side, François Delain was the one who spoke most vigorously. Nobody could be singled out, because the movement had no unity. It did not exist in Malville before 1976. It was with people like Valence that the locals had begun to organise the struggle against Super-Phoenix. And that concrete struggle was the only reality: we should accept all those who wanted to take part in it in the knowledge that we cannot go beyond it, because there is not one but several anti-nuclear movements.

It was a direct confrontation between the one who wanted orientations and an organisation and the one who sought to gather the most diverse forces around a priority objective. The sociologists, by their attacks on Valence, had committed themselves, which in turn provoked an attack on them by Claudine and Leforestier.

At the end of that afternoon, the group's internal crisis seemed to have only one meaning: the movement could not possibly exist. Perhaps the debate on science had been too abstract, had pushed the local militants too much to the side, restricted as it had been, in fact, to a dialogue between the agitator, one participant who was an engineer, and another who was an economist. But the reaction of the others did not necessarily lead to such an open conflict. The grass-roots militants rejected the tendency to develop a programme in which they saw the danger of a party being formed. Christophe tried to intervene, to adopt once more the role he had played during the first weekend, but it was too late. Esther, very conscious of the

136

distance between herself and Le Gall and of the need 'for the people who theorise far from the grass-roots to take the latter into account', defended the local action and the need for a consensus on concrete objectives.

The initiative had passed to Esther and Leforestier, who were the ones who now opposed Véronique's attempt to reintroduce her constant theme of the need to have the working-class movement take responsibility for the anti-nuclear struggle. Esther hoped 'that the workers who have seen the limits of the working-class movement will join *our* movement', and Leforestier showed that people who thought as he did wanted to create a new movement, and not just imprison themselves in a great refusal: 'In the working-class movement there were proletarians fighting the bourgeoisie. Today in the anti-nuclear domain there are other relationships than appropriation, other aims than taking the place of the middle classes. There are problems of the quality of life. And consequently there are people who don't define themselves solely as workers.'

Opposite Véronique, who denied the existence of an anti-nuclear movement and believed only in a mass action, in other words in the application of diverse forces to a particular objective under the aegis of the working-class movement for which that action was not the central battle, the rest of the group felt united in the affirmation of the independence and the originality of the struggle. But once this minimum agreement had been established, the separation was complete between those who had waged a crusade and those who were devising a strategy. As in the first weekend, anti-Statism joined forces with the search for the exemplary community against the makers of programmes who seemed to be reformist political manipulators or disembodied theorists. The afternoon drew to a close; Marie-Jeanne Vercors and François Delain left for Morestel; the group split up. Its collapse had been so sudden and the confrontations so direct that they could not be explained by some incident. In the middle of the session the group had experienced a brief illusion of consensus, and even the researchers had yielded to it. But the illusion had not lasted. It had been shattered in the space of a few minutes. The group's existence seemed threatened, and the idea of an anti-nuclear social movement seemed very remote from the results of a struggle in crisis.

Breakdown

After dinner, faced with the increasingly vigorous criticisms of Véronique and especially the offensive of Esther and Leforestier, the researchers committed themselves more and more directly. Zsuzsa Hegedus attacked Leforestier and Véronique head-on, and so strengthened the various resistances to the image of the social movement that she was defending. When the session began again, those resistances were so strong that

Christophe and Yves were on the defensive and Jean-Jacques felt excluded from a debate dominated by the absent figure of Valence.

The attacks against the project for a social movement were resumed. They came first from Véronique, who accused Jean-Jacques, Yves, and even Christophe of 'sidestepping the real problems by supposing them to be solved when they can only be so by a mass intervention of the working-class movement'. The social experimentation they dreamed of was easily recuperable and might even be proposed by modernist leaders; their struggle against the technocracy was dangerous because it did not try to see what was hidden behind the technocracy. Leforestier was more directly suspicious of the reformist orientation that Zsuzsa Hegedus was trying to impose on the debate, an attitude which provoked a reaction from Yves Le Gall, who rejected a political break of the Leninist type, which he considered dangerous, and defended democratic institutions. Yet again, Christophe defended a less extreme position, that of the CFDT, which does not reject the idea of a break with institutions but prefers to prepare it through concrete struggles and the fight for 'meaningful objectives of transformation'.

The internal imbalance of the group grew steadily worse, however. It was Leforestier who most often had the initiative. Véronique, almost silent during the afternoon, spoke frequently and energetically. Claudine pushed the attack against those who wanted to create a social movement so far that she provoked the breakdown of the group: 'We shouldn't construct a social movement which ends up like the working-class movement, which got concessions for the workers that duped them and trapped them more than they were a hundred and fifty years ago. Some big deal they got with their four weeks paid holiday! The workers were betrayed.' Christophe, scandalised by this attack on the trade unions, left the meeting for a while. Jean-Jacques, in exasperation, suddenly decided to leave, and with Yves Le Gall, whose departure had been expected from the beginning, travelled back to Grenoble through the night.

This departure was experienced as a dramatic crisis. Those who talked of consensus and ecumenicism like Esther, Leforestier and Claudine knew that their hopes were crumbling if Jean-Jacques, who had played such an important part in the Malville Committee of Grenoble, was leaving them just as he had withdrawn from the Committee after it had been taken over by the diversified tendency with its acceptance of violence. Jean-Jacques was a reformist but also very close to community ideas, suspicious of doctrines and parties, a leader of the ecology movement much more than the strategist of organised struggles. His departure affected the group much more deeply than that of Yves, who was more theoretical, more distant, and who had long since left an anti-nuclear struggle whose development he disapproved. Jean-Jacques, more sensitive and involved, had tried in the light of the Malville drama, which had left its mark on him, to transform

138

protest and refusal into a social movement. He was also the member of the group with whom the agitator had most identified, to the point of being convinced from the beginning that he would be the one through whom the group would achieve its conversion. But now this recognised leader of the group was leaving it as he had left the Malville Committee, torn, unhappy and bitter.

After his departure, the ones who were left – Christophe, Esther, Leforestier, Claudine and Véronique – broke up rapidly. But Michel Wieviorka, who had already shown his personal liking for Leforestier, stayed with them, and then alone with the latter until the early hours of the morning, trying to discover in him, after the departure of Yves and Jean-Jacques, a movement which might carry him beyond the break with society, which he had always claimed to be necessary, in the very direction that Jean-Jacques had taken. 'What you said tonight means to me that you see yourself in relation to the social movement and as an actor in such a movement.' Leforestier admitted that he was, in fact, unlike Valence, the working-class militant for whom the anti-nuclear struggle was only one field of action amongst so many others, but he did not respond to the advances: 'Myself, I've no desire to build anything.' He was above all suspicious of parties and organisations, a libertarian who gave himself entirely to protest and opposition. He also appealed to lived experience against 'ideology and theory'. He refused to condemn the use of violence because he wanted each individual to be free to choose and so recognised that it was impossible to give the movement general orientations acceptable to everybody.

The next morning Zsuzsa Hegedus in her turn tried to make Esther conscious of her own progress. She was more aware than Leforestier of the need to allow and organise the coexistence of various tendencies in the anti-nuclear struggle, and she was sympathetic to the simultaneously in-dependent and political line of the Amis de la Terre. Zsuzsa Hegedus asked her to reflect on the departure of Jean-Jacques, which she had in fact felt as a failure, and led her to recognise the need to define objectives and the usefulness of an alliance with the CFDT. But Esther very quickly broke free, and her tone was highly critical: 'The dynamics of the social movement that you want to create are basically reformist, and what's more its objectives are completely off target. It would be a first class funeral for the ecology movement. As for the intermediate objectives, I don't see them as being agreements between the CFDT apparatus and other apparatuses like the Amis de la Terre. What I see as an objective is a moratorium . . . to allow us to rebuild a mass movement.'

The meeting ended in an awareness of failure. Only Christophe was optimistic for the future of the struggle and satisfied with the group's work. Véronique, during the last round of the table, repeated her usual fears and accusations with a sincerity that was all the more convincing because everybody knew her militant attachment to the anti-nuclear action. Claudine was pessimistic; Esther felt more ecumenical than ever. It was Leforestier who concluded: 'At the beginning, we came across adversaries that we were more or less united against . . . then we came to problems of organisation, with some people, like myself, not wanting organisation. and then we skidded over some vague scheme between the CFDT and the Amis de la Terre. Then the break-up, we went through that too . . . We've come back to where we were in the autumn. Jean-Jacques has left over the same themes as then.'

The group had indeed relived the history of the struggle right up to the collapse. And as if the researchers had not felt the failure keenly enough, the two anti-nuclear sympathisers, a man and a woman, who had come to look after the group's meals, stepped in just as everybody was leaving to attack the sociologists who, in their opinion, had been trying to manipulate the militants. The accusation was made without violence and withdrawn immediately, but it symbolically marked the end of the meeting between the group and the researchers.

The meaning of the failure

Thus, after so many hours of discussion in the group, after so much effort by the researchers and so many confrontations with the Paris group, the Grenoble–Malville group seemed to be back where it had started, or rather back at the crisis of the Malville Committee. Those who had criticised or opposed Jean-Jacques spoke with increasing force. The call for a great cultural refusal and the necessary confrontation with the State was clearer than the will to create a social movement or to find a place in the political spectrum. Jean-Jacques left the group as he had left the Malville Committee, furious and despairing, convinced that the future of the ecology struggle required a break with elements which he considered to be destructive. It was not that Jean-Jacques was a political militant, but although he was sensitive to community themes, he had been offended by the doctrinaire spirit and the manoeuvring of the leftist groups who knew how to exploit the ecumenicism of many local militants. He was a liberal, humanist and moralist militant rather than an organisation militant.

Close to but very different from him, Yves Le Gall, an economist from Vive la Révolution, a short-lived movement for cultural revolution, who had experienced communal life and was a specialist in organic farming, was also extremely hostile to the spirit and the methods of the leftists and eager to live differently in a new social and political activity. He was more of a theorist than Jean-Jacques, but like him he was trying to define the institutional conditions for the production and expression of a new sensibility, new experiences and a desire for autonomy. The break-up of the group, hastened by the agitator's commitment, was experienced as anguish by Jean-Jacques, a man of action and collective life, and as liberation by Yves, who had had no part in the history of the Malville Committee. Both alike refused to link their counter-cultural refusal to political leftism, and both alike were determined to continue the action, but not with all the members of the group. They rejected on the one side the local militants, too intent on opening the struggle to everybody, and on the other militants like those from the LCR. Such was the meaning of their departure.

A few days after the weekend at Autrans, Zsuzsa Hegedus and Michel Wieviorka were invited to Grenoble to take part in a new meeting to which had been invited only Jean-Jacques, Christophe, Yves Le Gall, Leforestier and Esther. The meeting was dominated by a misunderstanding: Christophe and Jean-Jacques wanted to set up a new anti-nuclear group, linked to the Amis de la Terre and committed to seeking an alliance with the CFDT, close in other words to the line adopted by Roland Maire and Georges Flamand. The researchers, on the other hand, wanted to take advantage of this meeting to further the analysis, and were determined not to let themselves be identified with a particular militant action, especially since it excluded one section of the group they themselves had set up. The discussion showed at least that the new group, or its kernel – Jean-Jacques, Yves and Christophe – was equally remote from unanimism and avant-gardism. These militants from the ecology and anti-nuclear movement, without plan, without programme, but inspired by a sensibility which drew its strength from both refusal and innovative imagination, wished to rebuild the destroyed hope.

They gave their assessment of the intervention group and explained what they had learnt from its work. Firstly, in spite of Véronique, they had discovered that the struggle was directed against a new adversary. Everybody, from François Delain to Yves Le Gall, had recognised this transformation in the field of the social struggles, and we had followed Christophe's difficult, painful but decisive advance in this direction. In the second place, they had rid themselves, as was shown by the lengthy debate on science, repeated by Christophe during the fourth meeting, of the naive eulogy of alternative medicines and the appeal to the past. Yves Le Gall could not get over the ease with which the theme of modernity had been accepted by the group, when it was so generally resisted by the ecologists. No doubt this modernism would have to be protected against the dangers of a vaguely liberal conservatism, but it showed that the struggle can define a societal stake for itself instead of retreating into the creation of a utopia which would be no more than the projection of its refusal of the industrial and commercial society.

But none of this was in any way sufficient to give shape to the social

141

movement. Firstly because they were still unable to define the actor of the movement. At one time, the group came up with the idea that in a society of change the actor could no longer be defined by his origins, but should be defined by his future project. But the limits of such voluntarism are obvious. Wanting another future is not enough to create it, and there is no way of distinguishing a social movement from the day-dreaming of a handful of utopians or the language of a sect. Secondly, their ideas were not enough to constitute a social movement because the militants were keenly aware of their inability to organise an action, define their aim and create the means to achieve it.

What remained at the end of this difficult discussion was a strong collective will to be and to act, a demand that the militants addressed to themselves: probably in order to break with a past experience whose former warmth had dissipated, leaving only a bitter taste behind it. The intervention of the sociologists in Grenoble had not led to the disintegration of the will to act but the awareness of the need to break with forms of action and even with orientations that were now exhausted.

The members of this restricted group agreed on three main ideas. The first was that the movement, even if it did have to find allies, not to say protectors, must affirm its independence and its originality. Although linked to the working-class movement, it would not be a mere avatar of that movement. The second was that it should never dissociate lived experience and a project for society, in other words it should not be reduced to a general analysis or to general ideas, a point which had been made most consistently and most forcibly in Paris by Georges. The third was that it could not be content with the do-it-yourself experimenting of the fringe, but should propose realistic solutions to the economic and social crisis which meant paying rather more attention than before to people with an expertise that they did not want to put at the service of the technocracy. On such bases, the reconstruction of the struggle seemed possible.

This gesture of the people from Grenoble meeting at the house of the one who had left Autrans in despair a few days before did at least show their refusal to accept the threatening disintegration and their determination to give shape to a protest which would be both refusal and hope.

This temporary end to the work of the intervention groups did not call for a simple conclusion. It showed the disintegration of what had been the historical figure of the anti-nuclear movement, a mixture of cultural crisis and utopia, but also of a new definition of the fundamental social conflicts of our time. It also showed the militants' inability to free the social movement from a struggle that was in crisis and retreat. It did not yet define the forms that this social movement might take, but it indicated quite clearly that the latter could no longer live on the basis of a generalised cultural protest, that it must be helped and prepared by a specifically political approach, by learning to organise, by seeking alliances and above all by recognising itself as a protest against a mode of development, and no longer as the rejection of a technology or an industry.

It was our intention to accompany the anti-nuclear militants for as long as possible in their difficult attempt to give life to the movement whose presence they felt in their struggle, but we could no longer accept the idea of a struggle that would rise spontaneously, in spite of its crises and setbacks, towards a social movement. What had been the strength of the first demonstrations was now no longer able to further new struggles. It was not just a question of the normal transition from youth to maturity of a collective action. Between the first demonstration on the site at Fessenheim and the summer of 1978 the historical situation had changed. The protests born of May 68 had died away; the criticism of a growth which had seemed too assured had been replaced by anxiety over unemployment or repression; the parties of the Left could now no longer defend a programme which was based on an acceleration of growth. It seemed as if the period of ideas and feelings had been replaced by a time for calculation and caution. Finally, the debate for or against the nuclear industry seemed likely to be overtaken by events. Even the government, which was speeding up the nuclear programme, was also looking for alternative answers to the energy crisis, and, a few months later, the ecologists themselves, by accepting as a fait accompli the first government programme for nuclear plant, were to mark the end of their radical, absolute opposition to nuclear power.

We might venture to suggest that the anti-nuclear struggle of the years 1973–8 was over, not, however, to announce that its themes would disappear and that it had been no more than an ephemeral and confused resistance to the necessary development of an industry, but rather to alert its militants and other people too to the difficulty and the necessity of continuing the effort made by some members of the intervention groups to extract from the struggles of the past the ideas and the objectives which will be those of the social movement which, by other means and on other grounds, as well as on this one, will challenge the new forms of social domination. The main phase of the intervention had produced these two results, which were not contradictory: the exhaustion of the first forms of the struggle and the presence in them of a social movement borne by the militants who had played the central role in our groups and offered them the only coherent image of the anti-nuclear action.

PART THREE

FROM ANALYSIS TO ACTION

7

wwwwwwwwwwwwwwwwwwwwwwwwwwwwwwwwwwwwwwwwwwwwwwwwwwwwwwwwwwwwwwwwwwwwww

Permanent sociology

RETURN TO THE STRUGGLES

The evaluation groups

Since there was a danger that the intervention groups would too readily interpret their practice from the point of view of an analysis worked out by themselves, the latter had to be submitted to other groups of militants who had not been associated with the intervention. These groups were given a résumé of the research report, in the form of a special number of the *Gazette nucléaire*, one of the main militant organs of the anti-nuclear struggle. Meetings were organised between local militants, researchers and members of the intervention groups whose role was essential to establish a link between the analysis and the action, given their dual situation as militants and participants in the intervention proper. The meetings involved the following groups: the Amis de la Terre in Lille, the Réseau des Amis de la Terre meeting in Seignosse, ecology and anti-nuclear militants from Nantes and the region of Le Pellerin (two meetings), militants from Alsace meeting in Strasbourg, ecology and anti-nuclear groups, in particular from Cruas–Meysse and Saint-Etienne-des-Sorts, meeting in Montélimar, the CFDT union section from La Hague, anti-nuclear militants from the Malville region, ecologists and anti-nuclear militants from Grenoble, leaders of the ecology movement in Paris, members of the CFDT Energy Commission, scientists from the GSIEN, and the editors' collective of the *Gazette nucléaire*.

These meetings allowed us in the first place to correct and complete the analysis by supplying information on struggle practices different from those taken into account by the intervention groups. But if that had been their main function, they should have come before the intervention and not after. The role of the researchers was to ensure that they went much further and used the research to illuminate the action instead of just bringing fresh materials to the analysis. The mere existence of these meetings produced an effect of knowledge, since the militants were not accustomed to meeting for general discussion on the basis of a text which did not propose objectives to

147

them but an analysis of themselves and their struggles. The researchers and the members of the intervention groups wished to put the precise results of the analysis to the test by submitting them for study by the militants who would use them to evaluate and understand better their own practices. Such meetings are a success if they allow us to relate precise aspects of the struggle to the social movement, and to define its components and project level.

This part of the work came up against serious obstacles. Firstly, such an evaluation would have presupposed a lengthy preparation of the groups for such unusual work. There would have to have been a preparatory meeting with each one for the researchers to provide information about the research and its results before organising the session in which the group would evaluate its own practices. Then, and above all, the actors have an ideology and so resist the research. This resistance was often weak with the relatively isolated grass-roots militants, who were happy to be taking part in such a general reflexion. It was much stronger amongst those whose function was to express, in speech or in writing, the positions of the movement or of a particular association and who felt the research as a dispossession. This resistance from the ideologists of the movement was all the greater as the real struggle was more remote from the possible movement, so that it indicated the nature of that struggle. The evaluation groups realised the importance of this research for their action and gave the researchers a warm welcome. The example of the meeting in Nantes showed that they had recognised the problems of their action in the analysis of the researchers.

At the end of this meeting, which had brought out the internal divisions in the group, one of the militants turned against the research and attacked the very concept of social movement. Other participants immediately opposed him and pointed out themselves that the distance between their group and the analysis demonstrated the difficulty of setting up an anti-nuclear movement, and this in turn led them to ask for a second meeting during which important progress was made in the analysis. Neither was it any chance that the one who had attacked the research was a political militant from the extreme left for whom, as for Véronique Uri, the anti-nuclear struggle was only a mass battleground and a means to rejuvenate and revolutionise a working-class movement that had become reformist.

Almost all those who took part in these meetings not only recognised in the analysis presented to them a useful way of conceiving the problems of the movement, but also saw in these meetings a means of bringing its theory and practice closer together. For the most usual reaction was to acknowledge the distance between practical anti-nuclear action, especially at the local level, and the principles guiding that action. In this, the evaluation groups directly reached the same conclusions as the intervention groups, recognising both the importance of the stakes in the anti-nuclear struggle and the difficulty of organising concrete actions.

On the defensive

Return to the local action

In several groups, the militants recognised the distance between local defence and more general objectives. The violence of the confrontation between the militants of the two local committees in Le Pellerin in our presence showed that this distance could go to the point of conflict. Those who had called for a boycott of the municipal elections following the mayor's resignation were violently challenged by those who had called for support for those candidates of the Left who were prepared to oppose plans for power stations. The scissionists accused the boycotters of playing the game of the mayor who, according to them, had never been anti-nuclear but had used the people's opposition to the power station as a means of increasing his personal power. For their part, the boycotters accused the scissionists of playing the electoral game of a Left that had no real anti-nuclear position but was obviously ready to oppose the power station in order to win votes. Their objective was simple and straightforward: to prevent the building of a nuclear reactor at Le Pellerin. 'We don't see things the same way as the ecology Romantics. On the ground, we oppose the power station physically, and we're very glad to have the support of the politicians; it's a source of comfort for the struggle, because playing the foot soldiers , the martyrs, is all very well for public opinion, but where does it get you?'

These words, uttered in Le Pellerin, corresponded almost exactly to those of the militants from Saint-Etienne-des-Sorts or from Meysse: the opposition of the population to a power station has little connexion with the more general themes of the ecologists or even with nuclear problems. In Meysse it was the defence of a traditional way of life that had mobilised the commune. At Saint-Etienne-des-Sorts, it was the defence of the vineyards. 'The outcry would have been the same for a garter factory.' It was not nuclear power which mobilised them: workers from Marcoule who were suspicious of all opposition to nuclear power, as Bourguignon had often reminded us, had taken part in the opposition to the plant at Saint-Etienne-des-Sorts because they owned a few vineyards there.

In the groups, the ecologists were attacked by the local militants just as they were often rejected by the population. Their ever fragile alliance broke up before our eyes at Le Pellerin on the subject of the elections, as it had broken up at Cruas and at Meysse a year earlier. The inability of the militants to overcome this opposition through the analysis figured the failure of the anti-nuclear action itself. Defensive action had never mobilised people beyond a radius of ten kilometres, and, what was more serious, once the work on the reactor had begun, the mobilisation had disappeared completely. This was recognised even at Le Pellerin where the mobilisation at that time was nonetheless the strongest in France.

The opposition between a defensive action and a struggle related to a project was even greater at the level of the means of action. The former included the mobilisation of the population, pressure on the parties through elected representatives, and possibly violence. At Saint-Etienne-des-Sorts, as at Le Pellerin, it was the support of the politicians of the Left which seemed most effective in preventing the building of power stations. The militants who defended this position were aware of being used as a main striking force by the politicians, but that was no problem for them, because their objectives were limited and precise. The motives of the parties were not really important; the main thing was to force them to adopt and maintain an attitude of refusal. This action combined easily, as we have seen, with the possible use of violence. Since the aim was to prevent the building of a power station, all means were good.

The opposition between the defensive action and the ideas of the ecologists was expressed strongly at the meeting of the Amis de la Terre in Lille, a group which had split up after the failure of the mobilisation over Gravelines. 'The bottom line would be to put a reactor in each region and there'd be no more anti-nuclear movement', concluded Georges Flamand who led the group. The conclusion of all these meetings was clear: the action on the sites, the usual base of the struggles, was unable to raise itself to the level where it would meet the aspirations of the ecologists. The distance between the social movement and the defensive action was also shown in the reaction of the evaluation groups to the members of the intervention groups who tried to play a mediating role between the analysis and the action. Neither Jean-Jacques nor Kropo were able to play that role during these meetings. The distance between them and the groups increased, and, faced with the break-up of the groups, they had tended to move closer to the language of the analysis. Their failure symbolised that of the attempt to link the defensive action to a more general struggle.

The attempt to participate in general struggles
The Malville militants, on the other hand, hostile to the large rallies of which they had lost control, defended a struggle whose objective would be to create the need for, and the experience of, a real democracy. And they reacted against the conclusions of that part of the research which concerned them and which they thought too pessimistic. 'The document is entirely against us. You've stressed everything that could be negative or incriminating for us. By contrast, you've never analysed our real experiences through Malville 77. In spite of all the chaos, there was an attempt

to get a real democracy working and set up certain structures, certain kinds of representation, new forms of information. It worked more or less well, but in any case it was an experimental potential that was completely neglected after Malville 77.' These words had the support of all the militants, and the anti-nuclear explosion marked by the great gathering of 31 July 1977 was no longer criticised as ineffective but as the failure of what had been the real aim of the movement, the creation of a direct democracy and a self-management of the struggles.

The Alsace militants gave the same general meaning to their local struggle. The strength of their movement came precisely from its insertion into the local community and its capacity to unite political action and grass-roots defensive actions. However, this theme of the integration of community action and political action could not for long conceal the division between militants who go from local defence towards religious or humanist themes and others looking for the means to confront the forces which impose the nuclear power stations, who want, in other words, to organise a struggle against power. The latter are a long way from a cultural and moral protest which sustains exemplary actions and sees in nuclear power the effect less of a social and political power than of a crisis of civilisation. Despite the apparent unity of the community struggle, two logics can be separated out. The militant who had most vigorously defended the unity of the cultural and political actions recognised himself the impotence of the Alsatian struggle, closer to a moral protest than a social movement. The research was then examined for the means of passing from the regional level, where the Alsation struggle was located, to the national level, where the adversary who imposes nuclear power was to be found, and for the conditions which would allow this struggle to acquire a political capacity. But the Alsatian group was paralysed by its hesitation between the awareness of this distance and its desire to safeguard the strong community roots of its action.

In Nantes, the proximity of an important demonstration against the power station at Le Pellerin but also against unemployment in the region permitted the establishing of stronger links between a cultural refusal and a political and economic critique, links strengthened by the active intervention of PSU militants in local firms. The anti-nuclear militants were conscious of the need not to become imprisoned in the refusal of a technology and to present a general critique of the energy policy, but they also realised that the watchwords of their demonstrations, which appealed above all to the fear of accident, were remote from the demands of a political struggle. Here again the two levels of the anti-nuclear struggle remained separate.

Finally, the meeting in Lille, chaired by Georges Flamand, ended in the same defensive withdrawal. After defining very ambitious objectives for the

151

movement, they announced only very limited concrete propositions: to build a solar house and distribute solar water heaters, objectives which involved bringing pressure to bear on the local authorities but which were very remote from the general themes of social, political and cultural critique which had nonetheless been recalled and approved at the beginning of the meeting. This group, like all the others, recognised that such actions have an exemplary rather than a political value and lack the element of protest. Instead of being placed within a conflict, they are easily brought into line by the authorities and insufficient as a means of mobilisation. This weakness was felt less in Alsace where the struggles were situated mainly at the community and regional level, and more in Nantes and Lille where the distance between a socio-political project and exemplary action was clearly recognised.

The rejection of the analysis
If the meeting in Lille had revealed this impotence, the confrontation between the researchers and ecology militants which took place in Seignosse at the general assembly of the Réseau des Amis de la Terre showed that, confronted with the image of a social movement, the cultural withdrawal could increase its closure to the point of refusing to give its struggle a policy and a strategy. The attempt by Georges and Hannibal during this meeting to instigate an analysis of the movement's prospects on the basis of the results of our intervention encountered a strong resistance which produced reserved reactions and even a few misunderstandings when we presented the research on the fourth day. The creation of a socio-political movement and the research were criticised alike from the basis of a cultural withdrawal and an ecumenicism which were opposed to the elaboration of a political programme in the name of an intransigent attitude to nuclear power. Some militants were afraid that a research which tended to go beyond a cultural refusal and orient the struggle towards a more social and political conflict might be used as an argument by those who wanted to entice the ecologists towards the Socialist Party. Thus the confronting of ecology militants with the research showed that the struggle had little ability to go beyond its refusal, to define its adversary and place itself within a general social conflict. But it also showed that the transition from the anti-nuclear to the nuclear anti-politics was the chief condition for the existence of a social movement. The refusal to define a social adversary prevented any opening towards a political action at Seignosse, whilst in Malville and Nantes it was by agreeing to go beyond the cultural refusal that the militants defined the conditions for an anti-technocratic movement, thereby proving the existence of the social movement in their struggle.

The meeting in Paris with the leaders of the ecology movement showed even more clearly that the attitudes towards the research were a sign of the attitude towards the social movement and thus of the political capacity of the anti-nuclear action. 'I accuse Alain Touraine and his team of having driven a score of unfortunate ecologists up the wall and round the bend by setting them an insoluble problem and putting them in conditions where they could not solve it. Because although it is true that there are two adversaries in the anti-nuclear struggle, the anti-nuclear militants and the nucleocrats, there is no stake that both parties wish to seize control of. The anti-nuclear militants want no nuclear industry, or as little as possible, full stop.' This written declaration was handed over by Pierre Samuel, president of the Réseau des Amis de la Terre, to the research team at the very beginning of the session. Whereas the researchers were trying to find in the anti-nuclear action a social movement, in other words a conflict over a stake, which implies the at least potential presence of a societal counter-project, Pierre Samuel wanted to maintain this anti-nuclear action and the whole of the ecology movement in an attitude of refusal, in the direct and total opposition of two models of society.

For the present, these two meetings, the one at Seignosse and the one in Paris, had gone in the opposite direction to the ideas presented by the researchers, whose intervention aroused profound reservations, but they also confirmed the presence in the most important ecology organisation of both a will to create a movement of struggle against the dominant social and cultural values and the apparently insurmountable obstacles encountered by every attempt to define and organise a conflictual action. Every anti-nuclear action is divided between a general cultural resistance and a will to create a social movement directed against the holders of power, but when it is faced with practical choices, it swings towards the first. It feels more strongly linked to the fear of accident, the refusal of the large installations and the rejection of the theme of growth than it does to the search for a new kind of development or a new form of political intervention. Pierre Samuel's reaction reminded us of the central moment in the third weekend of the Grenoble–Malville group: in a discussion on science, this group, after coming close to the idea that science and technology are a stake disputed by opposed social forces, finally took refuge in the idea that we should oppose one science to another and subject it entirely to criteria of a social and political kind, an attitude which would in fact abolish all possibility of organising a conflictual action around the theme of the production and social utilisation of science.

Creating struggles

However, the evaluation groups did not remain imprisoned in these failures. Many of them, instead of retreating into a generalised cultural refusal or exemplary but limited initiatives, made a practical attempt to create, if not a social movement, then at least more limited collective forms of action, associating the anti-nuclear struggle with the struggle against the State, a democratic demand or trade union action. Would these attempts manage to overcome the opposition between cultural critique and political project by placing themselves halfway between? Would they lead to the definition of a political strategy?

The struggle against the State

The tendency which had shown itself during the intervention to be the furthest away from the social movement was the protest against the State. But the history of the Grenoble–Malville group had also shown the strength of the link between local defence and libertarian themes. During the permanent sociology, the anti-nuclear struggle was seen as a means of opposing the State only in Cruas where the link between local militants and libertarian or leftist groups had asserted itself yet again. Similary, violence as a means of struggle was defended vigorously only by the militants of that region. 'I'm not anti-nuclear. I'm a protester. For me, it's a way of getting back at the State which imposes a power station on me. It's an opportunity to oppose a government which refuses to listen to me, and the pigs who tossed grenades in my face in Malville. I protest in my own way and I'm getting more and more anti-nuclear.' This speech was as far away as it possibly could be from the language of the militants who were protesting against the nuclear policy in the name of a democratic society. It was a defensive, local, community action rather than a political one, quite indifferent to the general themes of the ecologists and blending easily with violence seen as the only effective means of fighting an oppressive State.

Nor did the Alsace militants exclude violence as a means of action. Their action, which was situated above all in the community, called for grass-roots democracy and thus did not reject violence because it was a fight against the State rather than a ruling class. Although more disposed to bringing pressure to bear on institutions, it accepted recourse to violence or to the violation of institutional rules. By contrast, the groups which most clearly recognised themselves in the affirmation of the social movement contained in the anti-nuclear struggle were the most opposed to the anti-Statist logic of violence. 'The anti-nuclear struggle in France has failed because of leftism', declared a militant from Grenoble. The militants from Malville agreed: violence and the struggle against the State had contributed to the demobilisation of the population and destroyed the positive elements of the struggle, namely the challenging of a social power and the search for a new form of democracy.

Thus the more or less libertarian call for a struggle against the State, far from helping to build a political strategy, was no more than the counterpart of a community defence too turned in upon itself to be capable of fighting effectively against the centres of social domination.

The link with the trade union struggle

How could the isolation and the limits of the local action be overcome? If links with left-wing councillors were recognised as a means of escaping from the fringe, the search for a political relay came up against a double obstacle: the rejection of the traditional parties and the political and organisational impotence of the anti-nuclear struggle itself. The Alsatians thought it was not possible to form an alliance with the parties because of their centralised mode of functioning, whilst in Grenoble it was the impotence of the movement itself which was blamed. The general refusal of a political opening towards the Socialist Party could be explained not only by the refusal to make a particular political choice but also by the fear that the movement, having no organisational capacity, would lose its autonomy if it had partners who were too powerful.

By contrast, all the meetings with the ecology or anti-nuclear groups confirmed that the latter felt the need for a rapprochement with the workers and in particular with the CFDT. It is true that in these groups, as in the intervention groups, this feeling was accompanied by the realisation that the workers were more often than not indifferent to the ideas of the ecologists. But the meetings with trade unionists in Paris and La Hague showed that of these two opposed forces, it was the first, the will to rapprochement, that was the strongest. In La Hague, when one of the leaders of the union section recalled the priority of an alliance with the CGT and thus of an orientation of union action towards directly economic themes, Haggar opposed the position violently and was listened to. He emphasised the dangers of a choice in which the CFDT ran the risk of losing its personality.

Cotentin, the most unionised of the CFDT members of the Paris group, also defended the idea of an opening, because it corresponded to the fundamental demands of the CFDT. He criticised his own organisation, recognised that union action 'cuts a bloke in slices' in just the same way as the authorities do, and was opposed to the institutionalisation of a movement which should remain a movement for liberation, fighting oppression and power and not just defending particular interests. He claimed that these aspirations of the workers were carrying the CFDT towards new movements of an anti-technocratic and anti-hierarchical nature rather than towards a defensive struggle. The institutionalisation of labour conflicts was useful and even necessary, but it ran the risk of contradicting the deeper aspirations of the workers, who wanted the working-class movement to regain the full rigour of its protest, its liberating role, in the service not only of certain professional categories but of all those who, in the workplace or elsewhere, were dominated by the holders of power.

Cotentin and Haggar were, in fact, reversing the usual themes of the debate. Instead of stressing what the CFDT could bring to the ecologists, they were reminding the latter that they should be capable of drawing the CFDT forward. But what exactly, in the deteriorating situation, were they proposing that might replace the strength of the workers' union? It was for the ecologists to create the conditions for the rapprochement, to define a project for society, to have a theory and a capacity for organisation which would lead the CFDT to turn more towards the future than the past. But the trade unions recognised that the future of the CFDT depended on the capacity of the new social movement to act: 'Either we'll get nuclear power or nuclear power will get us. If it is developed in this country, and if the CFDT is not only unable to stop it but actually comes to terms with it, that would mean that it has become an institution of the post-industrial era.'

At the confederate level, in the Energy Commission, there was an even greater awareness of the importance of the anti-nuclear struggle, especially since the Commission wanted the CFDT to defend a project for society and not let itself be imprisoned in a strategy of defensive negotiation. But at the time of their meeting with the researchers, these trade unionists doubted the strength of the anti-nuclear struggle and recalled, as had the militants of La Hague, the absolute priority of the problems of employment for the workers. They were as convinced of the need to fight the government's nuclear policy and its implications as they were reserved in their judgement on the organisation of the anti-nuclear struggles. They thought that support from the CFDT would help them to develop but they had little faith in the specific political capacity of the ecologists. The new initiatives the CFDT was to take after the Harrisburg incident did not contradict this judgement: they enabled various organisations to sign a joint agreement but they were not part of a more general protest movement and neither did the accident itself give rise to any such movement.

A final meeting with Haggar and Cotentin in September 1979 confirmed their pessimism. Trade union action had its own domain and could not be the centre of an anti-nuclear struggle. This was why, in Cotentin's opinion, he himself had played only a marginal role in the intervention group and why the trade unionists found the researchers' text so difficult to understand. Haggar's conclusion was that the anti-nuclear action should become the responsibility above all of political forces: 'As long as we don't have a strong political organisation to take charge of it all, the working-class movement won't get involved. The working class needs a welfare worker and that means a political organisation.'

Discovering the movement

Scarcely able as they were to set themselves limited objectives and a limited strategy, could the anti-nuclear groups recognise the presence of a social movement in themselves, as some of the Paris militants had done?

The groups which met to evaluate their own practice on the basis of the results of the intervention followed a process opposite to that of the intervention groups. The latter had been led by the researchers towards their conversion, and the mere fact of their participation in such a lengthy and constraining work indicated their awareness of belonging to a movement of the utmost importance. By contrast, the evaluation groups began with their defensive struggle and then rose towards the search for more open but still limited forms of action. At each level they acknowledged their failure. The defence of the sites was ambiguous; the anarchist action against the State divided or broke the action rather than strengthening it; the call for local and regional democracy was an important theme but less capable than the anti-nuclear struggle of creating a durable movement of central importance; the support of the CFDT, however great, could not prevent the proper domain of trade unionism from being production, whereas the anti-nuclear action was concerned with the living environment. This led some of these groups to look elsewhere for the meaning of their action and the possibility of developing it. On several occasions they discovered a social movement in their action, in other words they defined themselves in opposition to an adversary considered as the new ruling class and in relation to a stake which was the ability of society to choose its future. In so far as these attempts succeeded, in spite of the difficult circumstances in which they took place, they reinforced the conclusion of the intervention: the anti-nuclear struggle does indeed contain a social movement; it may not succeed in giving life to that movement, but if it does not define itself in relation to it, it is doomed to impotence and decay.

The adversary

A social movement is formed first by the definition of an adversary. The trade unionists were the ones who gave this definition its greatest precision. They denounced the 'industrial-military-State lobby' in the name of democracy. 'I'm a democrat,' said a CFDT official, 'and I consider that one function of the union movement is to oppose people who take it on themselves to choose for society and to impose those choices.' Similarly, a scientist explained the special strength of the anti-nuclear action in France by the concentration of State power and its support for the technocracy. In Nantes they referred to the book by Philippe Simonnot, *Les Nucléocrates*, and a trade unionist went so far as to say: 'Nuclear power is the consequence of a certain political and economic system.' In Malville a more elaborate definition of the adversary was given: 'All those structures which claim the right to make decisions in every field of knowledge and which use knowledge as a form of power.' The author of this definition added a moment later: 'I started off as anti-nuclear and even as anti-Malville, and now I'm anti-technocratic as well as anti-nuclear.' It is true that these analyses remained general, but they raised no objection. The anti-nuclear militants as a whole admitted that they were fighting a power which dominates a key sector of production and so imposes a certain way of life on the whole of society and maintains its reign through propaganda and police repression. It was enough to prove that the militants had no difficulty in going beyond a too general condemnation of industrial society and its values.

The stake

The importance of this definition of the adversary was that it directly controlled the recognition of the stake of the struggles. From the moment that its adversary was defined as a power based on knowledge, the anti-nuclear action became an attempt to liberate society's capacity for action on itself from the technocratic domination which seeks to identify itself with that capacity and to reduce it to its own interests. The militants were careful not to reduce their action to an anti-technocratic modernism which would quickly change into a reforming technocracy. The search for a struggle which would no longer be purely negative but would maintain the strength of protest in the anti-nuclear struggle led the Malville group to recognise a modernist attitude, turned towards the future, as the condition for a social movement. This movement would be one of protest because it is opposed to nuclear policy, but it is opposed to its adversary in the name of a counter-project which is both technical and social. The linking of these two elements enables the struggle both to go beyond nostalgia for the past and a neo-modernist project and not to be fixated at the level of pure protest. The movement is too weak to develop a 'realistic' counter-project; it must above all remain capable of refusal and protest, but the latter must be based on the conviction that the policy of the technocracy is opposed to a genuine modernisation and merely sinks us further into the crisis by refusing to abandon the vested interests and the ideologies of the industrial and capitalist society.

The meeting of the scientists brought an even clearer indication of the possibility of a social movement forming around such a stake. It was dominated by the dialogue between two opposed positions and by the efforts of the whole group, and especially of Roland Maire, who played the role of mediator, to overcome this opposition and so found a social movement that would be one of both protest and progress. To what were the participants opposed? To the role of science or to the power associated with the social use of knowledge? The two positions were drawn up against one another from the start of the meeting.

Jean-Philippe Pharisca maintained his own position, expressed several times during the intervention, and supported by several people: it was science itself which was in crisis. It was no longer playing its proper part, no

158

longer making great discoveries. Scientific work had become a game; its aim was no longer obvious. This feeling of crisis was nourished by the malaise of the researchers who no longer controlled their work, who felt dominated by the great scientific apparatuses and cut off from the outside world. The main concern for those who shared this opinion was not the problem of the organisation and the means of research, but of the very aim of science, of its social usefulness, which was doubtful and even disappearing.

This professional pessimism was strongly rejected by others who maintained their faith in science, in its capacity for innovation, in the watchword: know the world and dominate it. The problem for them was not one of science but of the association of science with power: nowadays knowledge has become the arena for the central conflict because it is the new centre of power. Decisions are taken in the name of knowledge, information and technology. Consequently, the scientists should assume their responsibility and challenge the adversary who was seeking to dominate the realm of knowledge: the technocracy.

Roland was the first to recognise the existence in the group of the problem which controls the formation of the movement: 'The two attitudes separating the scientists correspond to the separation between the trade union and the ecology attitudes in the movement.' The components of the group, like those of the struggle, could be integrated only if they recognised that the stake of this movement was to modify the relations between science and society. The group's capacity to do this, he said, would inform us of the capacity of the struggle itself to assume the stake of the social movement. The group responded to this invitation to seek a link between the two poles. They were aware that this integration was their own responsibility and that their success must demonstrate the possibility of creating a movement. 'If our sole purpose was to propose reform, we would tend towards a counter-plan; if we were no more than a force for criticism, we would tend towards nihilism. So the important thing is that there should be two tendencies and that each should feel the need for the other.' But at the same time the scientists recognised that it was not their task to integrate the movement, but rather to remind ecologists and trade unionists of what they had in common, to designate the social use of knowledge as the common stake of their complementary struggles. Rarely had a social actor analysed in such depth and with such precision its own specific role, both limited and fundamental, in the formation of an anti-technocratic social movement.

The Grenoble gamble

Still lacking in this discovery of a social movement was the militants' awareness of being themselves the chief actor in a historical drama. It was in Grenoble, in a group of militants different from the intervention group but meeting at the initiative of Jean-Jacques Rodrigo, that this awareness emerged. These militants had all taken part in the anti-nuclear struggle and then withdrawn from it. At the time of their meeting they were conscious of the practical inability of the struggle to link the achievements of the anti-nuclear action to a social counter-project. Confronted with the separation of the cultural critique and the political project, with the break-up of the anti-nuclear struggle into a current of opinion and a specifically political intervention, they reacted in an unexpected way. Instead of analysing these two components separately, they declared the existence of a social movement and the need to define a new actor. They asserted their determination to be that actor and stressed the need for a new theory of social relations which would play the same role as Marxism had. These militants recognised in their own action the movement that would take over from the working-class movement. This potential social movement would not be based on the force of a social or professional category but on a collective will, a collective need for self-management. The main conflict in our society would be between this self-managing project and its technocratic adversary.

This quasi-conversion of the Grenoble militants was helped by the part played in the group by the members of the intervention groups. It was Jean-Jacques and Christophe who first tried to associate conflicts, projects and actors. Jean-Jacques recalled the need to keep the struggle in the anti-nuclear field, because that was the heart of the conflict, and Christophe recalled the need for a societal project. And seeing the group's difficulty in defining the nature of the actor, Yves Le Gall declared: 'I'm not sure that the future, if any, of the social movement depends on its theoretical axis. It's a gamble on what we're capable of doing. But there's less to lose in gambling on a possible social movement than a gamble on the opposite. The backbone of the social movement is a theory. I think that if a movement is to emerge and have a part to play in the years to come, it must be built around a theory.' This group was acutely aware of the need to reconstruct social action and thought around the experience of the anti-nuclear struggle and its meaning for those who had taken part in it.

THE FUTURE OF THE MOVEMENT

The programming groups

During these meetings with various groups, the permanent sociology had already entered its final phase, the one which no longer confronts the analysis with real practices, present and past, but with the future projects of the struggle. But it was above all during fresh meetings with the intervention groups themselves that the programming groups were set up. In the present case, we brought a section of both intervention groups

160

together in Grenoble and much later held a meeting with each of the two groups. This phase marked the summit of the permanent sociology, just as the conversion had marked that of the intervention. It is to underline this parallelism that we speak here of *reconversion*. It was no longer a matter of rising from the struggle to the social movement but of incarnating the latter in a project for struggle, in a programme which would develop a strategy, a tactic and forms of organisation. The permanent sociology should not even stop there. The groups of militants, having thus devised a programme for struggle from their specific viewpoint of militant action, would receive information from the events they were to take part in and relay it to the researchers as a confirmation or invalidation of their analyses. This indicates what a permanent sociology extended over a protracted period of time can be, a movement back and forth between analysis and action.

The success of the method depends above all on preserving the separation and the complementarity of the procedures of action and analysis. It fails if the actor becomes researcher or the researcher becomes ideologist. Even more than during the intervention, the actor must be a militant and an ideologist as well as an analyst, and the main role of the researcher is to prevent the actors from reproducing their usual debates in these meetings, to help them to adopt an analytical attitude: a difficult task, especially at the moment of the reconversion, and especially if the latter should fail, if the idea of the movement cannot be transformed into a programme of action. In that case, the researcher is tempted to take the place of the group, to propose objectives and methods of action. That is acceptable if he does it simply to explore the possibilities of the struggle, but dangerous if he turns himself, no matter how unwillingly, into the leader of the group.

The absence of prospects

The sociological intervention had abstracted the militants from their action in order to analyse it in the light of its highest meaning. They must now come back to the action, but in order to define the likely prospects of a struggle which would assume responsibility for the social movement. This *reconversion* forces the militants beyond their real practice by asking them to create the objectives and the means which might raise the action to the level of the social movement. The groups' ability to transform themselves through the reconversion into *programming groups* figures the ability of the social movement to come into being in an organised political action. The distance between those who achieve the reconversion and those who fail represents the distance between the historical practice and the potential movement.

Questioned on the prospects for their action, the militants admitted that the anti-nuclear struggle was exhausted. The great wave of 1975–7 had

161

receded. Its strength had come from the convergence of the defence of the populations directly affected and the general themes of the ecology critique. Now, the separation of these components had appeared with as much force in the anti-nuclear struggle as it had in the research. The local actions were exhausted; in any case, it was declared in Cruas and Malville, the mobilisation collapsed as soon as building began. In Le Pellerin, where the mobilisation was strongest at the time of the research, there were no illusions: it was limited and precarious. The populations directly affected demobilised in the absence of prospects. In Malville, the only objective advanced was the moratorium, but the militants agreed that it was no longer topical, since the Left had not come to power, and even divided the population instead of mobilising it. The anti-nuclear movement needed victories, we were told in Grenoble, but it was incapable of defining an objective around which groups and a mobilisation could be recreated.

The exhaustion of the specifically anti-nuclear action sometimes sent the militants in search of other battlegrounds. Some, like Sophia or Jacqueline in the Paris group, saw computerisation or genetic manipulation as possible new fields of action, but nobody went beyond the expression of a vague desire to intervene in these new areas. 'We could see the movement disappearing,' concluded Georges Flamand, 'we'd suddenly come to a great hole. We could see where we had to intervene: the crisis, the ecologists, the CFDT; but we couldn't see the threads linking them together. If it's a matter of defining objectives, then we have no prospects of creating a great movement.'

Attempts at reconversion

A first strategy lay in extending the alliance with the CFDT, the importance of which was constantly recalled. The anti-nuclear action needed to be set in a more general economic perspective by showing first of all that investment in nuclear power creates very few jobs, and then that the technocratic power which decides on that investment is incapable of dealing with the crisis, because it is defending vested interests and an established power instead of looking for a new model of development which would imply the reduction of inequalities, the development of collective consumption and the fight against waste linked to the power of the monopolies.

The importance of this attempt lay in the fact that it preserved the central importance of the anti-nuclear struggle instead of diluting it in an ecological current of opinion that was unable to define its adversary and the grounds on which the decisive battles must be fought. So much was said by a CFDT leader himself: 'The anti-nuclear problem seems to me to be very important for employment and development . . . because it involves a whole policy of distribution, of the structuring of production, and of market domination. An attack on this non-traditional sector, if it were successful, could have consequences way beyond a slowing down of the nuclear programme, because it would be a victory against a completely coherent system of power.' But how could this insertion of the anti-nuclear struggle into an overall critique of economic policy be organised? The ecologists did not have the capacity to act at such a general level, which was more appropriate to the unions and the parties. 'We don't have the means to link the conflict with a counter-project for development', admitted the Alsatian militants. Whilst realising that they should respond to these problems, the political ecologists did not feel capable of taking on the task of creating a movement which would simultaneously oppose the government's nuclear policy and its economic policy.

Consequently, another strategy was proposed: the creation of a broad opposition front. After all, unemployed workers and populations threatened by a power station are both opposed to an economic and an energy policy and thus to a type of development which leads to the all-out growth of the nuclear industry and the abandoning of whole sectors of other industries. 'There are times when you have to be content with just saying no', said the Malville group. But the militants in general did not support what would amount to an anti-Statist strategy which, according to the Alsatians, could only appeal to a minority. Yet again, the militants were forced to admit the limits of their struggle.

The failure of these two global strategies sent them back to the idea of a programme of democratic demands. Unable to define the prospects for their struggle, the militants pointed to the achievements of the anti-nuclear action: the awareness of the people, the birth of new needs, for autonomy and control, against a power which imposes nuclear power stations and polluting industries. Their ability to act against the power stations was minimal, but the occupation of the site at Markolsheim, the struggle against Super-Phoenix and the reaction against the station planned for the Rhône valley had led to the creation of a network of solidarities against the authorities. This active rank and file was unable to wage a global war, but through local politicians it was trying to control the conditions of its own existence and its own future, and it would produce other struggles. Hence the importance attached by all these groups, as by the intervention groups, to the democratic organisation of the struggle itself.

Many of them thought that the chief originality of this action, which might be called political, was that it kept as far away as possible from the programmes and the counter-projects of the parties, and did not propose a new way of managing the economy, but, day after day, crisis after crisis, transformed the elementary, fundamental conditions of democratic life. In a country where the technocratic apparatuses are closely linked to the centralising State, the anti-nuclear movement was fighting both its own specific adversary and that omnipotent State, like a band of Lilliputians trying to overturn and immobilise Gulliver. The concentration of economic and political power should not lead them to adopt the same kind of organisation, but rather to scatter, like guerrillas fighting the formidable power of the invader through their mobility and their capacity to act from within the population like a fish in water.

The dead-end

But where was the spark to kindle this democratic movement? It was clear from their dejection that the militants were acutely aware of being the bearers of the new social movement and yet unable to bring it into the world. This was shown yet again in their attitude to the research. At the meeting between the most active members of both intervention groups, the militants began by refusing the researchers the right to come to a negative conclusion on the capacity of the social movement to materialise. But they had no justification to offer; they could only talk of deficiencies in the method or the historical circumstances. The pessimism of Hannibal, the departure of Yves Le Gall, whose proposal to become a pressure group on a part of the Socialist Party was once again rejected, or the refusal of Jean-Jacques to draw any conclusions at all showed that they were all aware of the dead-end they had come to.

What remained intact was the militant strength of the movement. For all that this meeting had produced no concrete results, it had clearly brought out the image of an autonomous and oppositional social movement with a great capacity for mobilisation. It was aware of its future. It sometimes even thought that it should first create the conditions for its existence by stripping off the straitjacket of earlier forms of social thought and action in order to reveal the image of the new conflict and be recognised as the only actor able to propose a way out of the dead-end of industrial society. The call for new ideas and a new theory of social relations showed the militants' awareness that that society would be renewed only through them.

But they also realised that the time had not yet come when their movement could become a political force, and most of them simultaneously welcomed the separation and deplored its consequences. They represented an incipient new social movement whilst the political scene was still occupied by parties or even trade union organisations which represented former social movements largely domesticated by decades of increasing institutionalisation of the conflicts that had given birth to them.

The greatness and the weakness of the anti-nuclear movement was that it was in a state of disequilibrium between a cultural refusal that it had already gone beyond and a political influence that it did not yet have. There could be no doubt that it was set in the space of social movements, but the latter can become reality only by linking the cultural protest to political pressure, whereas the anti-nuclear struggle was suspended between the two.

Should we say that the reconversion had failed? Yes, in so far as the struggle was unable to transform itself into a social movement. Those who still appealed to the mobilising force of the rejection of industrial values knew as well as the others the weakness of the struggle and its inability to undertake new actions. The wave of the great anti-nuclear demonstrations on reactor sites was spent. The convergence of a mass cultural protest and the intervention of ideological groups no longer existed and the hope of a coming victory of the Left had disappeared. But perhaps it was only one of the primitive forms of the anti-technocratic movement that was disintegrating. Perhaps the struggle, so visibly weakened by its lack of organisation and direction, could begin again in new forms if the weaknesses were eradicated through specifically political initiatives.

Unexpectedly, the accident at the American nuclear power station at Three Mile Island in the spring of 1979 was to offer the anti-nuclear struggle the chance of a new beginning. But whatever its future may be, our research leads us to consider as highly unlikely the renaissance of the simultaneously ideological and mass movement of the years 1974–7.

AFTER HARRISBURG

New directions

On 28 March 1979, the second reactor in the power station at Three Mile Island near Harrisburg in Pennsylvania suffered a serious accident in the cooling system. A combination of technical failure and human errors led to fears of a melt-down of the reactor core, which would have been followed by an explosion of the casing where a large hydrogen bubble had formed, and caused a large quantity of radioactive waste to be released into the atmosphere and the water. This accident, the most serious in the history of the civilian nuclear power industry in the United States, provoked extremely strong reactions in American public opinion and especially in the media, which used the occasion to publicise the dangers involved in the use of nuclear energy. In Europe, the event was the signal for large demonstrations. The most important took place in Germany, in Hanover, Hamburg and Frankfurt, where they protested against the federal government's plans to build an underground store for radioactive waste near Gorleben in Lower Saxony. Similar demonstrations actually caused the Swedish government to halt the production of reactors. In Belgium, the burgomaster of Huy decided to close down the Franco-Belgian power station in Tihange, a decision that was later overturned by the government. In Dunkirk, Monsieur Denvers, president of the Urban Committee, opposed the enlarging of the power station at Gravelines, and soon after, the Regional Council of the Nord-Pas-de-Calais under his presidency decided to set up a regional board of inquiry composed of ten elected representatives. In Narbonne, the municipality and the population rose up against the plans to build a power station at Port-la-Nouvelle.

Did this mean that the fear of an accident had given new life to the anti-nuclear action, especially on the sites of projected power stations? In France at least, that was not the case. A campaign launched by the Amis de la Terre in Paris, demanding a referendum on the construction of a power station at Nogent, aroused no echo. At Gravelines, after the first reactions to the Harrisburg accident, no further campaigns were organised, whilst in Malville the anti-nuclear militants felt increasingly frozen out by the population. Although a large demonstration against the power station at Le Pellerin had produced violent clashes with the police in Nantes on 10 March, no further initiatives were taken there between April and July. The nationally coordinated demonstrations at Whitsuntide had no success. Finally, an IFOP opinion poll published in *Le Sauvage* on 3 May 1979 showed only 27% of those polled hostile to the French nuclear programme, which was not much different from the findings of the opinion poll published in *Le Figaro* in December 1978. The shock of the event had not even visibly modified people's attitudes. A fact which *a fortiori* confirmed one of the conclusions of this research: the fear of nuclear power does not lead to anti-nuclear action. It was even possible that the very intensity of the media campaign had helped to fixate reactions at the level of emotion and fear and so prevented the formation of a collective action which can exist only if it is inspired by specifically political aims and organisations.

That fact was grasped immediately by the militants from the Amis de la Terre who had taken part in our intervention groups. At precisely the time when the media were spreading fear, they decided to revive the anti-nuclear action on the basis of more directly political themes and without making any appeal to the reactions of fear. The same approach was adopted by the CFDT, with which the ecologists were in constant contact. At the Annual General Meeting of the Réseau des Amis de la Terre in Grenoble (28 April–1 May 1979), they presented a text which constituted an open break with the usual cultural critique of industrial civilisation: 'Our function is to open the way to anti-technocratic conflicts, since the control of information and the technocracy is now the means to domination. Our function is to be the new Left, one that will reflect the conflicts of the future.' At the same time, they refused to transform the ecology movement into a party, so disarming those of their opponents waiting to accuse them of joining in the parliamentary game and sacrificing the movement's capacity for protest. This text admitted the failure of the militant action on the sites and the confusion created by the attempts to take part in elections. It concluded by demanding priority for a specifically social action, but one conducted in common with the CFDT and possibly with the Socialist Party.

The general assembly, which a few months earlier had given a poor reception to these same ideas, now gave them a favourable hearing, but the text which it adopted, and which contained a call for a national petition for the suppression of the electro-nuclear programme, the organisation of popular consultations, the drawing up of regional development plans and new measures for information and safety, remained totally anti-nuclear. The militants who had presented the text just quoted were assigned responsibility for negotiating with the CFDT, with the authorisation to make, if need be, one major concession: an undertaking not to challenge the first EDF programme for nuclear investment, in other words some thirty completed or partially completed sections, but with the order not to agree to the more limited objectives that might be proposed by the Socialist Party.

These negotiations were made easier by a most decisive commitment from the CFDT to the anti-nuclear struggle. At its Congress of Brest (11–13 May), it put the fight against the nuclear programme foremost amongst its preoccupations, together with the demand for the thirty-five-hour week and the defence of the abortion law. At the confederal level, Michel Rolant and Hubert Prevost conducted a campaign that was all the more vigorous because they wanted to use the initiative to counteract what many saw as the overly defensive image projected by the watchword of *recentrage* adopted by the Confederation. [The term *recentrage* conveys the idea of realignment, the attempt to find a new centre or focus, after a shift in the political situation. It may have defensive connotations. (Tr.)]

The Socialist Party, for so long reserved and preferring to act through parliament, finally rallied to the proposals of the Réseau des Amis de la Terre and the CFDT, with the result that these three organisations, together with the GSIEN, the CSCV (Trade Union Confederation for the Living Environment), the CIME (Interregional Committee of Ecology Movements), the Radical Left Movement, the PSU, the CSF (Trade Union Confederation for the Family) and the UFC-*Que Choisir?* (Which?-Federal Union of Consumers), signed a text in the form of a petition which represented a significant achievement for the anti-nuclear movement:

167

From analysis to action

For a different energy policy

For a democratic debate on energy

I oppose the choice of the 'all-nuclear' programme made by the government.

I demand the raising of the secrecy which surrounds all the decisions on energy, the setting up of decentralised and independent channels of information, and the strengthening of safety measures for the workers and the population.

I maintain that to meet the crisis we need a new kind of development based on the needs of the workers and the people and on regional realities. We must impose a policy for the conservation of non-renewable resources, the use of all the unexploited resources in France, and a policy based on the large-scale development of the new energies. This alternative policy will ultimately lead to the creation of hundreds of thousands of new jobs.

I demand the setting up of an extensive and free public debate on the energy policy of our country, and that implies:

Democratic consultation and decision for the major energy choices at the national and regional level.

The suspension of the present electro-nuclear programme until the completion of the public debate.

Paris, 25 June 1979.

This text was followed by an explanatory document which, in particular, made it clear that the call to suspend the power station programme did not concern the first EDF programme, and whereas the signatories demanded 'the abandonment of the plans to launch any industrial series of the fast-breeder', for Super-Phoenix they spoke only of suspension. Add to this the fact that the petition began with a declaration of hostility to the 'all-nuclear' programme but not to nuclear power, and it is clear that it belonged to a completely different perspective from the totally anti-nuclear texts of previous years. This greater moderation, which was a condition for an agreement with the CFDT, was above all linked to the priority attached to political objectives: 'For a different energy policy and for a democratic debate on energy.' To change the methods of production and consumption and especially of decision-taking, and to give a new form and a new content to democracy, such were the main objectives of a campaign whose aim was not only to collect several million signatures but also and above all to prepare new initiatives and give new life to the struggles. These objectives were political since they defined a general conception of social life, and the petition which defended them constituted the beginnings of a quasi-political current rather than a reinforcement of the anti-nuclear pressure, which all the opinion polls showed to be already situated at a much higher level. It would be surprising, moreover, if an anti-'all-nuclear' position, accepting the phases already in progress and consequently anticipating no action against the plants nearing completion at Gravelines or Tricastin, were to have more mobilising force than the more radical anti-nuclear campaigns of recent years.

So a hypothesis took shape: the anti-nuclear struggle had initially combined an incipient social movement and a cultural crisis. It had at that time been identified above all with demonstrations, often accompanied by site occupations, whose strength derived both from the moral conviction of the participants and from the action of groups closer to the far left than to the parliamentary left. This conviction, like the ideological language, prevented the struggle from being recognised as the bearer of a new social, anti-technocratic movement. Even the militants more readily defined themselves in terms of the fight against industry, the State or capitalism. After the failure of Malville, it was in our intervention groups that the idea of a new social movement began to emerge most clearly, but the initiatives of some of the members of those groups were not based on a collective movement: they rather broke with former practices and sought to revive the action through a change of strategy, replacing pure militancy and electoralism by a campaign of social and political action waged in agreement with the CFDT and with the support of the Socialist Party, the PSU and the Radicals of the Left. The compromise between the social movement and the cultural refusal had given way to another compromise – between the social movement and political intervention. The change did not correspond entirely to the objectives of those who had successfully completed their conversion during the intervention – Emmanuel Kropo, Roland Maire, Georges Flamand, Hannibal, Christophe, Yves Le Gall and Jean-Jacques Rodrigo – but it was perhaps the best result their action could achieve in a situation in which the anti-nuclear struggle, disoriented and divided, was losing its momentum.

It was not yet possible to pass a historical judgement on the real meaning of the agreement of 25 June, but the analysis of it was a direct justification of the recourse to the method of permanent sociology. The sociological intervention had produced a practical effect: it had helped certain militants to take more significant initiatives, to reorient the anti-nuclear struggle. It was now for the analyst to study those initiatives and their foreseeable consequences and discuss the conclusions with the actors themselves. Consequently, several months after the main phase of the permanent sociology, we met the Grenoble–Malville and the Paris groups again.

Final meetings

The groups and three of the researchers met in Grenoble on 9 July 1979 without Bourguignon, who was unable to attend, Valence and Leforestier, who had already left a group which increasingly rejected their points of view, and Véronique Uri, who seemed recently to have given up most of her militant activities, a development which could have been predicted from her growing isolation in the group and the diminishing influence of her themes, which could not be concealed by the force of her personality. There were present, then, on the one side Christophe, Jean-Jacques and Yves, who had played the main role in Grenoble in reorienting the anti-nuclear struggle after Harrisburg, in close relation to Hannibal, Emmanuel and Georges Flamand, and on the other side the local militants: Claudine, Marie-Jeanne, Esther and François.

At the beginning of the meeting, Claudine again repeated her attacks on our research report, even though the second version had taken account of her earlier criticisms. But instead of this intervention opening a fresh debate between 'culturals' and 'politicals', it unexpectedly brought the whole group together in the condemnation of a purely ideological political practice. The struggle should respond to the concrete aspirations of the young, said Marie-Jeanne; it should also offer practical solutions, said François. Esther stressed the need to break with the traditional parties. They were more limited outlooks than those of Emmanuel, Hannibal and Georges, but they explained the unexpected success of their ideas in the Réseau des Amis de la Terre. Although the new direction they were proposing caused some anxiety, it was accepted without too much difficulty because it broke with the doctrinaire spirit and tried to escape the confusion and division.

Thus the political development of the anti-nuclear struggle was mapped out. Associated initially with ideological groups, it had tried after Malville to free itself from those affiliations and seek allies rather than inspirers. Those allies were in their turn looked upon with suspicion by the militants even though the latter no longer believed in their own capacity to initiate local struggles and were trying now to see their movement as an expression of new political demands. Esther put it best: how could they recreate a political action on the basis of a lived experience? It was no longer a question of setting a cultural refusal against a political project. The problem now was to ensure that the refusal did not collapse into some vague, negative ideology but rather became a pragmatic reconstruction of political action based on practical initiatives and struggles.

How were we to interpret this opening from those who, during the intervention itself, had been most on the defensive and had even sided with Valence and Leforestier against Jean-Jacques? One explanation was that the transition from the cultural refusal to the social movement was no longer the main problem of the struggle and that the militants had no difficulty in passing from local defence to political pressure without rising towards the more demanding idea of a social movement. But there was more to it than that. Hardly anybody in the group was still confident that they could create a social movement and transform the anti-nuclear struggle into a direct action against technocratic power and the government's energy policy. Jean-Jacques Rodrigo hesitated to admit that the agreement of 25 June gave the anti-nuclear action a specifically political role. Christophe, whilst stressing that role and consequently the role of the CFDT whose militant and political capacity ought to help the Amis de la Terre to escape from its confusion, recalled the need to give priority to the forming of an anti-technocratic movement. Yves Le Gall, disappointed with the evolution of the Socialist Party since its Congress of Metz in April 1979, was more directly convinced of the need to create new political demands, new forms of grass-roots democracy. But at the same time they all emphasised the possibility of this democratic campaign resuscitating the specifically anti-nuclear action. The overriding impression, however, was that this group, which had not achieved its conversion during its first weekend and which, during the second, had caused the Paris group to lapse back into an attitude of defence and withdrawal, was swinging away so easily from a behaviour of cultural crisis towards a political intervention of a new type because it was acutely aware of the failure to form a social movement.

The following day in Paris the members of the other intervention group began by telling the researchers that it was the work undertaken together which had led them to take initiatives and commit the anti-nuclear struggle to a new direction. Militants and researchers were aware of the complementary nature of their approaches. Neither thought that the researchers had acted as advisers or ideologists. Both affirmed that the sociological intervention, through the knowledge it had brought, had given the militants, who had never ceased to act according to the aims of their struggle, a much clearer perception of the conditions that would allow that struggle to exist and develop. For the researchers, this recognition both of their independence and of their usefulness corresponded so completely to their intentions that they found in it the justification of their work.

The researchers, all four of whom were present, reproduced the same kind of intervention as in Grenoble. Michel Wieviorka defined the place of cultural protest in the struggle; François Dubet and Zsuzsa Hegedus spoke for the priority of the social objectives of the struggle and the need to preserve the central role of the directly anti-nuclear action; Alain Touraine drew an increasingly pronounced, and sometimes even exaggerated, picture of the transformation of a potential social movement into a real political force destined to intervene practically and directly in the mechanisms of political decision. The debate was tense. The members of the group were obviously aware of the nature of their initiative and of its implications. The discussion bore directly on the question of whether this reorientation was instrumental in the formation of an anti-technocratic social movement, or whether, whilst keeping its roots in that movement, it was moving away from it to respond to another logic of action, more specifically political.

Roland Maire, in harmony with the opinions he had already expressed in the intervention group, was closest to the position represented by Alain Touraine. Georges Flamand resisted that interpretation, as he had opposed François Dubet's definition of a social movement in opposition to cultural protest. The political direction he wanted the struggle to take was above all for him a means of restoring life to the cultural protest and the social movement. In his eyes, the main concern was still to create an anti-technocratic social movement, which was also Roland Maire's position. But after resisting Alain Touraine's analysis of the agreement of 25 June, they did not, in the end, reject it. Emmanuel Kropo recognised that the great novelty of the agreement was that it gave priority to objectives of democratisation, moving closer in this to Roland Maire. Hannibal, already torn during the group's conversion between the cultural protest and the social counter-project, refused more than ever to choose between the creation of a social movement and a political intervention. Ill at ease, he increasingly took refuge in silence as the evening advanced.

These resistances and this uneasiness gave the meaning of the meeting. The militants, who had all played an important part in the anti-nuclear struggle, were clearly not prepared to submit to the influence of any particular member of the research team. Even as Alain Touraine was pushing his hypothesis on the transformation of a social movement into political action to its furthest point, and in the most pressing manner, they refused either to accept or to reject it. Like their interlocutor, they accepted the idea that the creation of a social movement had failed and that it must be taken up again in an indirect way, in the political mode rather than as a direct form of the class struggle, but since they were all opposed to the idea of forming a political party, they wanted with all their heart both to cherish the hope that the anti-nuclear movement could be revived and to prepare to intervene in the political arena in some way or other, as Brice Lalonde had wished, to whose positions they were moving closer. This malaise, this refusal to choose, defined better than any doctrinal declaration the nature of the anti-nuclear struggle after Harrisburg and its reorientation by the agreement of 25 June.

The anti-nuclear struggle was circling around the social movement from which it derived its importance rather than being set within it. In that it was similar to the working-class movement in its beginnings, which was often related to manifestations of the crisis provoked by the brutal industrialisation and urbanisation and often involved in political campaigns, before finding its autonomous expression. The most active of the anti-nuclear militants expected that the highly active and open political operator which is the CFDT would help them to overcome their weakness and their dispersion and establish themselves as actors in the social struggles. Were we witnessing the degradation of a social movement into a political force or, on the contrary, the creation of a social movement through the support of political and trade union forces? It would be contrary to the spirit of this research to answer by indicating in what direction we thought the course of events would carry the anti-nuclear action. It is more appropriate to its method to say that this choice is the one that should be uppermost in the minds of the militants. The more consciously it is made, the greater will be the chances of strengthening the anti-technocratic social movement born of the cultural protest and trying today to organise and orient itself by intervening in the political arena.

vvv

The meaning of a struggle

THE PRESENCE OF THE SOCIAL MOVEMENT

In history

At the origin of the anti-nuclear struggle are to be found on the one hand the fear of the harmful effects of radiation in the factories and on the environment, either during the normal course of production, or as a result of an accident or sabotage, and on the other hand an appeal to the natural life associated with an increasingly strong rejection of an industrial civilisation which depletes natural resources, pollutes, overcrowds and fatigues human beings and sinks into contradiction and absurdity. This cultural critique may be directly associated with the fear of accident or contamination, as happened in the first public opinion campaigns, but it can also be independent of it and challenge a set of values and forms of social organisation. In that case, the link between the cultural critique of the ecologists and the defence against the nuclear power stations can be forged only through the creation of a critical analysis of the nuclear policy. Thus was born very early on the *political ecology*.

It was this tendency which prevented the anti-nuclear struggle from becoming a prisoner of its specificity and allowed it to conceive itself in general terms. It is not a pressure group, since those who take part in it challenge values and powers rather than defending purely private interests. It is not only directed against the Napoleonic State, since it has developed in liberal or social-democrat countries as much as in France. As our research draws to a temporary close, the strength of conviction of the anti-nuclear militants is even more visible than at the beginning. In 1976 and 1977, the struggle was going from success to success and its actors were carried along by those victories. In 1978 it was receding everywhere, divided, disoriented, sometimes disheartened. And yet its militants are borne along as strongly as ever by the conviction of having fought and of fighting still for a fundamental cause, for the survival of the planet, for the defence of liberties, for the search for happiness.

The meaning of a struggle

As the opposition to the nuclear programme grew and the movement of opinion began to transform itself into a political campaign, the least social themes, such as fear, were increasingly incorporated into a critique of a mode of decision-taking, of power and of a type of social organisation. The influence of the CFDT was decisive here since it never declared itself anti-nuclear but hostile to the nuclear policy. One of the strongest proofs of the transformation of the struggle and its increasing remoteness from the fear of nuclear power is the decreasing importance of the military theme in its action. Although there is still a strong connexion in the attitudes of individuals between the memory of Hiroshima and the fear of the nuclear power stations, the organised action has remained in the civilian domain, especially when it was conducted on the site of future reactors and mobilised a large number of participants. It is only with some scientists, in other words personalities intervening as individuals and at the level of public opinion, that the fear of the proliferation of nuclear weapons has again assumed central importance. The collective action is directed towards political and social objectives. Even the theme of the 'plutonium society' is no longer accepted so readily by the organised militants, even though books such as the one by Robert Jungk are enormously successful with the general public in their denunciation of the risks created by the nuclear industry for freedom and democracy.

The anti-nuclear action has gradually moved away from the idea that society is modelled by technologies and has discovered that it is, on the contrary, the choice of an energy policy which is determined by the mode of decision-taking in society. It is not plutonium which creates the tech-nocracy, but the technocratic power which imposes the 'all-nuclear' policy. As for the police regimes, it would – unfortunately – be too optimistic to believe that they are the product of the most modern technologies. This fundamental reversal of ideas still encounters a great deal of resistance, but it is sufficiently well established for the anti-nuclear campaigns conducted by the press and the specialised associations to make little appeal to fear nowadays and to be above all political in nature, in other words challenging decisions and power.

Even more clearly, the anti-nuclear action cannot be isolated from a whole range of protest campaigns, such as the consumer movements, which challenge technocratic power and the moulding of social demand by the apparatuses of production and management: the call for a conception of health which is not controlled solely by medical or hospital apparatuses; the defence of the freedom of information against the broadcasting monopoly of State radio and television; the struggle for regional autonomy and local democracy against the authoritarian and centralising administrative apparatus; the women's revolt against the masculine dominations of power, war and money. In all of these areas, struggles are being waged

175

which extend beyond their specific object and so have a general meaning of both cultural mutation and a redefinition of social conflicts.

In the intervention

This evolution of the struggle was re-enacted during the intervention itself. The members of the groups advanced in the analysis of their action, partly on the initiative of the researchers, by starting from the hypothesis of the social movement. Whereas at the beginning, faced above all with EDF or CEA directors, they had reacted in a weak and confused way, from the first weekend in the case of the Paris group and during the third for the Grenoble–Malville group, they successfully completed a conversion which led them to examine their struggle from the point of view of the social movement. From that moment, and right to the end of the phase of permanent sociology, they questioned themselves constantly and with increasing urgency on the way of giving life to the social movement and raising the level of their struggle. This conversion did not take in the whole of the group; on the contrary, it widened the distances between its members to the point of causing real divisions. This fact, however, gave added force to the central hypothesis that a social movement was present in the anti-nuclear struggle, since it was that hypothesis which provided the clearest definition of the behaviours and attitudes of each participant, beyond any superficial similarities. It was the work of conversion accomplished by the researchers and the groups which gave the best understanding of the real conflicts which have moved through the anti-nuclear struggle. It can be said that the intervention groups' capacity for conversion demonstrated, better than any historical event, the presence of a social movement in that struggle.

The discovery of the social movement was progressive, difficult and limited, indicating both its presence in the struggle and the difficulty of inducing the latter to start from the demands of the former.

It was the definition of the adversary that was worked out most clearly. The members of the group tended at the beginning to denounce either the authoritarian State or the capitalism of the large monopolistic firms, with the trade unionists tending naturally to the second, and the ecologists to the first. But they both succeeded in going beyond their ideology and naming their adversary in a new way, as the technocratic power created by capitalism but now capable of surviving it.

It was much more difficult for them to recognise the stake of the struggle, that is to go from the declaration of its own specific objectives to the discovery of the stake common to both antagonists and which both were trying to control in order to give it opposite social directions. The working-class movement had believed as much as the capitalist movement in

176

progress through industry, but its social interpretation of that cultural orientation was the opposite of the interpretation placed on it by the capitalist domination. Were the anti-nuclear militants capable of recognising the cultural orientations which they shared with the pro-nuclear technocrats but which they interpreted in a socially opposite way? This recognition was possible, and even seemed too easy to those who distrusted the new social movements and refused to see them as anything other than a modernising reformism favouring the interests of a new ruling class. But that judgement was profoundly false because the commonality of cultural orientations between protesters and dominators, far from proving the treason of the former, actually provides a foundation for their conflict with the technocrats.

This recognition of the stake of the struggle was difficult to bring about in the intervention groups, which were inclined to set balance against growth or traditional medicines against hospital medicines. It was achieved only when the groups, aware of the crisis of the specifically anti-nuclear protest after Malville, discovered that the critique of the government's economic policy and the search for another way of solving the economic crisis were much more useful themes for directing the anti-nuclear action. The result was to make the ecology critique as much if not more modernising than the policy of the ruling class and the State, but in the opposite direction. The adversaries recognise that what is involved is the transition to a type of society in which information and communication will play the central role, but whereas the pro-nuclear technocrats interpret this idea as the need to reinforce the high technology industries, the ecologists emphasise the need to create a society which is able to fight against its own disintegration and the destruction of its natural environment, and which is therefore in a position to function as a network of communications. This means doing away with the centralisation, authoritarianism and hierarchy which impoverish communication and distort or withhold information.

This swing of ecologist thought towards the alliance of modernisation and democratic protest did not take place without reticence. Many were afraid, and rightly so, of being drawn into an increasingly limited reformism, but, as the work advanced, the reticence diminished – to the point where the most active members of our groups, at the time of the Harrisburg accident, rejected the anti-nuclear campaigns which appealed only to fear and were thus purely defensive.

Much more difficult still than the discovery of the stake was the discovery of a definition of the actors themselves. Only the Grenoble–Malville group produced a clear formulation of the question: in whose name are we fighting? However, the intervention as a whole did provide the elements of an answer to a question which is not so simple as it seems. For the dominated actor is not a collective ego, a self-conscious identity. In order to defend itself against the dominant class, it leans first on that which seems most able to resist social power: it defends its work force in the case of the working-class movement, and nature in the case of the ecology movement. Next, however, it goes over to the counter-offensive by calling upon its capacity for action and production, the union of the workers in the case of the working-class movement, and what one what might call the self-management of needs in the case of the new social movements. The distinctive feature of the latter is that social domination embraces much more than work, extending to almost every domain of social activity, so that it is no longer possible to appeal to tradition, to a local or professional culture, or to a specific community, as the artisans were able to do, or the miners, the steelworkers, or the fishermen, living in a working-class environment that was both homogeneous and isolated from the rest of society. Hence the difficulty for the new social movements of defining a membership group in whose name they could speak: a society which has an almost unlimited capacity for action upon itself, where 'acquired status' is becoming more important than 'transmitted status', can no longer have social movements able to call upon real groups, like a village defending itself in the name of its culture, language or religion against the foreign and infidel invader. Hence, too, the constant call for exemplary action. The anti-nuclear movement cannot be reduced to a political action. It is a voluntary action, and above all a different way of living, acting and thinking. It is not simply the weakness of the movement which leads it to emphasise the appeal to an ethic of conviction and to quasi-religious forms of behaviour, but the fact that it must rely entirely on will since it cannot rely on a community rooted in traditions.

So emerges the image of an anti-technocratic movement at the heart of a society of information and communication that the technocrats are seeking to programme in the interests of the apparatuses which they manage. Against them it defends needs which cannot be reduced to mere demands manipulated and imposed by the masters of supply.

But the anti-nuclear struggle is not simply a social movement. Like every social struggle it combines many different meanings and acquires importance only in so far as it is capable of subordinating its most immediate objectives to those of the social movement within it. In the same way, the working-class movement was formed by integrating demands and pressures into a class struggle. But the case of the anti-nuclear action is special. It too must insert the defence of local interests into a more general social and political struggle, but in addition, as well as being a social movement, it contains a *cultural movement*. It does not only try to seize control of cultural orientations introduced and dominated by the new ruling class; it is itself a direct creator of those new cultural orientations; it is a movement as much of innovation as of protest. At the same time as it combats the technocracy, it creates models of knowledge, of economic activity and of ethics which are post-industrial but which are also wary of the modernising attitudes of a new ruling class. It is virtually impossible for an organised action to integrate these two orders of meaning with any kind of cohesion. Hence the weakness of the anti-nuclear struggle, which has always remained a current of both innovation and protest rather than organising itself into an action of a political or trade union type able to define a strategy and a tactic. Hence above all the vital importance of the movement and the impossibility of reducing it to a sectorial struggle and restricting it to the limited domain of associations. The anti-nuclear struggle is a historical event which reveals for the first time the blurred yet brilliant image of the new social movement which will give the political life of the programmed societies its meaning. Because it is not yet at the heart of those societies but announces their coming, it is incapable of organised action. Because it is still the agent of a cultural mutation as well as the agent of a new social conflict, it is placed at the gateway to the world in which we are already learning to live, hope and struggle. It invents the battlefield even as it begins the fight. It conveys the new historicity as much as the new class struggle.

This first conclusion is not yet a judgement on the present state of the anti-nuclear struggle. We shall try in a moment to define the distance which separates the latter from the anti-technocratic social movement contained within it, but we can already state that any analysis which sets aside the idea of social movement is false, as would be an analysis of the results of the intervention which did not start from the central fact of the group's conversion. It must be added, however, that the elements which constitute the social movement are not directly integrated with one another. They even seem to be floating, separated from one another in the midst of other meanings of the struggle. The call for exemplary action turns in upon itself, the anti-technocratic struggle is claimed by the leaders and the trade unionists, and the cultural innovation of the ecologists seems to pass through the anti-nuclear struggle rather than to take root in it. Consequently, the remainder of this conclusion must examine the historical reasons permitting or preventing the crystallisation of the movement which still hangs in suspension in the struggle.

But let us return to the main point. A social movement is taking shape in a domain which is no longer that of work, which is not only that of consumption, which is that of production and economic development. It is new in that it no longer opposes workers and bosses but the population and the great apparatuses which determine their way of life and their collective future, which impose their decisions on the whole of the community in the name of technical rationality and economic necessity. At a time when trade unionism is torn between the fight for job security and the desperate defence of declining industries, the anti-nuclear movement, even through its deficiencies and impotence, carries an entirely new protest and hope. In spite of its weaknesses and its disorganisation, it has brought out the figure of the new social movement with such clarity that it has already transformed our social experience and thought. The force of its convictions, the originality of its analyses, and the strength of its mobilisation bear witness to its importance, as the first unions and the first riots in the large industrial towns bore witness before 1848 to the birth of a working-class movement which, however, did not find its unity and its capacity for political intervention immediately.

Analysing the student struggle, we found that it contained traces of a possible social movement, but we recognised that after coming to life in 1968 it had become more and more unreal, and a struggle unable to recognise its true meaning was thus condemned to decline into a limited syndicalism or to disappear. That conclusion was too fragile, however, to give us confidence in our own procedure, to verify our central hypothesis on the appearance of a new social movement. Our situation at the end of this second intervention is very different. Although we have reservations about the ability of the anti-nuclear struggle to organise, we are convinced that it reveals the existence and the nature of the new social movement. Today the political arena is covering over with a new flora; later will come new gardeners; we should savour while we can the heady scents of these wild flowers and unruly weeds, so invigorating after so much deodorant and disinfectant. The functionaries and the doctrinarians of the former social movements rub their eyes in bewilderment: these struggles are not in the place reserved for them; they do not speak the language learnt in the last century; they are badly organised, and still unable to separate what is best in them from what is most confused.

It is not in the name of personal preferences or ideologies that we announce the visible presence of a new social movement, nor is it as the devoted interpreters of the actors and their ideology, but after an intervention in which we questioned the anti-nuclear struggle at length, placing ourselves far from its practices and its representations, on the summit of a distant social movement. For we have seen the actors of this struggle, gathered in our intervention groups, acting and thinking in response to our question, which thus makes sense, literally.

THE STATE OF THE STRUGGLE

The end of a period

The importance we have just attributed to the anti-nuclear struggle may turn against it. The bearer of so many hopes, it is so clearly inferior to its mission. This risk of disappointment is serious in a research programme where some of the researchers tended to stand back from the real struggle and adopt the viewpoint of the social movement that it contains. The most active members of the Paris group twice accused the researchers, and especially Alain Touraine, of yielding to that disappointment, above all during the meeting between the two groups at Autrans. The accusations were not justified, as was shown by the next stage of the research, the stage of permanent sociology, during which the leader of the research programme tirelessly repeated his attempts to bring out the social movement at the heart of the struggle, at the risk sometimes of seeming to take directly upon himself the search for new objectives for the action. But it is easy to understand the origin of the accusations: it is a fact that the distance between the potential social movement and the real action was very great in the anti-nuclear struggle at the time when we studied it and that the researcher could not, would not, conceal that distance, which everybody, and himself first of all, felt as a distance between the group and him, between the militant and the analyst. What is more, the problems facing the struggle were acknowledged from the very beginning of the intervention by many of the militants, especially in the Grenoble–Malville group where on various occasions most of the participants voiced the most pessimistic conclusions on the future of the anti-nuclear action. Within the intervention itself, the success of the conversion in the Paris group during its first weekend and of the semi-conversion of the Grenoble–Malville group during the third was bought at a heavy price: the virtual breakdown of the groups and the comparative isolation of the sub-group of those who had gone over to an analysis of the struggle in terms of a social movement. The division was between those for whom the anti-nuclear action was above all a refusal and those who saw it primarily as a social and political project. It would be wrong to say that one part of the groups had rejected the conditions for political action and retreated into a cultural withdrawal, because such a formulation introduces a value judgement. We should rather say that the division had shown the practical impossibility of uniting the two indispensable components of a popular social movement, its defensive action and its counter-offensive action. Without the first it is in danger of becoming no more than a programme of a modernising counter-elite, whilst without the second it is no more than the front line of a cultural refusal with neither homogeneity nor durability.

The result of the crises was the tendency for the social movement to disintegrate, for its principles of identity, opposition and totality to come apart. In the extreme case, the first can close in completely upon itself to produce a sect, the second can lead to pure conflict, either in the form of violence or, on the contrary, of pressure and negotiation, and the third can transform itself into a pure cultural ideology detached from all social conflict. These disjointed components of the social movement, which

181

cannot unite in practice, tend to mingle together inside a doctrinaire discourse. Such was the force of leftism and the explanation of its at first sight surprising links with local defence and humanist protest. Leftism is the negative legacy of May 68 whilst the impulse towards new practices and new orientations for the struggle is its positive legacy. In leftism the theory is stronger than the political action which, in its turn, controls the social struggle. It is a caricature of Leninism, an avant-garde with no mass movement and no real struggle for power. Leftism gave the anti-nuclear and other struggles the conviction of its militants, who were at one and the same time the bearers of new ideas and feelings and the prisoners of a language so out of key that it often seemed to be no more than a series of metaphors, preventing the movement from finding a definition, a direction and an organisation.

What was broken after Malville 77, in the test of reality, was the capacity of this discourse to impose itself on militant demands and practices. Words and things came apart, and through the interstices appeared the void of thought, method and organisation, felt acutely by many members of the intervention groups even before the researchers. This collapse was also a liberation because the false efficacy of the leftist theory and mobilisation was limited to purely symbolic protest whilst its doomsday mentality prevented it from embarking upon any kind of prolonged action. It was a political position which, being unable to analyse social relations, could only reiterate its total rejection of all social organisation, treating each occasion as if it were the final catastrophe and so refusing itself any kind of strategy and permanence.

The example of the student struggle, which we examined before the anti-nuclear struggle, reveals the end of leftism even more clearly. The university strike of 1976, turning its back on the May 68 themes of the link between knowledge and power and the need to liberate knowledge from the hold of the technocrats, was the act of self-destruction of a student movement imprisoned in the contradictions of the leftist language. There is no guarantee that the exhaustion of leftism will allow the anti-nuclear movement to develop, but if it does not break with that doctrinaire diversion from action, the movement surely has no future.

An uncertain future

This impression was reinforced by all the interviews with anti-nuclear groups during the phase of permanent sociology. The action on the sites, which remained strong in those places where the threat seemed most direct, had eluded the grasp of revolutionary militants (who came from outside and left as quickly as they had arrived) only to imprison itself in local problems. Thus the most specifically anti-nuclear action, instead of using its ability to turn the conflict against a precise adversary as a means of going beyond a generalised ecological protest, became the least elaborated level of the struggle, where a community simply defends itself against an aggression from outside. Conversely, the attempts to transform a specifically anti-nuclear action into a counter-project of economic policy merely widened the gap between the local resistances and the attempts at the summit to establish links with the parties and the unions. The mass action could not easily be revived by incorporating the anti-nuclear theme into a political strategy for overcoming the crisis, because the latter is located at a higher level, that of the new class struggles and the political projects.

The agreement of 25 June 1979, because it was signed in particular by the CFDT and the Socialist Party, committed the anti-nuclear action to a more political path and pushed it to organise itself better, but also brought the risk of depriving it of the support of many of those who had led the great anti-nuclear demonstrations. Its signatories in the Réseau des Amis de la Terre saw it above all as a means of reviving the anti-nuclear action, but we ourselves interpret it more cautiously as a sign of the distance between a grass-roots movement and a political intervention and consequently of the difficulty of setting up the social movement without an intermediary. We can go even further. In five years' time nuclear power stations will provide almost half of electricity production, and even now the tripartite agreement accepts a production programme representing about a quarter. Can it really be hoped that an action against a technology which is already so solidly implanted will be able to retain its full force?

The working-class movement lasted because it fought not industrialisation but industrial relations in the factories. The anti-nuclear movement has a future only if it ceases to fight an industry and directs its forces against a ruling class, the technocracy, and attacks it in every domain of social life. If it cannot attain such a high level, which is that of the social movement, and which would presuppose a solidly organised action and the capacity to protest against precise forms of social organisation in the name of well-defined interests and needs organised into a force for demanding change, then can it not at least impose new demands on the political system and contribute to the reconstruction of the political left on profoundly transformed bases? If the anti-nuclear militants follow such a course of action, they can play an important part in French political life, provided they are able to maintain their autonomous capacity for mobilisation. But such a role has nothing at all to do with the anti-nuclear struggle of the past few years and even less with the social movement whose presence we had recognised in struggles where it mingles with forms of behaviour related to the crisis in the values of industrial society. Our research finishes, or at least this book is closed, at a time when the anti-nuclear action of the years 1974–8 has come to an end and when perhaps a new phase and a new form of struggle is beginning. It is the duty of the researchers to address themselves to the anti-nuclear militants and to summarise their results for them as follows: the anti-nuclear wave has receded since the drama of Malville, but it has contributed greatly to transforming our way of living and thinking. It was produced by a cultural movement which is carrying us out of the industrial civilisation. It also contains a social movement, but this mixture of cultural revolution and social conflict has not allowed that movement to take shape. Now it is in association no longer with behaviours of cultural crisis but with forces for the transformation of political life that the anti-technocratic social movement will try to create itself. This is a frequent alternation in history: social movements try to make their entrance on the stage of history both from the bottom and the top, by the transformation of ideas and customs and by action on the institutions and the State. The main problem for the militants in the years to come will be to disengage the anti-technocratic social movement from the political strategy with which it will be combined, just as at the time of our intervention the central problem was to disengage this movement from the cultural revolution with which it was associated. The intervention groups, become programming groups, were perfectly aware of the two dangers between which they must pick their way: they no longer believed in effervescent demonstrations, but neither did they want to transform themselves into a party. They wanted to preserve the mixture of cultural revolution and social movement which had mobilised them by giving the anti-nuclear struggle a greater capacity for political action.

Is it possible for the social struggle to be revived through a specifically trade union initiative? The CFDT's denunciation, followed by the CGT, of serious deficiencies in very many of the power stations in 1979 led to a strike at the Gravelines and Tricastin plants where the reactors were to be loaded. But this action in defence of the workers cannot easily be extended into a general anti-nuclear campaign. The distance between the trade union and ecology components of the struggle is not easy to overcome. And yet the militants are convinced that their action should be developed on the basis of concrete demands.

If the anti-nuclear struggle remains attached to past forms of action or is transformed into a specifically political force, it will disappear. But if, on the other hand, it is able to go beyond both cultural protest and political intervention and win recognition for the new figure of the class struggle in the political arena, then it will contribute to the formation of a new social movement. It is not for us to predict the future but to point out to the militants the condition for the success of the project from which their struggle draws its meaning, which is to create, in the post-industrial, programmed society, the anti-technocratic social movement which will oppose the domination of the apparatuses wherever it seeks to impose itself.

The meaning of a struggle

A revolution in the revolution

How can we define the situation of this struggle and explain how the anti-technocratic social movement is both present in it and powerless to direct its action? Firstly by pointing out that we are not firmly established in a post-industrial society but merely standing at the entrance to it and that our political and social life is still dominated by the problems of the industrial society. This is a customary time-lag, and one which dominated the whole of the nineteenth century, already directed by industrial capitalism and yet still dominated by the categories and the problems of a pre-industrial, mercantile society. This precocity of the anti-nuclear movement explains the mixture in it of a cultural movement and a social movement, its tendency to utopia, and the predominance in its action of the protest against the ends over the search for the means.

But there is more to it than this. If this still shapeless and invertebrate movement is to exist, it must also have a strong will and intention to be a social movement. In which direction is that intention turned? Because the programmed society is only just beginning to take shape, the new social movement can define itself only in relation to other social movements, or at least in relation to the doctrines and forms of political intervention which accompany their institutionalisation. Hence this precise hypothesis: the ecology and anti-nuclear movement, in a word the political ecology, is constituted by opposing the degraded forms of the working-class movement which fill the ideological and political stage. It is a dialogue not between action and reality but between a young social movement in search of itself and the preceding movement which is now domesticated or changing. Like a revolutionary movement striving to resuscitate the revolution which has grown cold, and within which it is itself developing, like the students of 68 who wanted to place their uprising within the working-class movement, even though the latter was more concerned with collective bargaining and political influence than protest, the political ecology takes shape in response to a working-class movement which has lost itself to communist power, social-democrat influence or the devout belief in a technical and scientific revolution bringing social progress with it. It criticises the working-class ideology as the working-class movement criticised the bourgeois liberties. Its intention is to be both the successor and the adversary of the working-class movement just as the latter both opposed and continued the work of the bourgeois revolutions.

This gives the real meaning of the close links between the political ecologists and the CFDT. The latter is much more than a minority trade union confederation. In spite of its advances in metallurgy and other industries, it is a trade unionism of the modern sectors of the economy, where operators and technicians are able to wage limited battles for professional status but can also inspire a new social movement by fighting the appropriation of knowledge by the apparatuses and joining with the users in their struggle against them. The CFDT, as was agreed by all the confederation members who took part in our intervention groups, will avoid reformism, and also the domination of the CGT which represents the classical model of union action, only if it joins in the new protests in the name of self-management.

The political ecology is primarily a critique of the ideology of the working-class movement. It directly opposes its definition of the societal stakes of the conflicts. It does not believe that its role is to help the capitalist or industrial society to give birth to a more advanced socialist society. It combats all industrialised societies, be they capitalist or socialist, in the name of a will to live differently, and to do so immediately. It refuses to define its adversary by the ownership of the means of production or by its purely economic role. It is not opposed to ownership but power. And finally it does not accept that a party should speak in the name of a class or that a specific social category should be the representative of the universal and of the meaning of history. It is established, in other words, on the rejection of the definitions that the working-class movement gives of itself, its adversary and the stake of their conflicts.

At the risk of offending those who might read these lines too quickly, we shall say that ecology is a working-class anti-movement. This was understood and expressed best by Brice Lalonde who wanted to break with what calls itself the Left because he claimed that ecology alone was the real Left. And it should be remembered that the intervention groups only once came into conflict with an interlocutor. They were interested and disturbed by the language of the military strategists of the nuclear weapon and embarrassed by the moderation of the technocrats, but they came into brutal confrontation with the representatives of the Communist Party, especially in Paris. The anti-nuclear militants did not feel rejected by the working-class world – and opinion polls confirm that feeling – but condemned by the communist leaders attached to the dogma of the liberation of the workers through the growth of production and the progress of science and technology. It would be pointless to conceal this division which was one of the clearest signs of the transition from the industrial society to the programmed society. It would be deeper still if the ecologists were not aware, like every new social movement, that they need political allies and protectors.

The meaning of a struggle

Defensive and utopia

This revolution in the revolution cannot control all the practices of the struggle. Hence the constant dissociation, in this social pre-movement, of a utopia which announces a social movement and a defensive action which is also part of it but which invariably extends beyond the defence of particular interests and so refers back, at least in counterpoint, to a general protest.

Not everybody experiences the change of culture and society as a discovery and a struggle. Most people feel it as a crisis; in other words their behaviour contains no reference to historicity and they no longer define their adversary in terms of social relations but as an order, a State which controls, manipulates and excludes. Such indeed is the representation of society which dominates today, in this interval between the old and the new social movements, in this movement which is more one of protest than of conflict. Because the old form of class relations is disintegrating and its new form is not yet clearly recognised, the protesters denounce a Power without any social definition, in other words the State. That is why they side so strongly with Soviet dissidents, with citizens fighting a totalitarian State. In countries where the defence of the citizen is more assured, the struggle against Power is necessarily more limited or less dramatic, and so the political struggle seems almost without object since it is not content with supporting parties or unions concerned mainly with negotiations in which the rank and file play hardly any part. The resulting vacuum fills up with a motley of all the refusals, from the critique of industrial values to the resistance to all change in social organisation and the habits of life. The building of a new social movement is difficult because it must sink its foundations into this shifting sand if it is not to become a mere intellectual exercise or the faith of a sect. The birth of a social movement can never be separated from forms of behaviour which manifest the crisis and the destruction of the former culture and society, including their forms of social conflict. If the seed falls upon stony ground . . .

Each one of the constituent elements of the social movement – identity, opposition, stake – can thus be divided into two concrete figures whose complementarity can be discovered only by the analysis. To the utopian movement is added and opposed a defensive struggle. The actor is defined by the struggle as a particular group, a local population, an association, and by the protesting utopia as the species, humanity in so far as it belongs to nature. The adversary is defined by the defensive struggle as a 'thing', factory or plutonium, which threatens the community or the biological organism, and by the utopian movement as Power, omnipresent and diabolical, a new image of death. And finally the stake is defined by the defensive struggle as the survival and thus the protection of the balances necessary to life, but by the utopians, as Pierre Samuel clearly saw, as autonomy, that capacity for free actions which can also be called self-management but which the adversary interprets in the opposite sense as adaptation to change.

Offensive and defensive ecology are thus set one against the other, and communication is difficult between the community withdrawal and the ecological counter-project. But each half of the movement feels its infirmity and tries to acquire what it cannot produce by itself. That is why the partisans of the exemplary community, as we saw time and again during the intervention, so readily accept the ones who speak of the need to break with the State and who are prepared to use violence, whilst the supporters of the counter-project stress the need to maintain the link between the political struggle and community life, the social conflict and cultural experience. The internal life of the anti-nuclear struggle consists of this nexus of complementarity and opposition between these two halves of the social movement, always separate, often opposed, and constantly in search of a still impossible unity.

Three project levels

The historical manifestations of the anti-nuclear struggle can be defined by the degree to which they integrate this defensive action and this utopian movement.

A first manifestation is that of local defence, where the defensive action prevails almost completely over the utopia. A community defends itself against the outside world in a struggle which accepts all meanings and all interpretations. Where defence prevails there also appears what the militants call ecumenicism, the concrete expression of this refusal to identify the struggle with a social relation and even less with a particular political ideology. The local militants struggling against a plan to construct a nuclear power station are naturally inclined towards this type of action.

Opposite this form of the struggle is found no longer utopian protest but, in a more complex way, the social movement capable of taking up and transforming the defensive forms of behaviour. To define it we must recall that a social movement does not only emerge in its own domain, that of social action and, at the highest level, of historicity: it can appear in another region 'of society', in behaviours of opposition to order, of response to a crisis or of pressure for change. In each one of these cases the social movement appears only in broken form, split up into at least four fragments. Since we are here concerned with a social movement which reveals itself through crisis behaviours, we shall describe directly the fragments of a social movement acting in that region of society. In the first place, it transforms behaviours of crisis and anomy into revolt and violence. Secondly, in a complementary way, it appeals to the social movement, over its own practices which are dominated by the crisis, by overdeveloping an ideology of the class conflict. In the third place, it tries to escape from the crisis by choosing modernisation, like people who emigrate to escape unemployment. Finally, it tries to protect itself from the crisis by defending the integrity of a concrete community, a reaction which can transform the movement into a sect. The strongest and most fecund movement is not the most unified and organised but on the contrary the most divided.

Between these two opposed forms appeared another during the research and especially in its phase of permanent sociology. We might call it the *populist* manifestation. A local or regional community, in Alsace in particular, tries not only to defend its integrity against an enemy from outside but also to manage its own change, to retain its identity while transforming itself. To stay the same whilst becoming different is the hope which defines the populist movements. It is a call to the people, which is not addressed to the people in general but to a given people with its customs, language or religion, to defend itself against a State which is both internal domination, an agent of the ruling class, and a foreign power. It is a defence which by no means excludes recourse to all the institutional means, political and juridical, of opposition to heteronomous change. These regional movements are often associated with the anti-nuclear struggle, and where, as in Alsace, they encounter resistance, the banner of ecology replaces the regional flag. It is in Alsace that the anti-nuclear movement can best be called popular because there more than anywhere it is inspired and directed by local leaders most of whom live in villages rather than in Strasbourg or Mulhouse, and because it calls upon a people which is to be found as much in Switzerland or Germany as France and which wishes to preserve its culture not out of sheer traditionalism but out of communal spirit and the will to direct its own history instead of being manipulated by the power politics of the States.

The anti-nuclear struggle in Alsace is profoundly different from what it is in Paris, where it is closer to the divided utopian figure, or the Nogent region or Cruas–Meysse, where it is composed mainly of local defence. After the reverses of Malville and the elections, it has maintained itself more solidly in Alsace than elsewhere, effectively supported by a dense network of voluntary associations. But, whatever its historical importance, it should be understood simply as an intermediary between local defence and the anti-establishment utopia of the political ecologists. Only the utopia enables us to situate the other forms of the anti-nuclear struggle, and especially the local defence movements, which have never been turned in upon themselves, so little indeed that it was usually the revolutionary militants who brought them to public attention by making places like Malville or Braud-et-Saint-Louis the centre of militant action which on other occasions has been turned to the defence of the farmers on the Larzac threatened with expropriation by the army, or the workers of Lip fighting to prevent the closure of their firm by setting up a cooperative.

We have come back to the beginning: the anti-nuclear struggle is primarily a social movement, but one which still exists only as a *social pre-movement*, torn between local defence and utopia, between counter-culture and a social and political counter-project. Is this distance between the potential social movement and the observable form of the struggle especially great? It is most certainly greater than it was in the working-class movement in 1908 or 1936, but it is smaller than the distance between the possible student movement and the forms of struggle used in the 1976 student strike in France. At times the researcher was in despair over this distance and at other times enthusiastic at being constantly brought back by his analysis to the potential social movement whose still hidden sun already illuminates a new society and new social struggles. But after stressing so often what separates the nuclear fear from an anti-nuclear movement, we must, at the end of this research, rather stress its prophetic role. Without that fear, without that reaction of defence, which spread only after the brutal acceleration of the nuclear programme, the struggle would not have gone beyond the limits of an intellectual critique and local reactions. It was the fear that caused most people to heed warnings that were not just arguments. It was the fear that spotlighted the importance of the stake and helped to name the new adversary while the ideologists were trying to reduce it to former figures.

The movement is not formed by renouncing that fear but by transforming it into a will to act. It will be a long and difficult transformation, and one which will not succeed without a break with certain forms of action or without remaining faithful to the reaction which has designated the nuclear industry as the first field of confrontation with technocratic power.

The possible transition to politics

This transformation may take place. It has not taken place yet, and the history of the research brings out the breaks more clearly than the continuities. The ones who were successfully converted in Paris and Grenoble were those who recognised the presence of the social movement in the struggle. They were also the ones who after Harrisburg successfully concluded the agreement signed by the Amis de la Terre with the CFDT, the Socialist Party and other organisations. They believe that this more political approach will revive the anti-nuclear protest. It is too early to say whether they are right. In any case, they do not confuse the social movement with a political action. None of them wishes to reduce the anti-nuclear action to a political current which would manifest itself in elections or on television. They all give priority to direct social conflict with the technocrats, but they believe that a conflictual action presupposes organisation and that the agreement they have signed is important above all because it reveals the capacity for decision of the Réseau des Amis de la Terre and so represents a decisive progress in the organisation of the ecology current. That is why they became very actively involved in the campaign against the loading of the Gravelines and Tricastin power stations in the autumn of 1979, seeing it as the expression of a direct social conflict which must in their eyes always remain at the centre of the anti-nuclear action.

But another development must be envisaged: the formation of a new political current trying to insert itself between the parties, either to influence one of them, in this case the Socialist Party, or to prepare itself for the 1981 presidential elections or others. The receding of the specifically anti-nuclear action may be accompanied by the reinforcing of an ecology current taking advantage of the feeling of many voters that the parties, their language and their leaders are out of tune with the present state of public opinion. Such will be the meaning of the debates to come: there will be a great temptation to abandon the realm of social conflicts and enter the arena of political struggles, especially since it will be difficult to wage the same strong social actions as before and since political intervention might seem more likely to mobilise the population. The research, which has shown the presence of a social movement in the struggle, must conclude that in the coming years the main problem for the militants will be to preserve the priority of the social movement over political pressure, even if the latter is a form in which the movement must inevitably manifest itself.

A PROPHETIC MOVEMENT

The strongest criticisms of the anti-nuclear action and our own hypotheses are made in the name of a firm belief in science as the instrument of human liberation: reason must replace tradition and prejudice just as the law of the State must replace the upper classes and their traditional power. These criticisms come from rationalist lay scientists and left-wing politicians and trade unionists attached to the belief in the liberating power of the development of the forces of production. Their resistance is all the greater since even recently there seemed to be unanimity in extolling the peaceful use of nuclear power whilst condemning or fearing its military use. But within the space of a few years the confidence in a new and abundant source of energy associated with a keen awareness of the benefits of economic expansion and the progress of education has been replaced by a more or less well argued rejection not only of nuclear energy but of many new techniques, medical discoveries, and more generally of work and growth. These defenders of science and reason have the feeling that a wind of madness is blowing through our society and they explain it by the effects of the brutal change in the economic situation: after thirty years of exceptional expansion, we are seized by a great doubt as the growth that we had come to look upon as natural shudders to a brutal halt, creating a moral crisis from which we must, however, escape as fast as possible if we are to overcome the economic crisis.

This lay scientistic optimism has been and will be the object of debate, but it is condemned by our research more clearly than by any argument. The anti-nuclear action does not correspond to the image given of it by those who claim to be the inheritors of rationalism. It contains no more irrationalism than the belief in progress, which is blind to many crises, destructions and colonisations. It is neither stronger nor weaker than the scientism inherited from the last century; it is attached to a different image of development. But people are unable to see this because the image is introduced by forces of opposition, whereas scientism, which was for a long time progressive, fighting the ruling class and traditional ideas, is now the ideology of the technocrats. The working-class movement believed in progress and work but it also halted or slowed down production and fought against what the masters of industry called the rationalisation of work. In the same way, those who today are the bearers of a new model of knowledge and economic activity combat an ideology which identifies with the interests of the ruling class and which encloses itself in an arbitrarily restricted vision of rationality. Is it irrational to say that we still do not know the effects of radiation or how we are going to store radioactive waste for thousands of years? Is it irrational to say that blind confidence in nuclear energy blocks the attempts to use the new energies or the necessary transformation of our mode of consumption? Is it irrational to denounce the secrecy, the wrong calculations, the repression, all eternal instruments of absolute, that is to say irrational, power? It would be as false to reduce the anti-nuclear struggle to a tide of irrationalism as to see in it only the action of scientists fired by a vision of the world which is new, and wider than the old one. It is a social and cultural movement in which social protest and cultural innovation are not separable, a great historical phenomenon which brings progress through rupture and creation through refusal. It is this mixture which deceives both those who see the movement only as a wave of irrationality and those who reject the cultural orientations of industrial society in the name only of balance and identity, dreaming of stability in a world whose accelerated changes frighten them. The anti-nuclear movement is not only the expression of a new science or a new ethic. It participates in the great mutation which is taking us from the industrial society to the post-industrial society which I have called programmed. This transition is not continuous and smooth; it produces behaviours of crisis, refusal and regression as well as stirring and prophetic utopias. This explains why the movement is weak and splintered, because it is itself wracked by this same discontinuity and the contradictions that come with it. But even more significantly it explains the greatness of an action whose historical importance is in no way diminished by its weaknesses, for the weaknesses of an action are less important than its creativity. The anti-nuclear struggle is helping us to build our future. On the threshold of the programmed society, it brings first a strategy to escape from the crisis, in other words to enter the post-industrial society, and above all a prophecy which announces the new conflicts of that society.

How can something which has been called a great refusal or a utopia now be called a strategy for entering the post-industrial society? Because its radical critique of industrial society rejects solutions to the crisis based on hyper-industrialisation. It calls upon us to transform our representation of the world, our economic organisation and our ethic. It takes us from one field of historicity to another and calls upon us to increase our society's capacity for action upon itself. Is it possible for a country or a region of the world to enter a new society without being carried towards it by new values and new sensibilities as much as by new forms of social organisation? The political ecology explodes limited or sclerotic forms of organisation, information and communication. It replaces hierarchical organisation by the dynamic of networks, the idea of a humanity building on the destruction of nature by that of a community controlling its relations with its environment as well as its own internal functioning, and the priority of capital and output by the priority of communication and interdependence. It refuses to believe that social life is controlled by economics or by any other determinism, because it represents social life as the product of social activity itself. If it is accepted that we are on the threshold of a great social transformation, can we really believe that it is only by acting on investment that society will be able to undergo the mutation without breaking up in that difficult venture? Was the entry into the mercantile economy and then into industrial society successfully completed in Western Europe without a revolution in our representations of the world and human action as well as our forms of economic action? Ecology participates in a transformation of our representations of the world as well as defining new cultural values and corresponding to an economic activity dominated by the production, transmission and use of complex masses of information. This great transformation was already at work in May 68, as also in the great movement of counter-culture that began in the United States. It traverses the ecology movement and the anti-nuclear action, but it does not imprison itself within the limits of a particular struggle. Tomorrow the anti-nuclear fire may be extinguished; the cultural revolution will light new fires elsewhere.

But the anti-nuclear movement is not only charged with cultural innovation. It also carries the definition of a new social movement. It may come down to a defensive, conservative action, or even to the selfish preservation of habits or privileges, but beyond its weaknesses it announces the uprising of the populations against the technocratic apparatuses, be they public or private. It is opposed to the kind of life which favours the reinforcing of their power and prevents democracy, in other words the capacity of those populations to impose their collective will on the material and symbolic instruments which organise their personal and collective practices. It is true that the anti-nuclear struggle sometimes hesitates to make the transition, that it still sometimes calls for an uprising against the specific dangers of nuclear power, but, as we know, these campaigns in the name of danger and fear are dying out and the struggle is learning to name its real adversary: not nuclear energy or plutonium but the *nuclear policy* and the *technocratic power* which decides it.

What name shall be given to this struggle which contains a movement for which it is no more than a feeble agent? It is a *prophecy*. Like all prophets the anti-nuclear movement speaks in the name of a necessity and of principles which must control all forms of human behaviour. Like them it stands outside organisations – in this case parties, like churches in the case of the religious prophecies. Like them it creates strong affective relationships between those who follow the new word. It is true that the prophets of tradition spoke in the name of the sacred, but in a society which has eliminated transcendence, the meta-social guarantors of the social order, the image of God or the Prince, are replaced by the appeal to historicity and creativity. Max Weber, who has given the classic account of prophecy (*Economy and Society*, Vol. 2, pp. 447–50) marked out the place of this new prophecy in advance when he opposed *ethical* prophecy and *exemplary* prophecy. The first reveals a law and gives commandments, like Moses, Zoroaster or Mohammed, the prophets of a Middle East which saw the triumph of the concept of one god, whilst exemplary prophecy appeals to a conduct which is its own witness of its purity or saintliness. This prophecy, which is that of the Buddha and corresponds to civilisations which do not believe in one god, is close to the prophecy of the anti-nuclear movement, which is nonetheless alien to all religious belief but has the same attachment to exemplary action, the same attraction to the search for wisdom, and the same hostility to submission to the Law. And even if there are no ecology or anti-nuclear prophets (although Illich is not far from fulfilling that function) the men and women who inspire the movement radiate a charisma which makes them if not prophets then at least the bearers of a prophecy. The researchers, at the moment of the conversion of the intervention groups, were defined as prophets of the social movement, and the term brought sneers from those who made no attempt to understand it. Is it not obvious that the word would be meaningless if it were not the movement itself which was prophetic, since the researchers at a given moment had the role of speaking to the militants locked in their struggle from the point of view of the movement and in its name? It was for them only a role, and one which the group took from them as soon as it had achieved its conversion, as soon as it was itself speaking in the name of the movement contained within their struggle, as soon as it was speaking prophetically itself.

There is no more distance between the defence of a site, the criticism of official information or the fear of contamination on the one hand and the anti-nuclear prophecy on the other than there was between the defence of a trade or a job and the socialist prophecy which illuminated the industrial society. And this terminology which is religious only in appearance helps us not to be deceived by the visible weakness of the real struggles, to recognise in them the invention of a culture and a society through the prophetic protest.

The anti-nuclear movement is neither cultural refusal nor pressure group. If it is not yet a social movement capable of political expression, it is because it still combines within itself, almost as much as the May movement from which it was born, cultural revolution and social struggle, and because the political forces are unable to give it the means to influence institutional decisions. It is precariously balanced between positions of principle and concrete but limited actions, a situation which prevents it from playing a specifically political role but which should not prevent us from seeing that it works upon public opinion and carries it towards new problems and new answers.

The former social movements are dying out or changing into instruments of management or co-management, whilst the industrialisation of almost every sector of social activity and the accelerated spread of mass culture are extending the field of power but also of the struggles which oppose it. It is in such conditions that the anti-nuclear movement and the political ecology which accompanies it are transporting us on to a suddenly transformed stage. From the Opéra to Woodstock, from the public of subscribers to the multicoloured crowd, social and cultural life is becoming more public, more open. It can no longer be properly illuminated by the light of former theories, and the general staffs can no longer impose their strategy on that crowd. One can understand the irritation of the old revolutionary intellectuals who, in this agitation, lose the thread of their theory and mislay their historical references. The anti-nuclear movement cannot become a party, not because its object is too specific, but on the contrary because it is a disturbance which displaces the ideas and the forms of action of the opposition parties, because it is carried forward by the immense transformation of the experiences, ideas and feelings created by mass industrialisation, the birth of the programmed society and the crisis of the hegemonies.

If the anti-nuclear struggle is not yet a socio-political force, it is because it is more: the double movement of a change of culture and a transformation of the social struggles.

And now the time has come not to put an end to this research but to hand it back to the actors so that they may continue this permanent sociology of which we have seen only the beginning. Truly permanent because the social movement of which actor and analyst speak is taking shape at the same time as the programmed society and will dominate our social history for a long time to come. We are writing above all for the actors: may they transform our analysis into action, invent a new culture and give life to a new social movement.

Chronology

MEETINGS

	Paris	Grenoble–Malville
1	24.4.78 closed meeting	21.4.78 closed meeting
2	28.4.78 M. Rubline, mayor of Saint-Laurent	28.4.78 M. Daurès, EDF
3	28.4.78 M. Gauvenet, Head of Security, CEA	28.4.78 M. Thiriet, CEA
4	29.4.78 closed meeting	29.4.78 closed meeting
5	12.5.78 M. Boiteux, Managing Director, EDF	12.5.78 M. Durand, county councillor, Morestel
6	12.5.78 M. Metzger, Communist Party	12.5.78 M. Blachère, Communist Party
7	13.5.78 General Buis	13.5.78 M. Briot, CGT
8	13.5.78 closed meeting	13.5.78 closed meeting
9	19.5.78 M. Y—, government backbencher	19.5.78 General Poirier
10	19.5.78 closed meeting	19.5.78 closed meeting
11	20.5.78 M. X—, from the Nogent-sur-Seine region	20.5.78 M. Philippe Lebreton, biologist, ecology and anti-nuclear militant
12	26.5.78 Mme Solange Fernex, ecology militant from Alsace	26.5.78 M. Brice Lalonde, from the Amis de la Terre
13	26.5.78 M. Cherruau, reporter	26.5.78 M. Brice Lalonde
14	27.5.78 closed meeting	27.5.78 M. Sigoyer, anti-nuclear militant

WEEKEND SESSIONS

1	9/10/11.6.78 Versailles I	9/10/11.6.78 Autrans I
2	24/25.6.78 Autrans II	24/25.6.78 Autrans II
3	1/2.7.78 Versailles II	1/2.7.78 Autrans III
		9.7.78 Grenoble

Chronology

October–December 1978	Meetings in Cherbourg, Lille, Seignosse (RAT)
January 1979	Meetings with the intervention groups in Paris and Grenoble
January–March 1979	Meetings in La Hague, Nantes and Le Pellerin (2), Strasbourg and Mulhouse, Montélimar (Cruas-Meysse, Saint-Etienne-des-Sorts), Malville and Paris with leaders of the ecology movement (P. and L. Samuel, Ph. Saint-Marc, B. Lalonde), the CFDT Energy Commission and scientists from the GSIEN and the *Gazette nucléaire.*
July and September 1979	Meeting with the intervention groups to discuss a new version of the research report.

RESEARCHERS

Zsuzsa Hegedus and Michel Wieviorka worked with the Grenoble–Malville group and Alain Touraine and François Dubet with the Paris group.

Principal abbreviations used in the text

~~~~~~

AFL-CIO	American Federation of Labor and Congress of Industrial Organisations
CEA	Atomic Energy Commission
CENG	Grenoble Centre for Nuclear Studies
CFDT	French Democratic Trade Union Confederation
CGT	General Confederation of Labour
CIME	Interregional Committee of Ecology Movements
CLIN	Local Committee for Nuclear Information
CNRS	National Centre for Scientific Research
COGEMA	General Company of Nuclear Materials
CRIN	Regional Committee for Nuclear Information
CSCV	Trade Union Confederation for the Living Environment
CSF	Trade Union Confederation for the Family
CUSPAN	University and Scientific Committee to Stop the Nuclear Programme
EDF	French Electricity Generating Board
GSIEN	Grouping of Scientists for Information on Nuclear Energy
IFOP	French Public Opinion Institute
LCR	Revolutionary Communist League
ORSEC-RAD	Emergency Service – Radiation
ORTF	French Radio and Television
PEON	Commission for the Production of Electricity of Nuclear Origin
PSU	Unified Socialist Party
PWR	Pressurised Water Reactor
RAT	Network of the Friends of the Earth
SNCF	French National Railways Company
UFC	Federal Union of Consumers

Bibliography

Les Amis de la Terre *L'Escroquerie nucléaire*, Paris, Stock, 1978

Les Amis de la Terre, Commission Energie *Tout solaire*, Paris, Jean-Jacques Pauvert, 1977

Anger, D. *Chronique d'une lutte*, Paris, Jean-Claude Simoen, 1978

Barbichon, G. in Tubiana, op. cit.

Bookchin, M. (ps. Herber, Lewis) *Ecology and Revolutionary Thought*, with *Toward an Ecological Solution*, New York, Times Change Press, 1970

Bupp, I. C. and Darian, J.-C. *Light Water – How the Nuclear Dream Dissolved*, New York, Basic Books, 1978

Cavanna, H., Kende, P., Matalon, B. and Pitts, J. R. *Les Origines de l'angoisse et du sentiment de malaise à l'égard de l'avenir*, Paris, CORDES, undated

CFDT *Nucléaire, Energie: Nos conditions*, Paris, Montholon Services, 1975
  Energie, Nucléaire: Choisir notre avenir, Paris, Montholon Services, 1979

CFDT Syndicat de l'énergie atomique *L'Electro-nucléaire en France*, Paris, Ed. du Seuil, 1976

Chaudron, M. and Lepape, Y. *Le Mouvement écologique dans la lutte anti-nucléaire*, Paris, CORDES, No. 1, 1977

Chiva, I. in Tubiana, op. cit.

Claude, C. *Voyage et aventures en écologie*, Paris, Editions sociales, 1978

Colloque interdisciplinaire et international *Un Lieu de contrôle démocratique des sciences*, Namur, 1977

Colson, J.-P. *Le Nucléaire sans les Français: Qui décide? Qui profite?*, Paris, Maspero, 1977

Comité nucléaire environnement et société *Rapport au parti socialiste: Pour une autre politique nucléaire*, Paris, Flammarion, 1978

Commoner, B. *The Closing Circle: Confronting the Environmental Crisis*, London, Cape, 1972 (originally published New York, Knopf, 1971)

CUSPAN *Plutonium sur Rhône: le Super-Phénix*, Grenoble, PUG

De Montbrial, T. *Energy: The Countdown. A Report to the Club of Rome*, New York, Pergamon, 1979

Dumont, R. *Utopia or Else . . .* (Tr. from Fr. Menkes, V.), London, Deutsch, 1974
  Seule une écologie socialiste, Paris, Robert Laffont, 1977

Durand, M. and Harff, Y. *La Qualité de la vie. Mouvement écologique, Mouvement ouvrier*, Paris, Mouton, 1977

Fagnani, F. and Nicolon, A. (under the direction of) *Nucléopolis. Matériaux pour l'analyse d'une société nucléaire*, Grenoble, PUG, 1979

200

Bibliography

Faivret, J.-P., Missika, J.-L. and Wolton, D. *L'Illusion écologique*, Paris, Ed. du Seuil, 1980

Fournier, P. *Y en a plus pour longtemps*, Paris, Ed. du Square, 1976

Friedmann, G. *Le Travaille en miettes*, Paris, Gallimard, 1956

Gazette nucléaire Special Number, Dec. 1978–Jan. 1979, *Le Mouvement*, and the collection as a whole

Gorz, A. *Ecology as Politics*, (Tr. from Fr. Vigderman, P. and Cloud, J.), Boston, South End Press, 1980

Gorz, A. and Bosquet, M. *Ecologie et politique*, Paris, Ed. du Seuil, 1978 (The first part, *Ecologie et liberté*, was originally published by Galilée, 1977)

Gravelaine, F. and O'Dy, S. *L'Etat EDF*, Paris, Alain Moreau, 1978

Gremion, P. *Le Pouvoir périphérique*, Paris, Ed. du Seuil, 1976

GSIEN *Electro-nucléaire: Danger*, Paris, Ed. du Seuil, 1977

Guedeney, C. and Mendel, G. *Angoisse atomique et centrales nucléaires*, Paris, Payot, 1973

Harry, J., Gade, R. and Hendee, J. 'Conservation: an upper middle class social movement', *Journal of Leisure Research*, I, 3, 1969

Hervé, A. *Animal-Man* (Tr. from Fr. Singleton, S.), New York, Quist, 1976

Illich, I. *Energy and Equity*, London, Calder and Boyars, 1974

Institut économique et juridique de l'énergie *Alternatives au nucléaire*, PUG, 1975

Jund, T. *Le Nucléaire contre l'Alsace*, Paris, Syros, 1977

Jungk, R. *The Nuclear State* (Tr. from Ger. Mosbacher, E.), London, John Calder, 1979

Knelman, F. *Nuclear Energy: The Unforgiving Technology*, Edmonton, Alberta, Hurtig, 1976

Lalonde, B. and Simonnet, D. *Quand vous voudrez*, Paris, Jean-Jacques Pauvert, 1978

Lalonde, B., Moscovici, S. and Dumont, R. *Pourquoi les écologistes font-ils de la politique?* (interview by J.-P. Ribes), Paris, Ed. du Seuil, 1978

Lamour, P. *L'Ecologie oui, les écologistes, non*, Paris, Plon, 1978

Le Henaff, Y. *Aspects techniques, écologiques, économiques et politiques de l'énergie nucléaire*, Paris, APRI, 1977

Lebreton, P. *L'Ex-croissance. Les chances de l'écologiste*, Paris, Denoël, 1978

Lenoir, Y. *Technocratic française*, Paris, Jean-Jacques Pauvert, 1977

Lovins, Amory B. *World Energy Strategies: Facts, Issues and Options*, Cambridge, Mass., Ballinger Pub., 1975

McKinley and Olson, C. *Unacceptable Risk: The Nuclear Power Controversy*, New York, Bantam Books, 1976

Mollo-Mollo, Ps. (Philippe Lebreton) *L'Energie, c'est nous*, Paris, Stock, 1974

Morgan, R. *Nuclear Power: The Bargain We Can't Afford*, Washington, DC, Environmental Action Foundation, 1977

Moscovici, S. *Society Against Nature* (Tr. from Fr. Rabinowitz, S.), Atlantic Highlands, Humanities, 1976

Hommes domestiqués et Hommes sauvages, Paris, '10/18', 1974

Nelkin, D. *Nuclear Power and its Critics*, Cornell UP, Ithaca, NY, 1971

'The political impact of technical expertise', *Social Studies of Science*, V, 1975

Nelkin, D. (Ed.) *Controversy. Politics of Technical Decisions*, Beverly Hills, Ca., Sage, 1979

Bibliography

Nelkin, D. and Pollack, M. 'The politics of participation and the nuclear debate. A comparative study', *Public Policy*, 1977

Nicolon, A. *Analyse d'une opposition à un site nucléaire: le cas du Blayais*, Paris, ADISH, IREP, 1977, reprinted in Fagnani and Nicolon, op. cit.

Nicolon, A. and Carrier, M.-J. *Les Partis et syndicats face au programme électro-nucléaire et la contestation*, Paris, ADISH, IREP, 1977, reprinted in Fagnani and Nicolon, op. cit.

Puiseux, L. *L'Energie et le désarroi post-industriel*, Paris, Hachette, 1973
  La Babel nucléaire, Paris, Galilée, 1977

Québec Science *Face au nucléaire* (collective work), Québec Science, 1979

Que Choisir? Special Number, 1978, *Au soleil de l'an 2000. Peut-on stopper le nucléaire*

Rossel, J. *L'Energie nucléaire*, Paris, Pierre Faure, 1977

Samuel, P. *Ecologie: Détente ou Cycle infernal?*, Paris, '10/18', 1973
  Le Nucléaire en question, Paris, Entente, 1976

Simonnet, D. *L'Ecologisme*, Paris, PUF, 1979

Simonnot, P. *Les Nucléocrates*, Grenoble, PUG, 1978

Skills, D. L. 'The environmental movement and its critics', *Human Ecology*, III, I, 1975

Thiriet, L. *L'Energie nucléaire: Quelle politique pour quel avenir?*, Paris, Dunod, 1976

Touraine, A. *The Voice and the Eye* (Tr. from Fr. Duff, A.), Cambridge, CUP, 1981

Touraine, A., Dubet, F., Hegedus, Z. and Wieviorka, M. *Lutte étudiante*, Paris, Ed. du Seuil, 1978

Tubiana, M. (Ed.) *Colloque sur les implications psychosociologiques du développment de l'industrie nucléaire*, Paris, Société française de radioprotection, 1977

Vadrot, C.–M. *L'Ecologie – Histoire d'une subversion*, Paris, Syros, 1978

Weber, M. *Economy and Society* (ed. G. Roth and C. Wittich), New York, Bedminster Press, 1968